THE NEW DECADE SERIES

FOR ORGANS, PIANOS & ELECTRONIC KEYBOARDS

E-Z PLAY TODAY

362

SONGS OF THE
1920s

ISBN 978-1-4950-6267-4

HAL•LEONARD® CORPORATION

7777 W. BLUEMOUND RD. P.O. BOX 13819 MILWAUKEE, WI 53213

For all works contained herein:
Unauthorized copying, arranging, adapting, recording, Internet posting, public performance,
or other distribution of the printed music in this publication is an infringement of copyright.
Infringers are liable under the law.

E-Z Play ® TODAY Music Notation © 1975 HAL LEONARD CORPORATION
E-Z PLAY and EASY ELECTRONIC KEYBOARD MUSIC are registered trademarks of HAL LEONARD CORPORATION

4	Ain't Misbehavin'
6	All Alone
8	Always
10	Among My Souvenirs
12	April Showers
14	Baby Face
16	Back in Your Own Backyard
22	Basin Street Blues
24	The Best Things in Life Are Free
19	Bill
26	The Birth of the Blues
28	Blue Skies
30	Button Up Your Overcoat
32	Bye Bye Blackbird
34	California, Here I Come
36	Can't Help Lovin' Dat Man
38	Charleston
40	Charmaine
42	Crazy Rhythm
44	'Deed I Do
46	Everybody Loves My Baby (But My Baby Don't Love Nobody but Me)
48	Fascinating Rhythm
50	Five Foot Two, Eyes of Blue (Has Anybody Seen My Girl?)
52	Honeysuckle Rose
54	How Long Has This Been Going On?
56	I Can't Believe That You're in Love with Me
62	I Can't Give You Anything but Love
64	I Cried for You
66	I Wanna Be Loved by You
68	I Want to Be Happy
70	I'll Get By (As Long as I Have You)
72	I'll See You in My Dreams
74	I'm Sitting on Top of the World
76	If I Could Be with You (One Hour Tonight)
78	If I Had You
80	If You Knew Susie (Like I Know Susie)
82	In a Little Spanish Town ('Twas on a Night Like This)
84	It All Depends on You
59	It Had to Be You
86	Just You, Just Me
88	Let a Smile Be Your Umbrella
90	Liza (All the Clouds'll Roll Away)
92	Look for the Silver Lining
94	Louise
96	Love Me or Leave Me
98	Lover, Come Back to Me
100	Mack the Knife
102	Make Believe
104	Makin' Whoopee!

106	The Man I Love
108	Manhattan
110	Me and My Shadow
112	Mean to Me
115	Mississippi Mud
118	Moonlight and Roses (Bring Mem'ries of You)
120	More Than You Know
126	Mountain Greenery
123	Muskrat Ramble
128	My Blue Heaven
130	My Heart Stood Still
132	My Man (Mon homme)
136	Oh, Lady Be Good!
138	Ol' Man River
140	Puttin' on the Ritz
142	Ramona
144	Rhapsody in Blue
148	Rockin' Chair
150	'S Wonderful
152	St. Louis Blues
160	Say It with Music
157	Second Hand Rose
162	Sentimental Me
164	Side by Side
170	Sleepy Time Gal
172	Softly as in a Morning Sunrise
167	Some of These Days
174	Somebody Loves Me
176	Someone to Watch Over Me
182	The Song Is Ended (But the Melody Lingers On)
184	Squeeze Me
186	Stardust
188	Swanee
190	Sweet Georgia Brown
192	Sweet Lorraine
194	Tea for Two
196	Thou Swell
198	Three O'Clock in the Morning
200	Tip-Toe Thru' the Tulips with Me
202	Toot, Toot, Tootsie! (Good-bye!)
204	'Way Down Yonder in New Orleans
206	What'll I Do?
208	When My Baby Smiles at Me
179	When You're Smiling (The Whole World Smiles with You)
210	Whispering
212	Who?
214	Who's Sorry Now
216	With a Song in My Heart
218	Yes Sir, That's My Baby
220	Yes! We Have No Bananas
222	You're the Cream in My Coffee
224	**Registration Guide**

Ain't Misbehavin'
from AIN'T MISBEHAVIN'

Registration 7
Rhythm: Fox Trot or Swing

Words by Andy Razaf
Music by Thomas "Fats" Waller and Harry Brooks

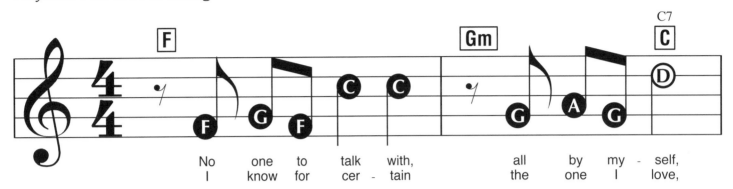

No one to talk with, all by my - self,
I know for cer - tain the one I love,

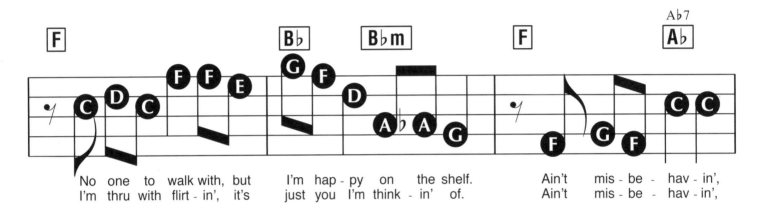

No one to walk with, but I'm hap - py on the shelf. Ain't mis - be - hav - in',
I'm thru with flirt - in', it's just you I'm think - in' of. Ain't mis - be - hav - in',

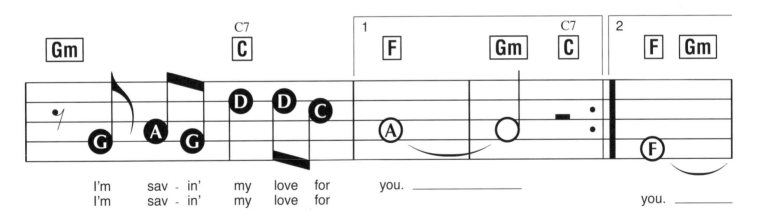

I'm sav - in' my love for you.
I'm sav - in' my love for you.

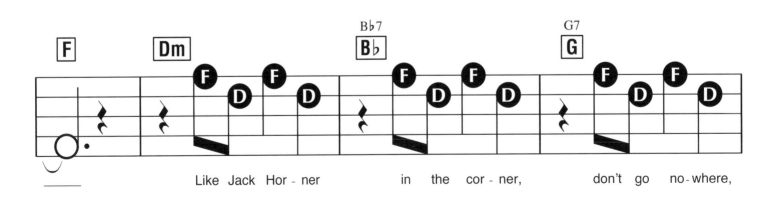

Like Jack Hor - ner in the cor - ner, don't go no - where,

© 1929 (Renewed) CHAPPELL & CO., INC., EMI MILLS MUSIC INC. and RAZAF MUSIC CO.
All Rights for EMI MILLS MUSIC INC. Administered by EMI MILLS MUSIC INC. (Publishing) and ALFRED MUSIC (Print)
All Rights for RAZAF MUSIC CO. Administered by BMG RIGHTS MANAGEMENT (US) LLC
All Rights Reserved   Used by Permission

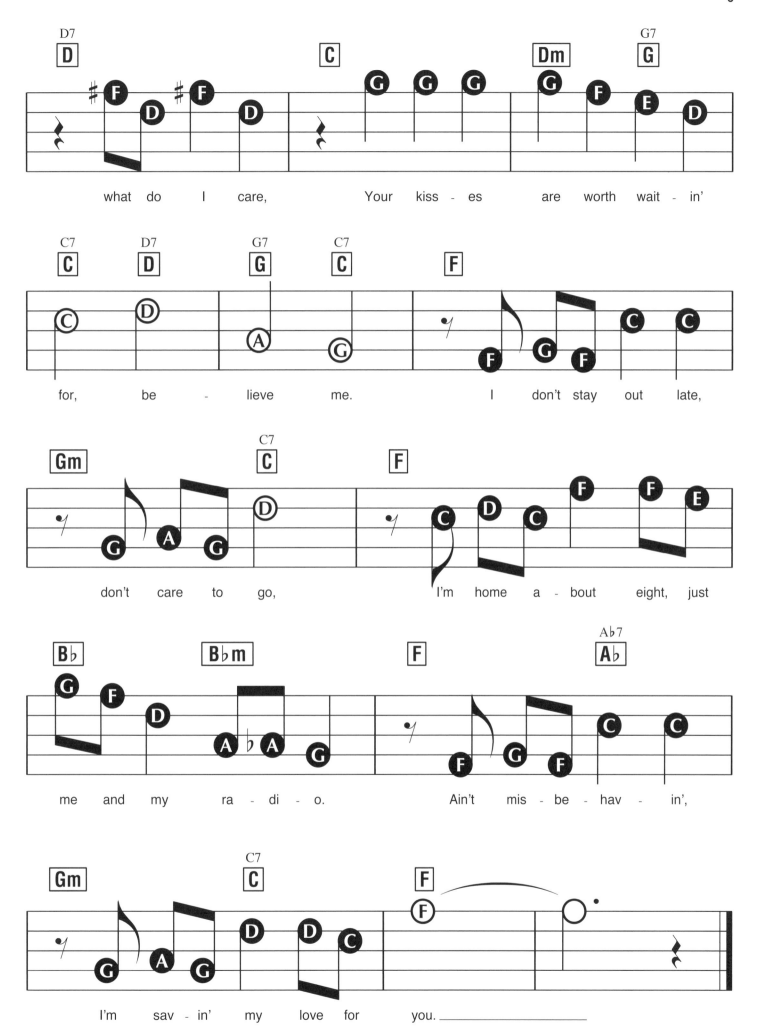

All Alone

Words and Music by
Irving Berlin

Registration 5
Rhythm: Waltz

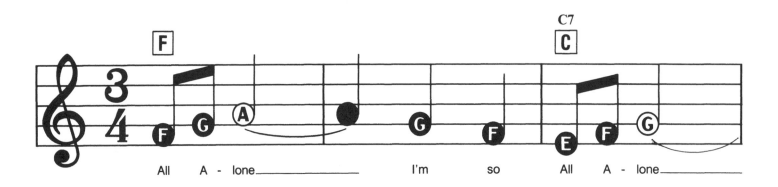

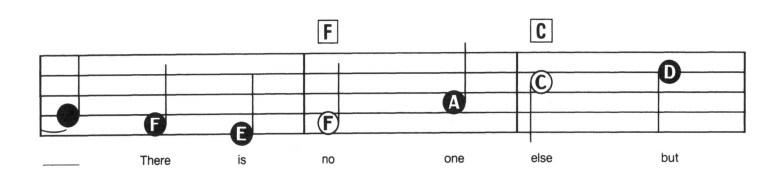

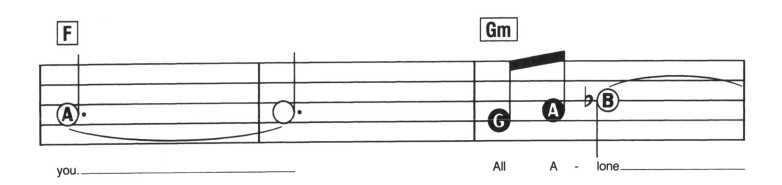

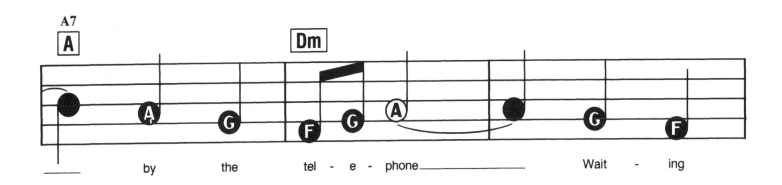

© Copyright 1924 by Irving Berlin
Copyright Renewed
International Copyright Secured   All Rights Reserved

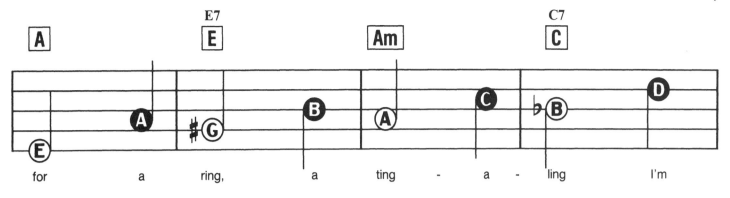

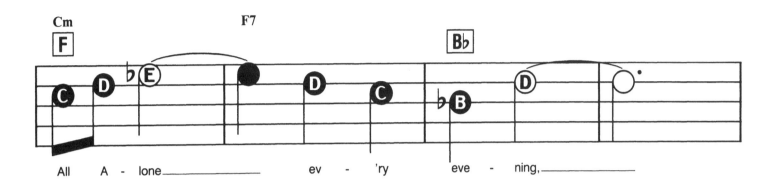

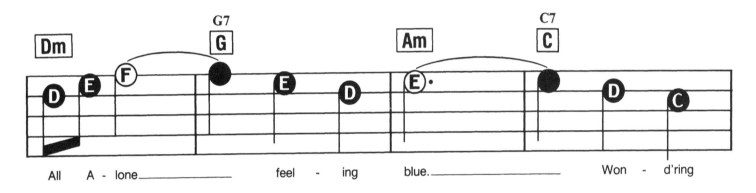

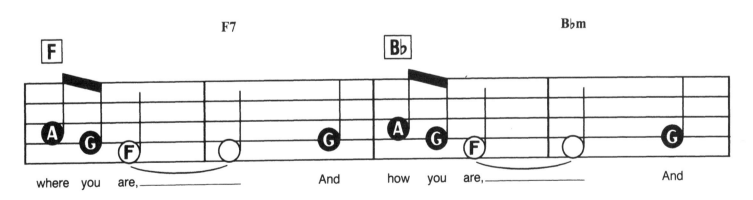

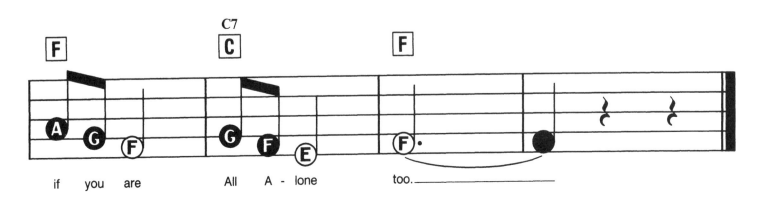

Always

Registration 2
Rhythm: Waltz

Words and Music by
Irving Berlin

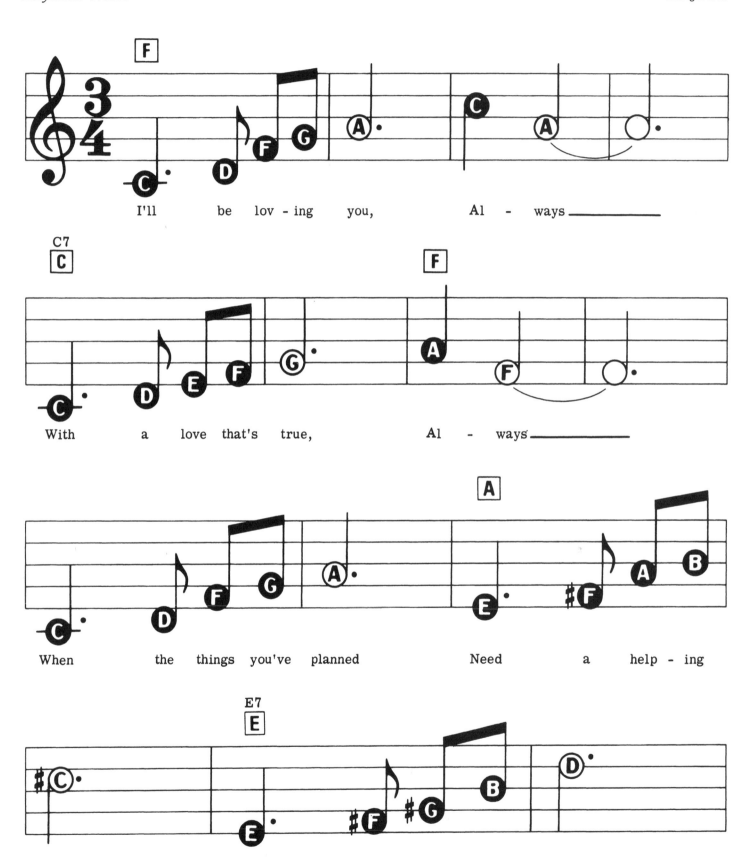

© Copyright 1925 by Irving Berlin
Copyright Renewed
International Copyright Secured   All Rights Reserved

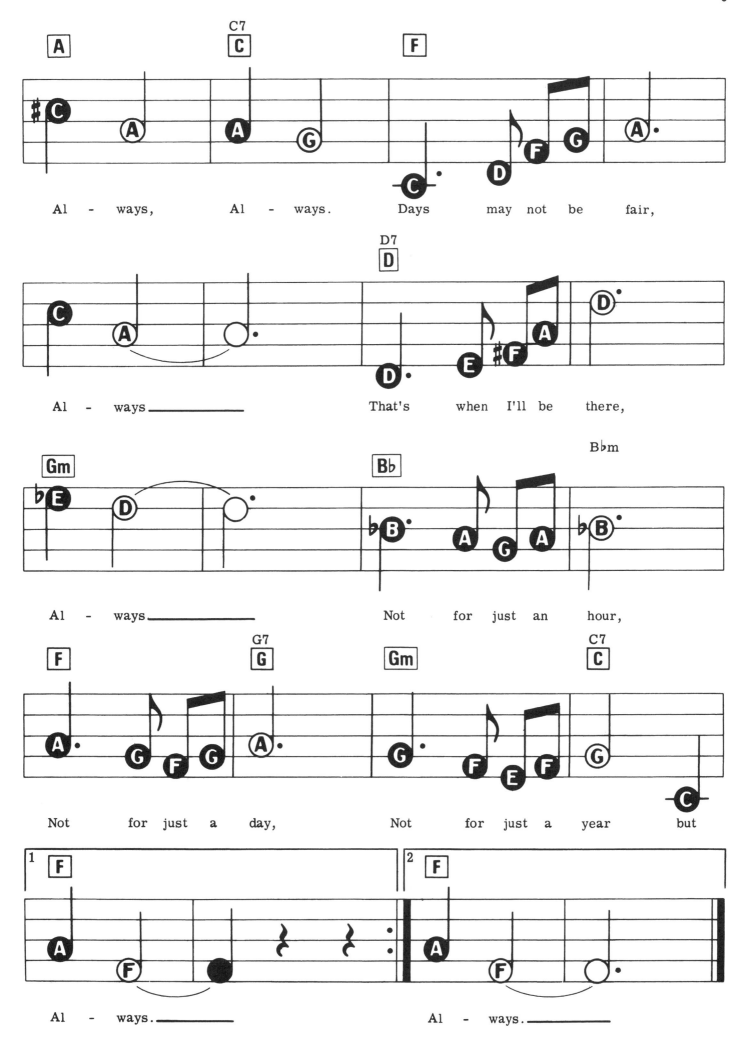

Among My Souvenirs

Registration 1
Rhythm: Fox Trot

Words by Edgar Leslie
Music by Horatio Nicholas

© 1927 (Renewed) CHAPPELL & CO., INC. and HERALD SQUARE MUSIC INC.
All Rights Reserved   Used by Permission

11

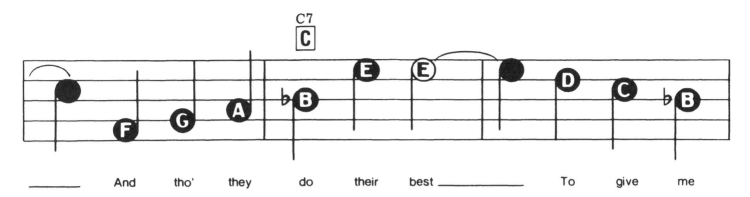

And tho' they do their best _____ To give me

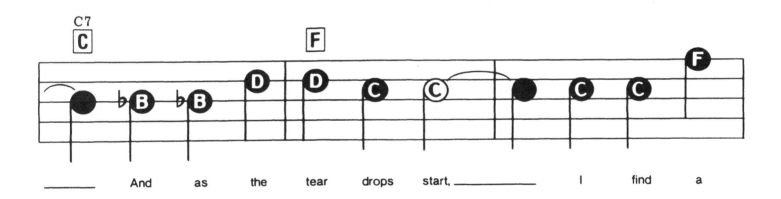

con - so - la - tion, I count them all a - part,_____

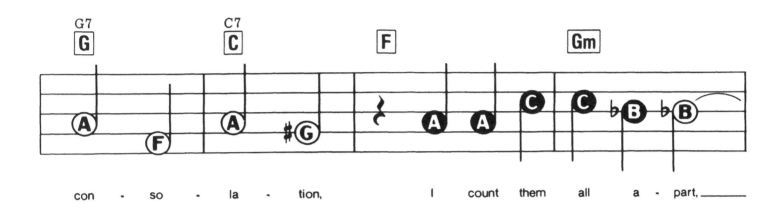

_____ And as the tear drops start,_____ I find a

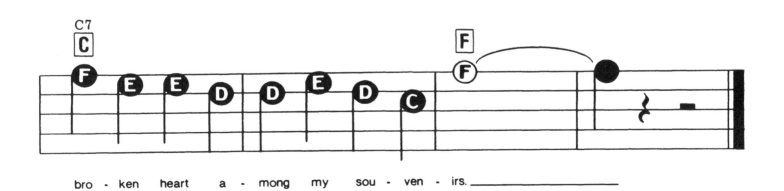

bro - ken heart a - mong my sou - ven - irs. _____

April Showers
from BOMBO

Registration 9
Rhythm: Swing

Words by B.G. DeSylva
Music by Louis Silvers

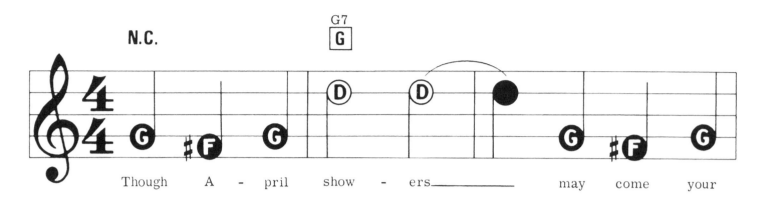

Though A - pril show - ers_____ may come your

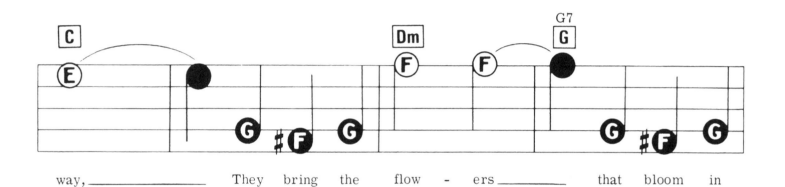

way,_____ They bring the flow - ers_____ that bloom in

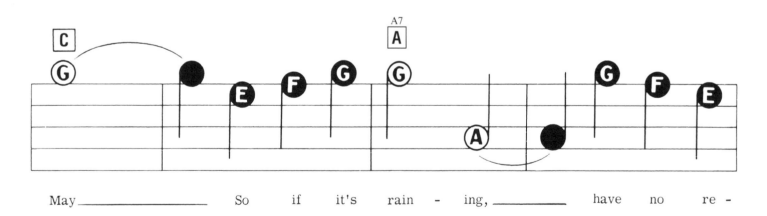

May_____ So if it's rain - ing,_____ have no re -

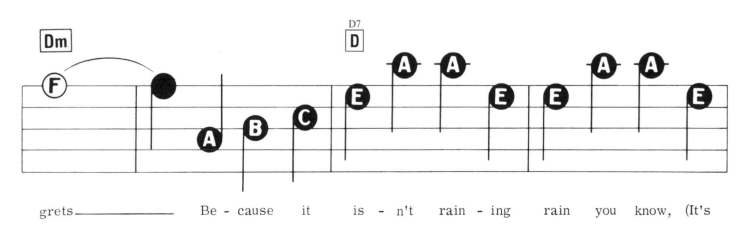

grets_____ Be - cause it is - n't rain - ing rain you know, (It's

Copyright © 2010 by HAL LEONARD CORPORATION
International Copyright Secured All Rights Reserved

13

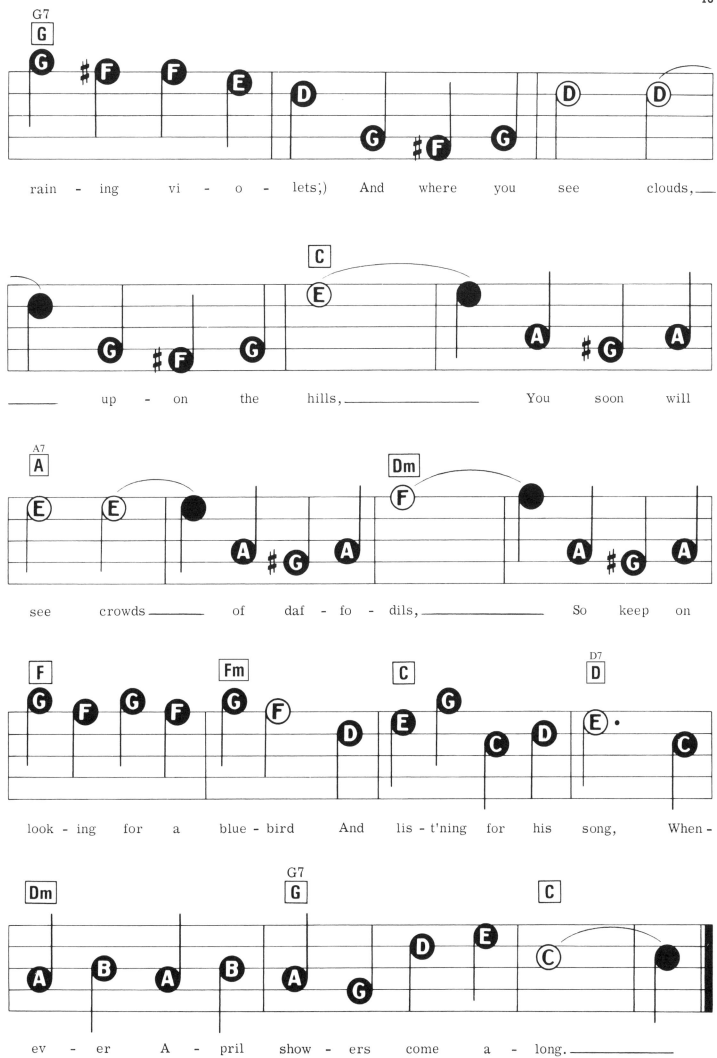

Baby Face

Registration 7
Rhythm: Fox Trot or Swing

Words and Music by Benny Davis
and Harry Akst

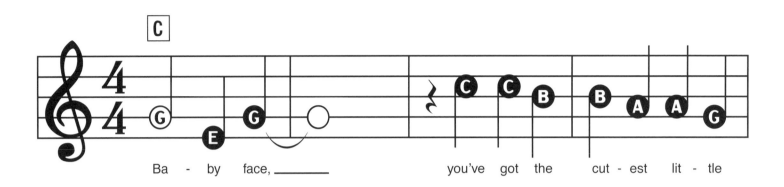

Ba - by face, _____ you've got the cut - est lit - tle

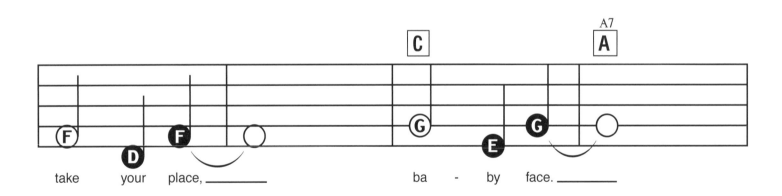

ba - by face. _____ There's not an - oth - er one could

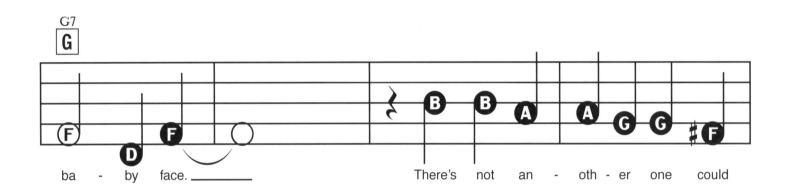

take your place, _____ ba - by face. _____

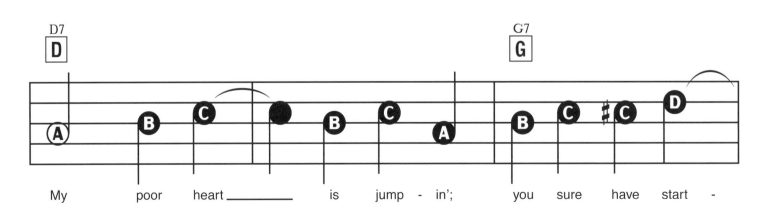

My poor heart _____ is jump - in'; you sure have start -

Copyright © 1926 (Renewed) B & G AKST PUBLISHING CO. and BENNY DAVIS MUSIC
All Rights for B & G AKST PUBLISHING CO. Administered by THE SONGWRITERS GUILD OF AMERICA
Harry Akst Reversionary Interest Controlled by BOURNE CO. (ASCAP)
International Copyright Secured   All Rights Reserved

15

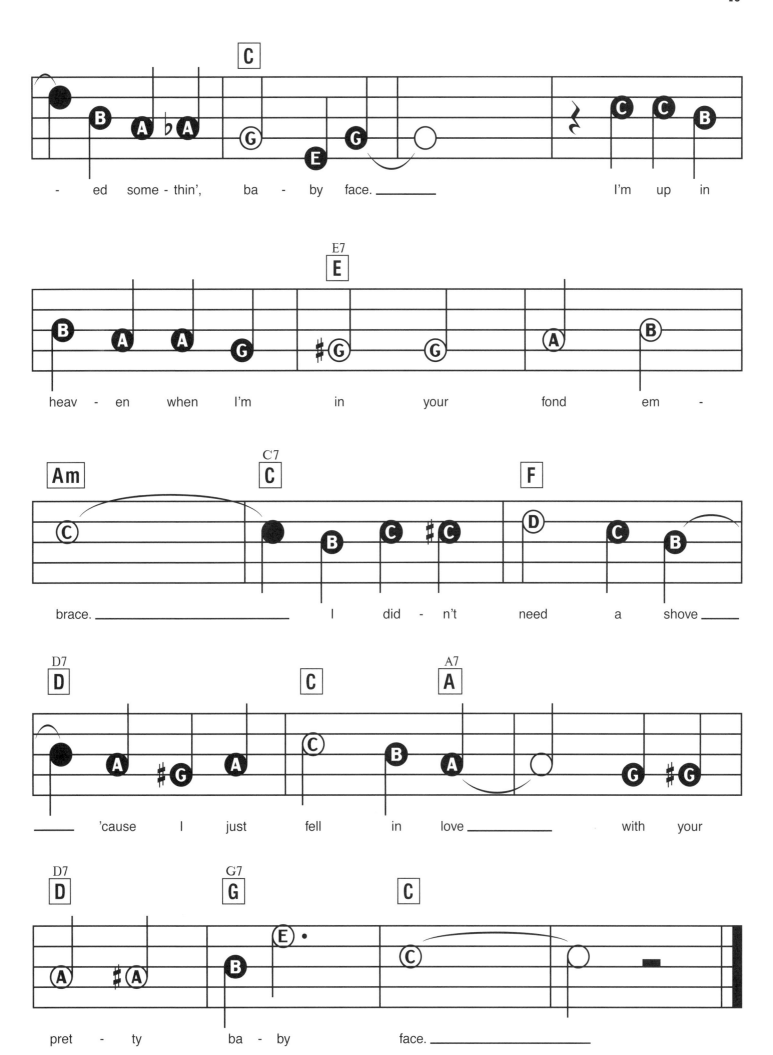

Back in Your Own Backyard

Registration 10
Rhythm: Swing

Words and Music by Al Jolson,
Billy Rose and Dave Dreyer

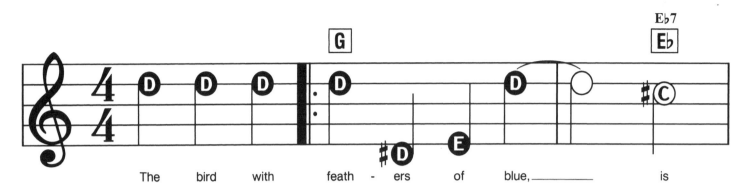

The bird with feath - ers of blue, _____ is

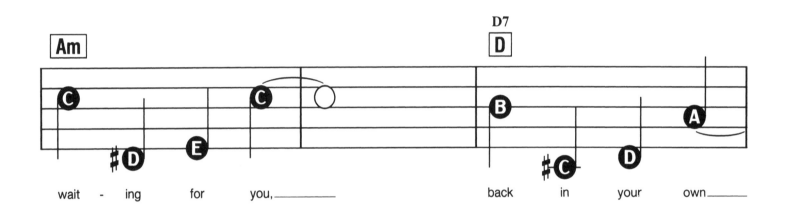

wait - ing for you, _____ back in your own _____

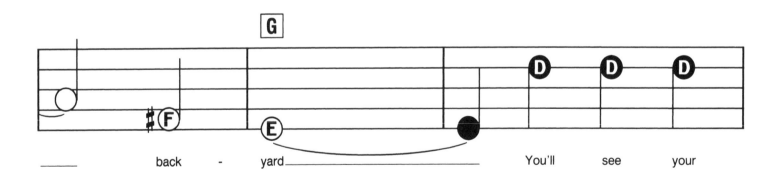

_____ back - yard _____ You'll see your

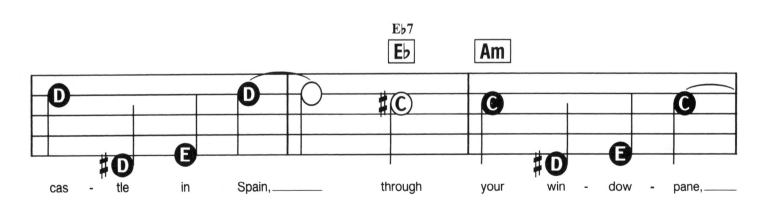

cas - tle in Spain, _____ through your win - dow - pane,

Copyright © 1927, 1928 by Bourne Co. (ASCAP) and Larry Spier Music, LLC
Copyright Renewed
International Copyright Secured   All Rights Reserved

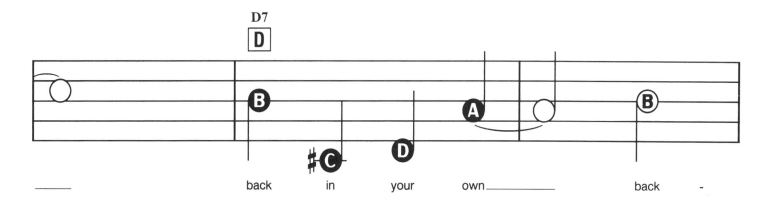

back in your own_____ back -

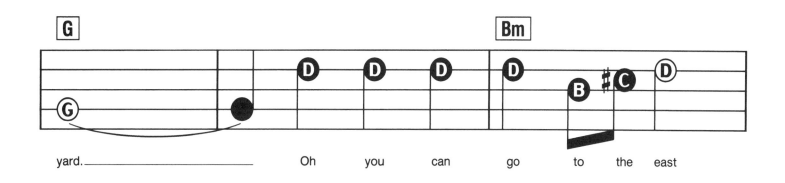

yard._____ Oh you can go to the east

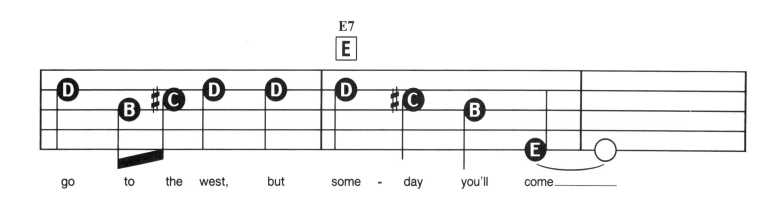

go to the west, but some - day you'll come_____

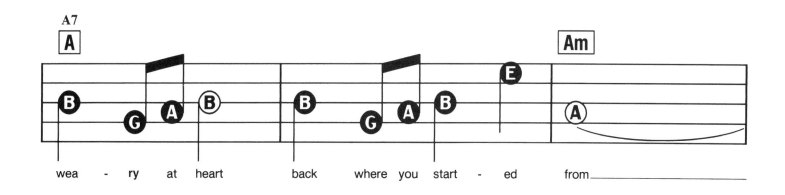

wea - ry at heart back where you start - ed from_____

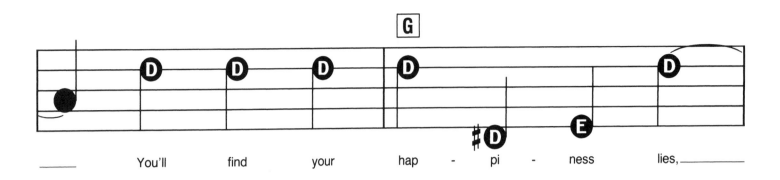

You'll find your hap - pi - ness lies,

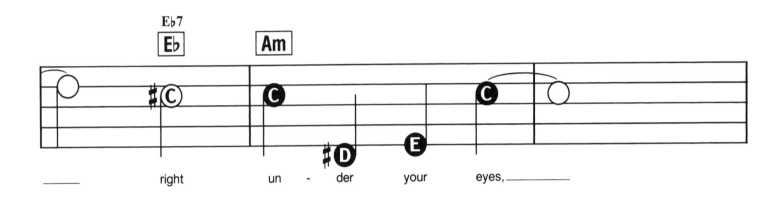

right un - der your eyes,

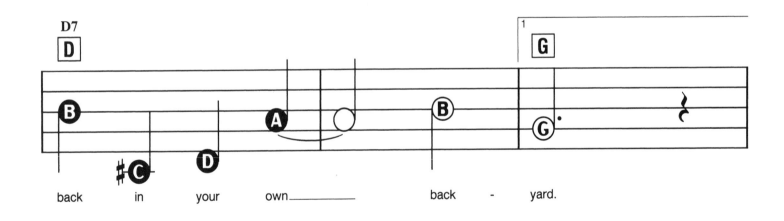

back in your own back - yard.

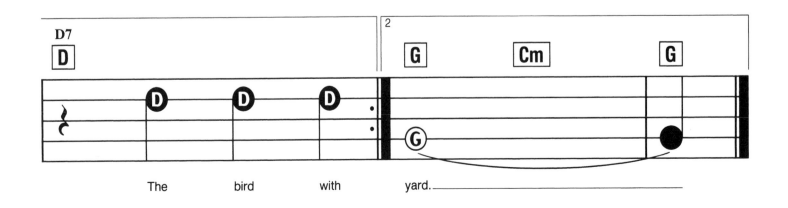

The bird with yard.

Bill
from SHOW BOAT

Registration 1
Rhythm: Swing or Fox Trot

Music by Jerome Kern
Words by P.G. Wodehouse and Oscar Hammerstein II

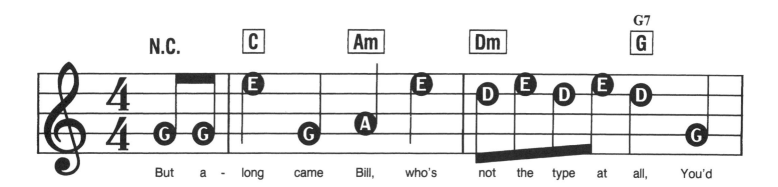

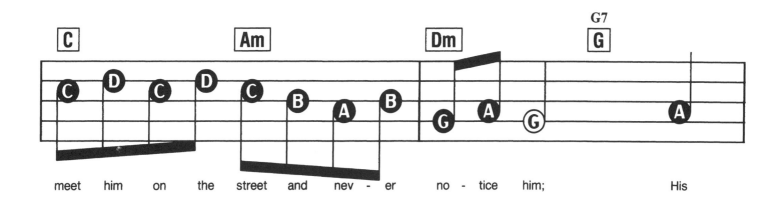

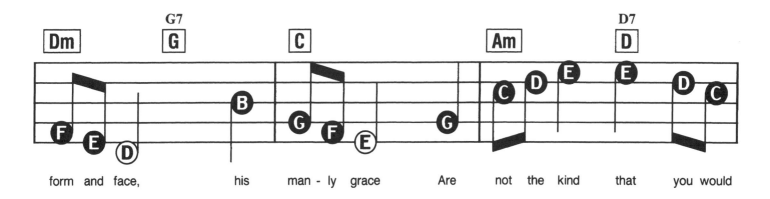

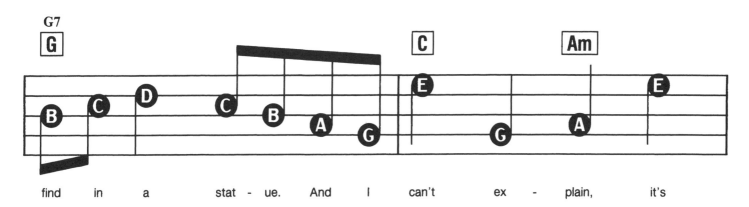

Copyright © 1927 UNIVERSAL - POLYGRAM INTERNATIONAL PUBLISHING, INC.
Copyright Renewed
All Rights Reserved   Used by Permission

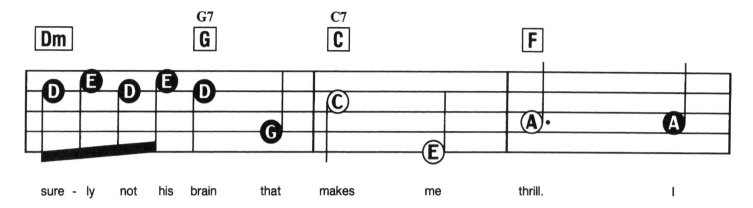

sure - ly not his brain that makes me thrill. I

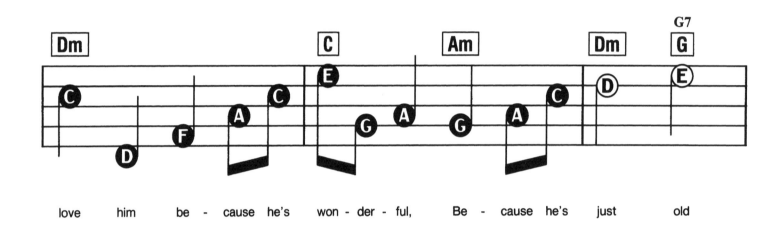

love him be - cause he's won - der - ful, Be - cause he's just old

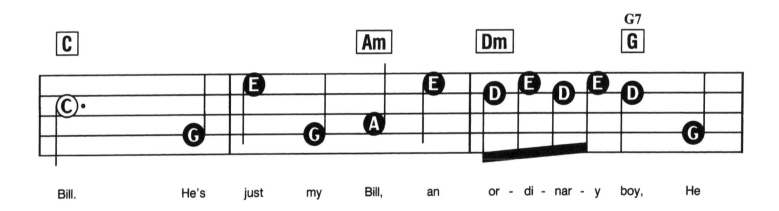

Bill. He's just my Bill, an or - di - nar - y boy, He

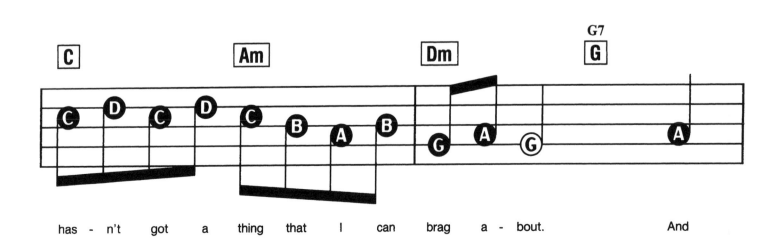

has - n't got a thing that I can brag a - bout. And

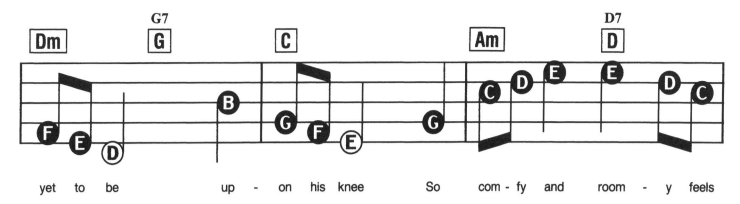

yet to be up - on his knee So com - fy and room - y feels

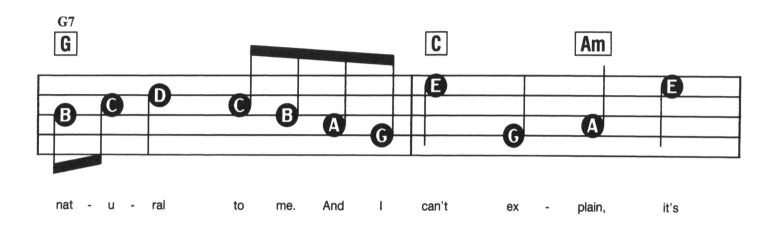

nat - u - ral to me. And I can't ex - plain, it's

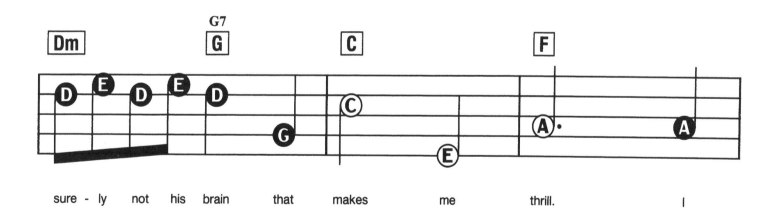

sure - ly not his brain that makes me thrill. I

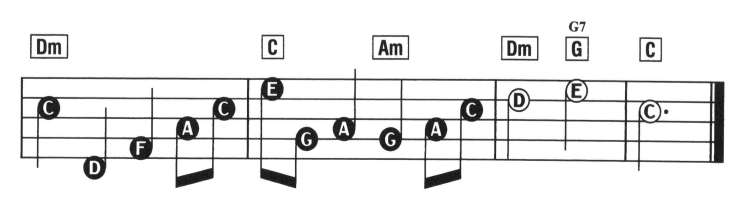

love him be - cause he's I don't know, Be - cause he's just my Bill.

Basin Street Blues

Registration 1
Rhythm: Swing or Fox Trot

Words and Music by
Spencer Williams

© 1928, 1929, 1933 (Renewed) EDWIN H. MORRIS & COMPANY, A Division of MPL Music Publishing, Inc.
All Rights Reserved

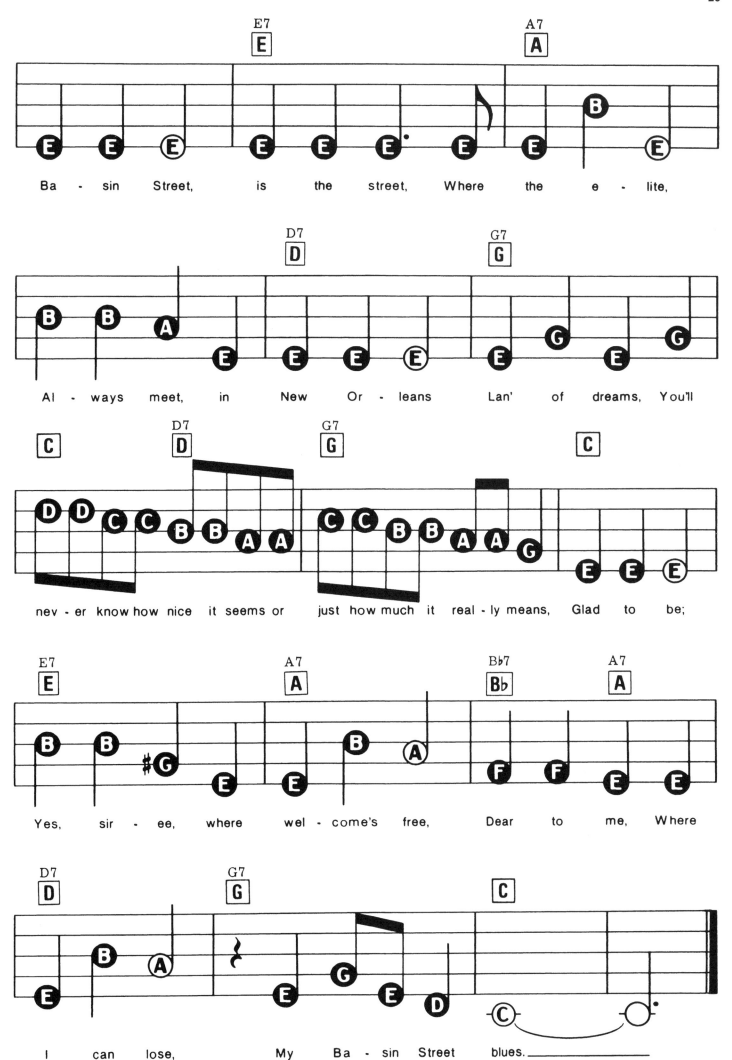

The Best Things in Life Are Free
from GOOD NEWS!

Registration 8
Rhythm: Fox Trot or Swing

Music and Lyrics by B.G. DeSylva,
Lew Brown and Ray Henderson

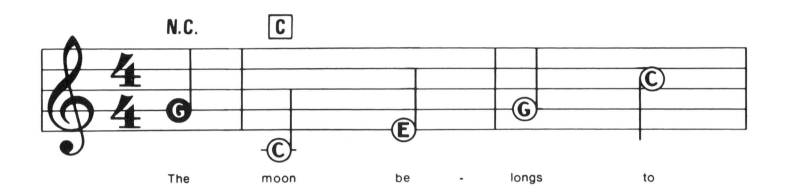

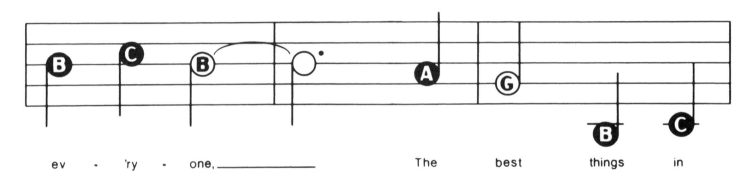

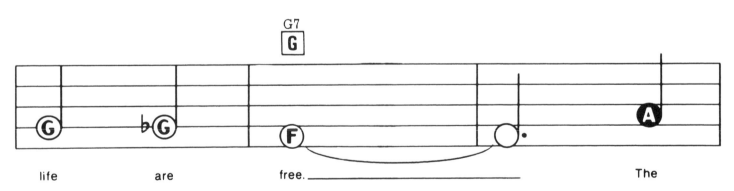

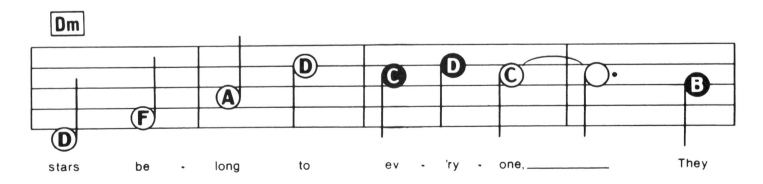

Copyright © 1927 by CHAPPELL & CO., INC., STEPHEN BALLENTINE MUSIC PUBLISHING CO. and RAY HENDERSON MUSIC CO.
Copyright Renewed
International Copyright Secured   All Rights Reserved

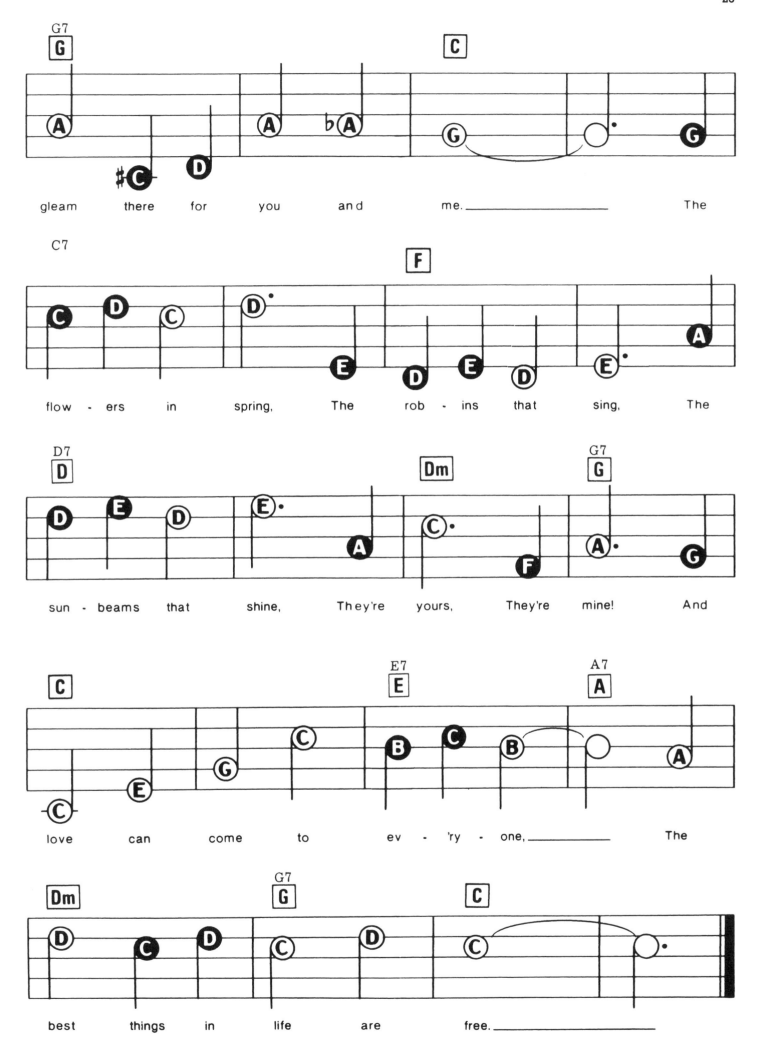

The Birth of the Blues
from GEORGE WHITE'S SCANDALS OF 1926

Registration 7
Rhythm: Fox Trot or Swing

Words by B.G. DeSylva and Lew Brown
Music by Ray Henderson

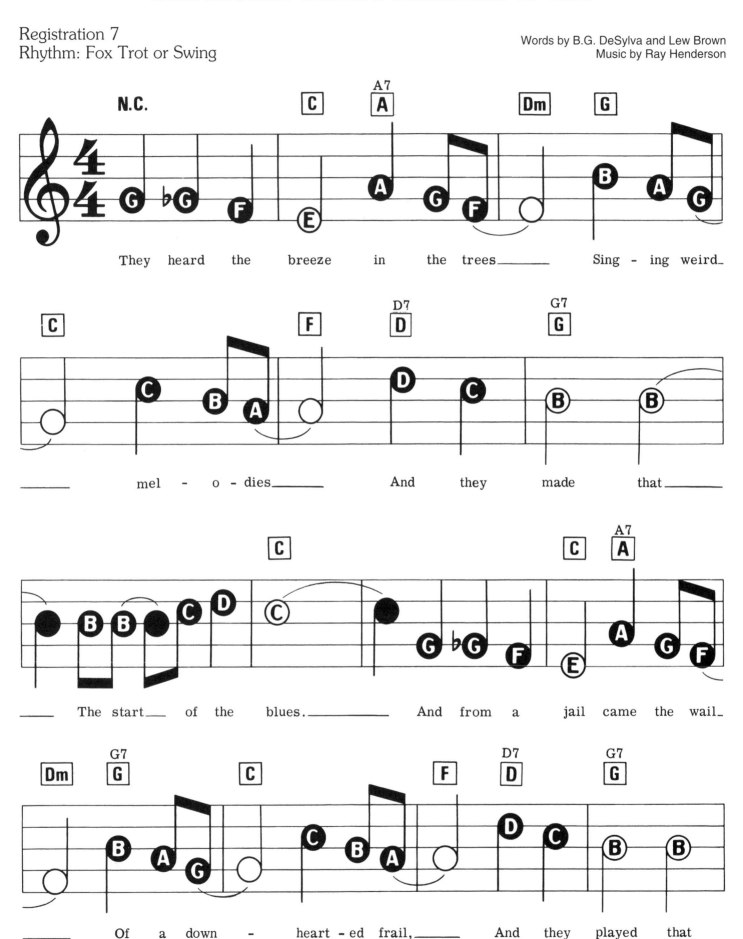

Copyright © 1926 Stephen Ballentine Music, WB Music Corp. and Ray Henderson Music
Copyright Renewed
All Rights for Stephen Ballentine Music Administered by The Songwriters Guild Of America
International Copyright Secured   All Rights Reserved

27

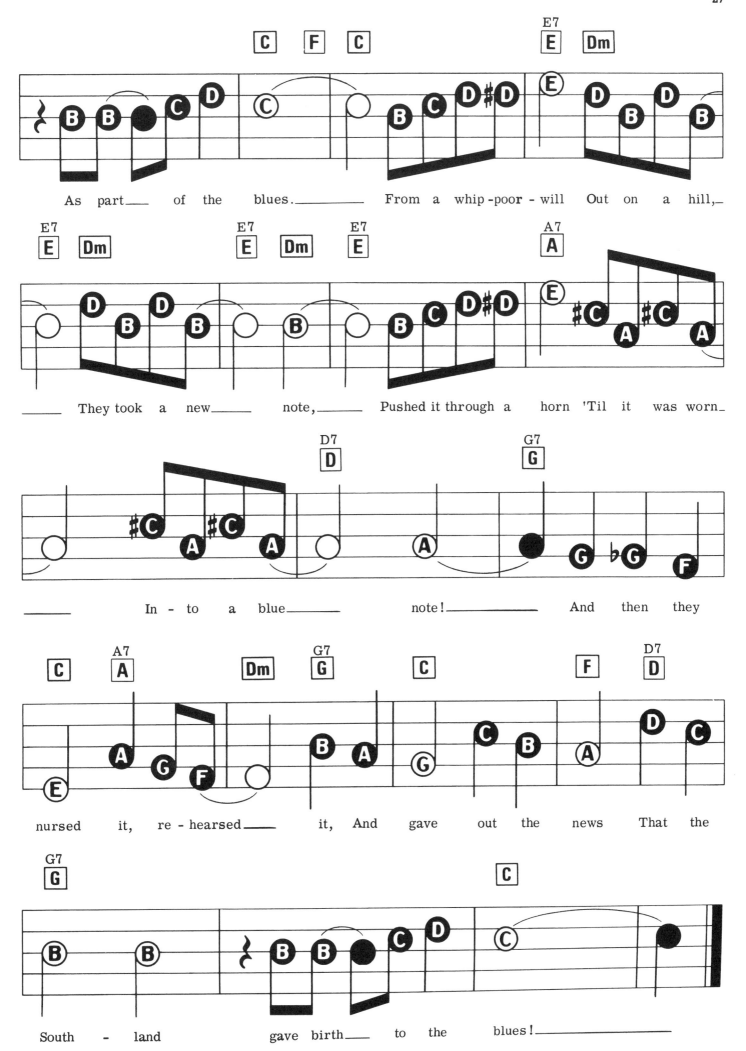

Blue Skies
from BETSY

Registration 8
Rhythm: Fox Trot or Swing

Words and Music by
Irving Berlin

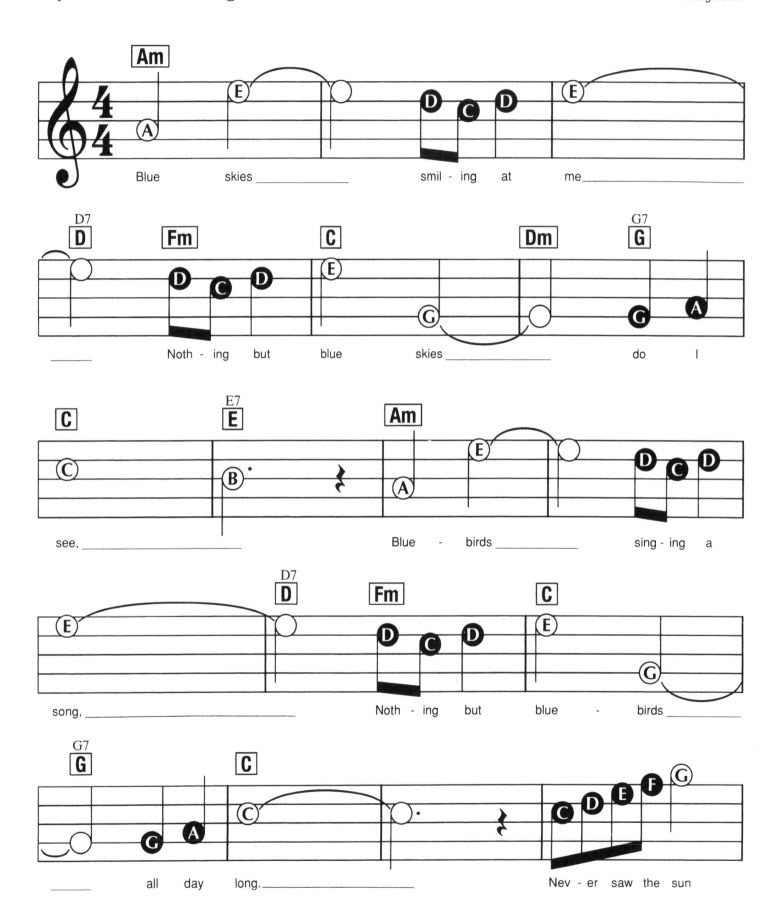

© Copyright 1927 by Irving Berlin
Copyright Renewed
International Copyright Secured   All Rights Reserved

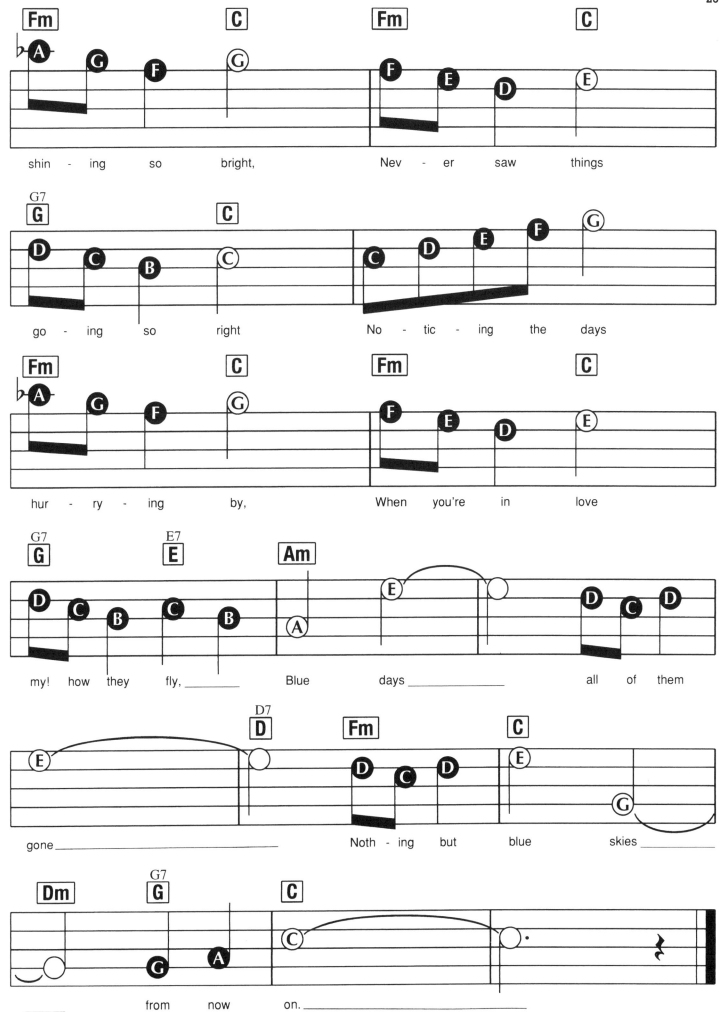

Button Up Your Overcoat
from FOLLOW THRU

Registration 5
Rhythm: Fox Trot or Swing

Words and Music by B.G. DeSylva,
Lew Brown and Ray Henderson

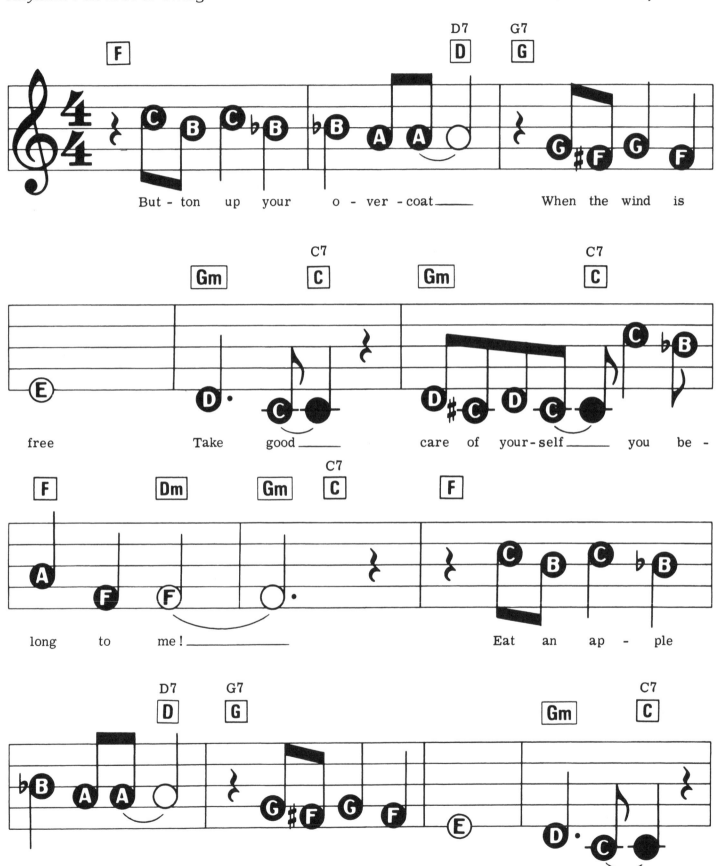

Copyright © 1928 by Chappell & Co., Stephen Ballentine Music Publishing Co. and Ray Henderson Music Co.
Copyright Renewed
International Copyright Secured All Rights Reserved

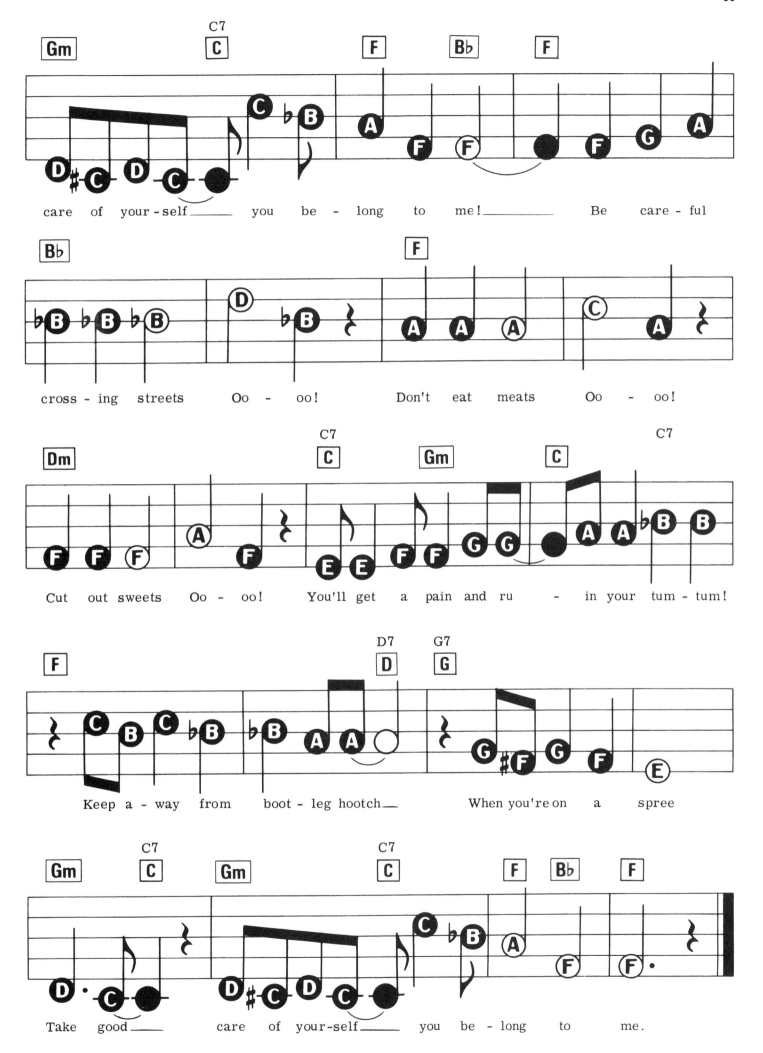

Bye Bye Blackbird
from SHOW BOAT

Registration 2
Rhythm: Fox Trot or Swing

Words by Mort Dixon
Music by Ray Henderson

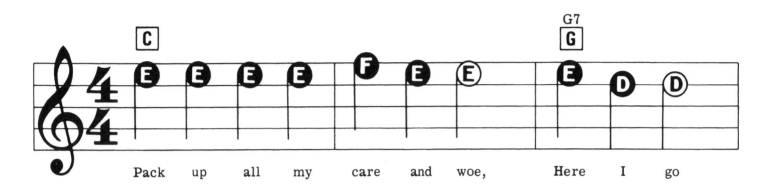

Pack   up   all   my   care   and   woe,   Here   I   go

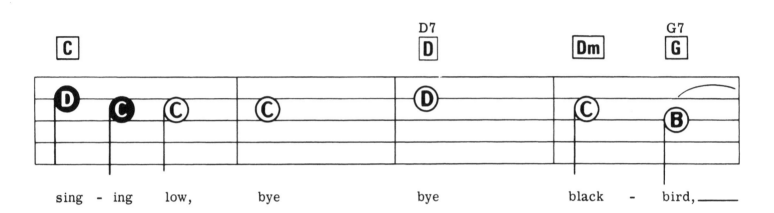

sing - ing   low,   bye   bye   black - bird,_____

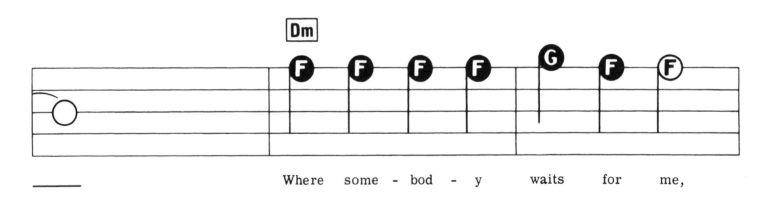

_____   Where   some - bod - y   waits   for   me,

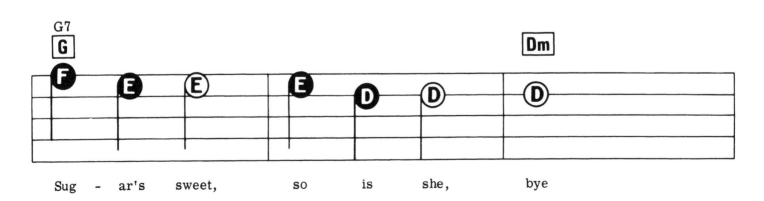

Sug - ar's   sweet,   so   is   she,   bye

Copyright © 1926 BMG Gold Songs and Ray Henderson
Copyright Renewed
All Rights for BMG Gold Songs Administered by BMG Rights Management (US) LLC
All Rights for Ray Henderson Administered by Ray Henderson Music
All Rights Reserved   Used by Permission

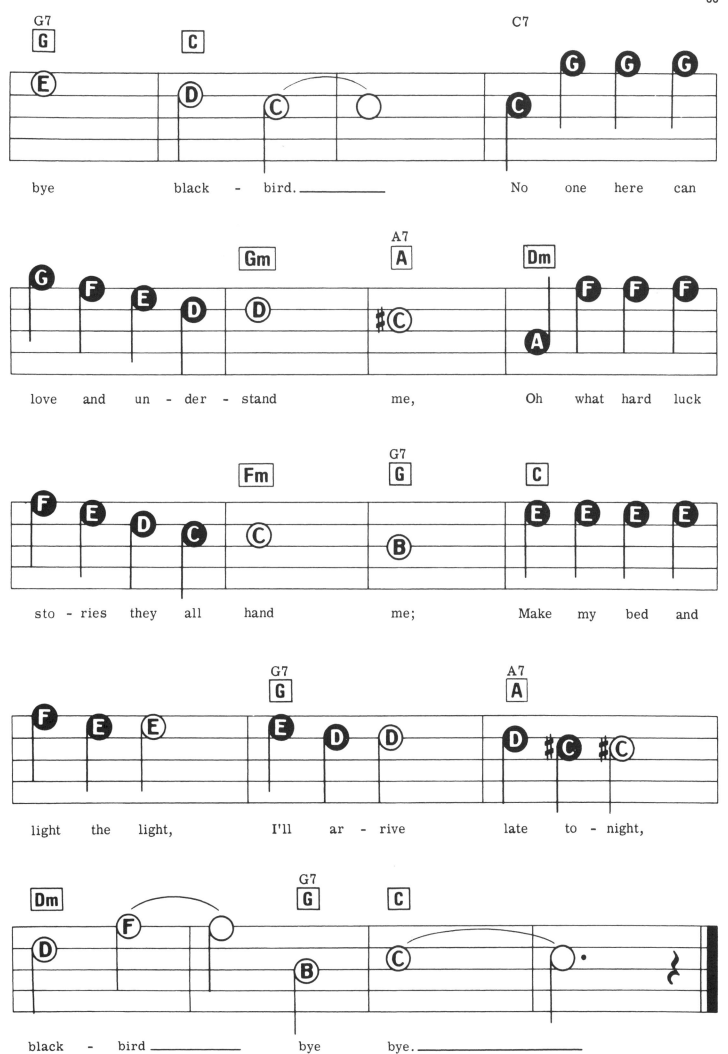

California, Here I Come

Registration 5
Rhythm: Swing or Jazz

Words and Music by Al Jolson,
B.G. DeSylva and Joseph Meyer

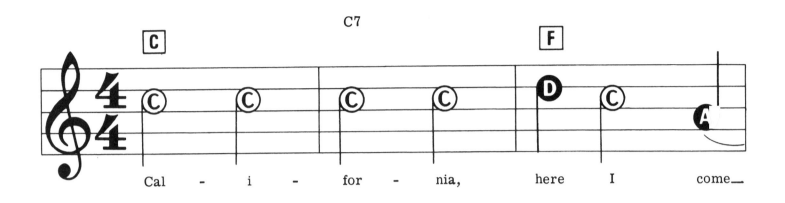

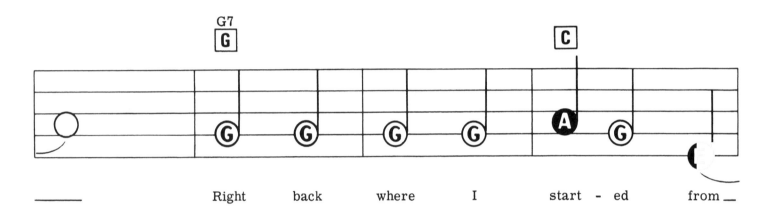

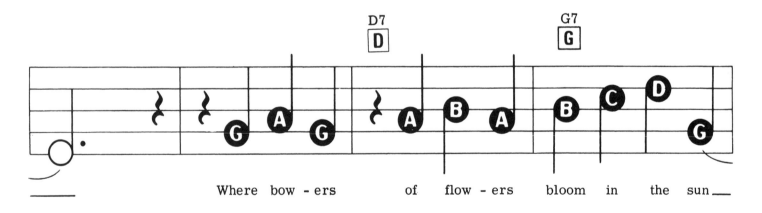

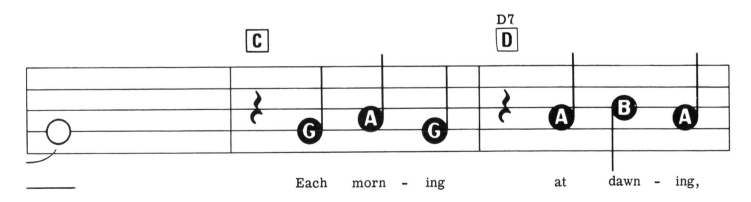

Copyright © 1924 (Renewed) JoRo Music Corp., New York, NY, Stephen Ballentine Music, New York, NY and Warner Bros. Inc.
International Copyright Secured   All Rights Reserved

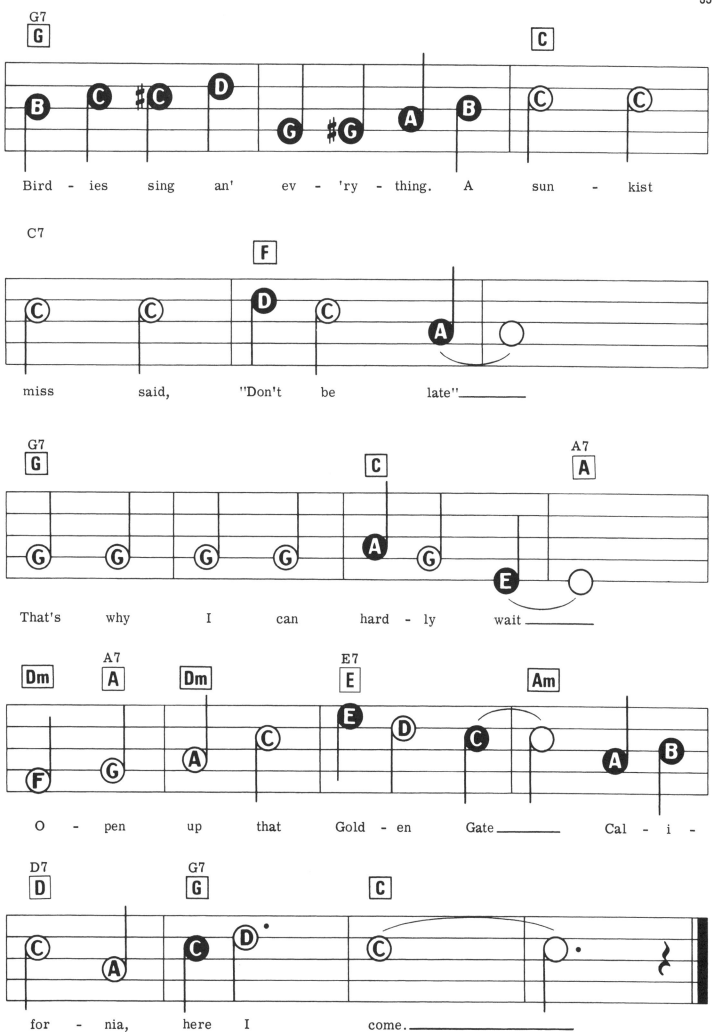

Can't Help Lovin' Dat Man
from SHOW BOAT

Registration 5
Rhythm: Ballad or Swing

Lyrics by Oscar Hammerstein II
Music by Jerome Kern

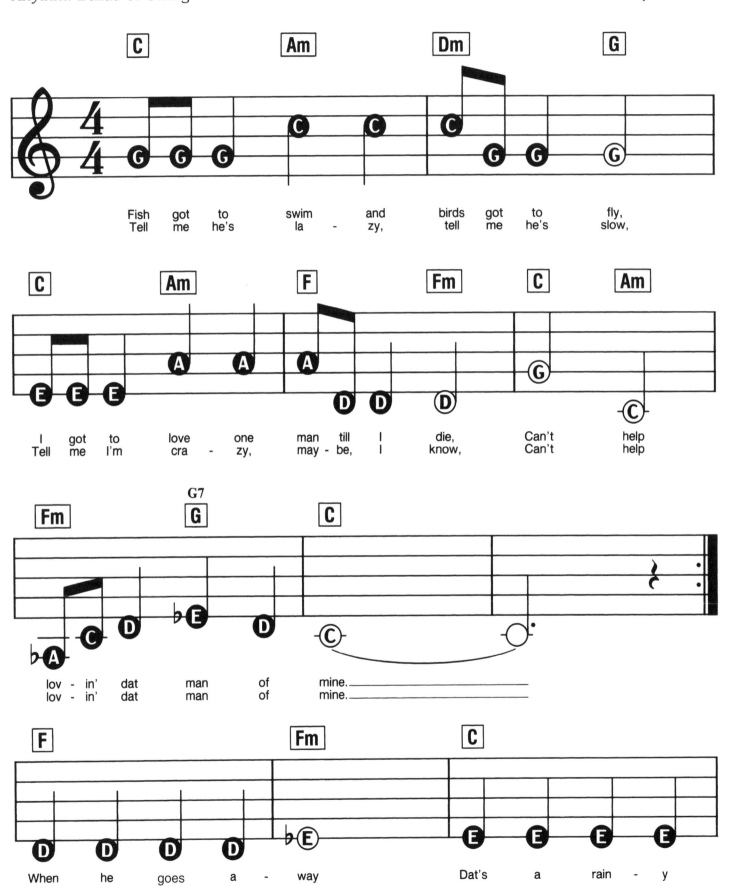

Copyright © 1927 UNIVERSAL - POLYGRAM INTERNATIONAL PUBLISHING, INC.
Copyright Renewed
All Rights Reserved   Used by Permission

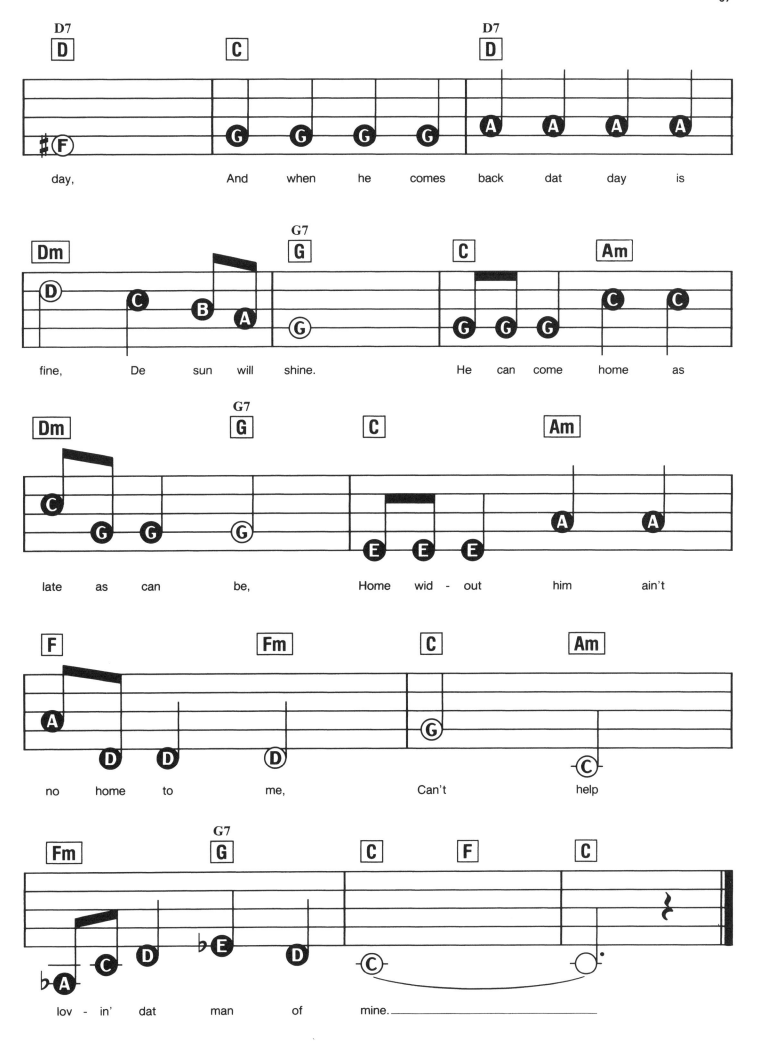

Charleston

Registration 2
Rhythm: Fox Trot

Words and Music by Cecil Mack
and Jimmy Johnson

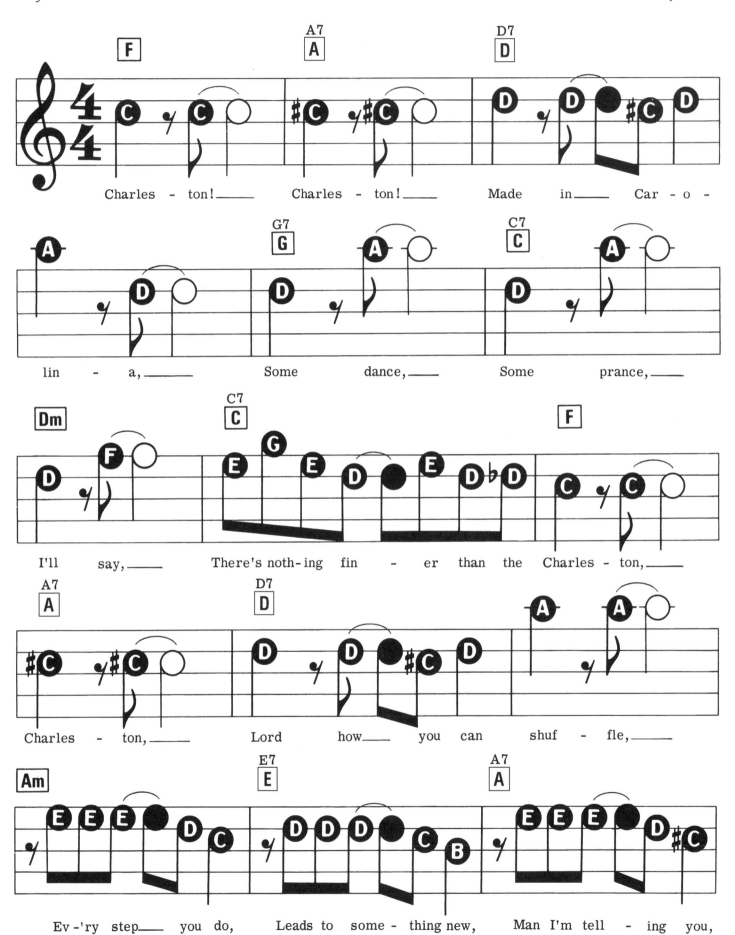

© 1923 (Renewed) WARNER BROS. INC.
All Rights Reserved   Used by Permission

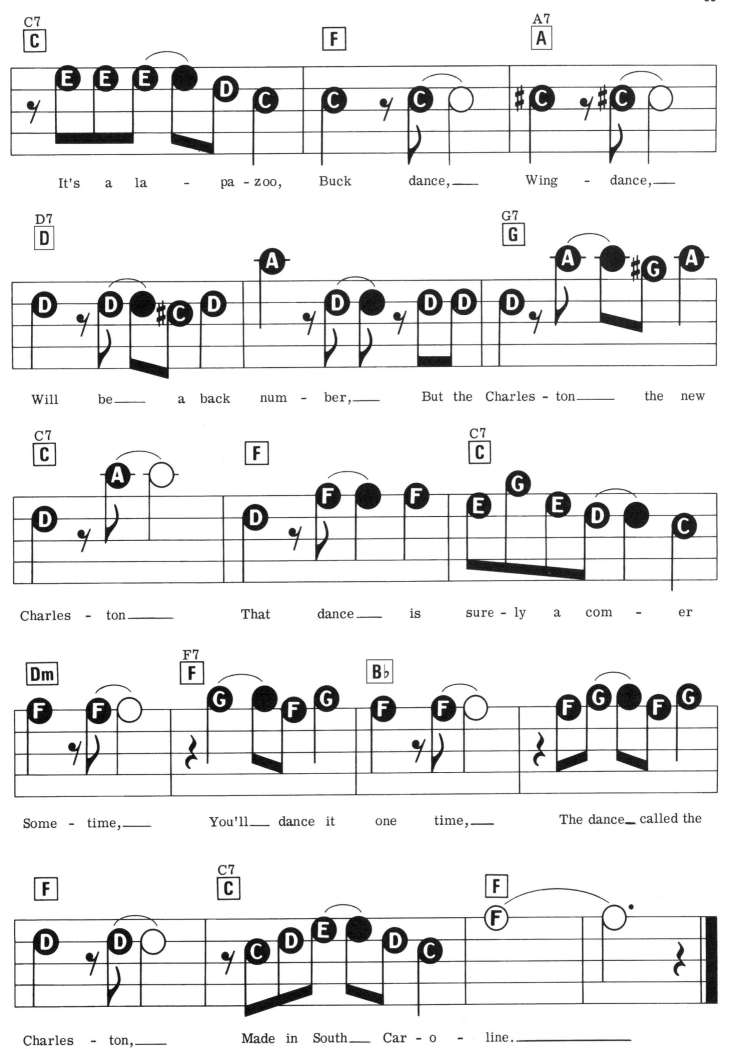

Charmaine

Registration 8
Rhythm: Waltz

Words and Music by Lew Pollack
and Erno Rapee

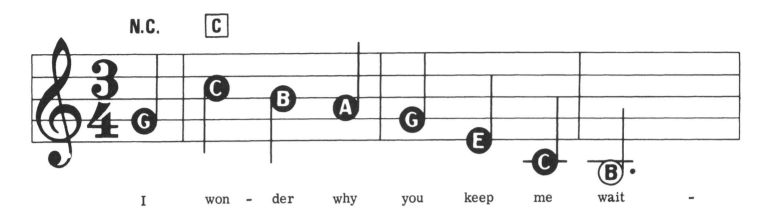

I won - der why you keep me wait -

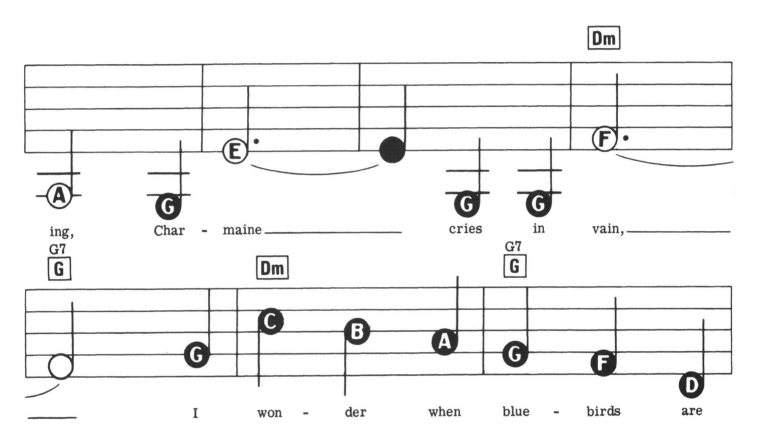

ing, Char - maine _____ cries in vain, _____

I won - der when blue - birds are

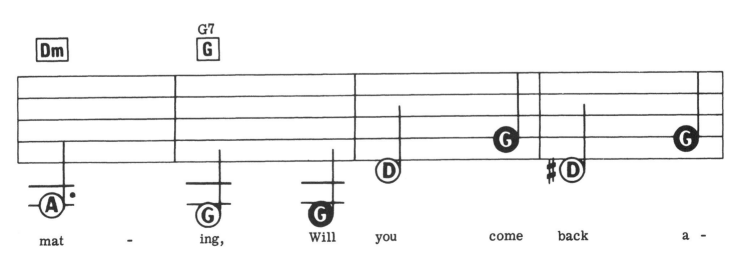

mat - ing, Will you come back a -

Copyright © 1927 BMG Gold Songs and Rapee Music Corp.
Copyright Renewed
All Rights for BMG Gold Songs Administered by BMG Rights Management (US) LLC
All Rights Reserved   Used by Permission

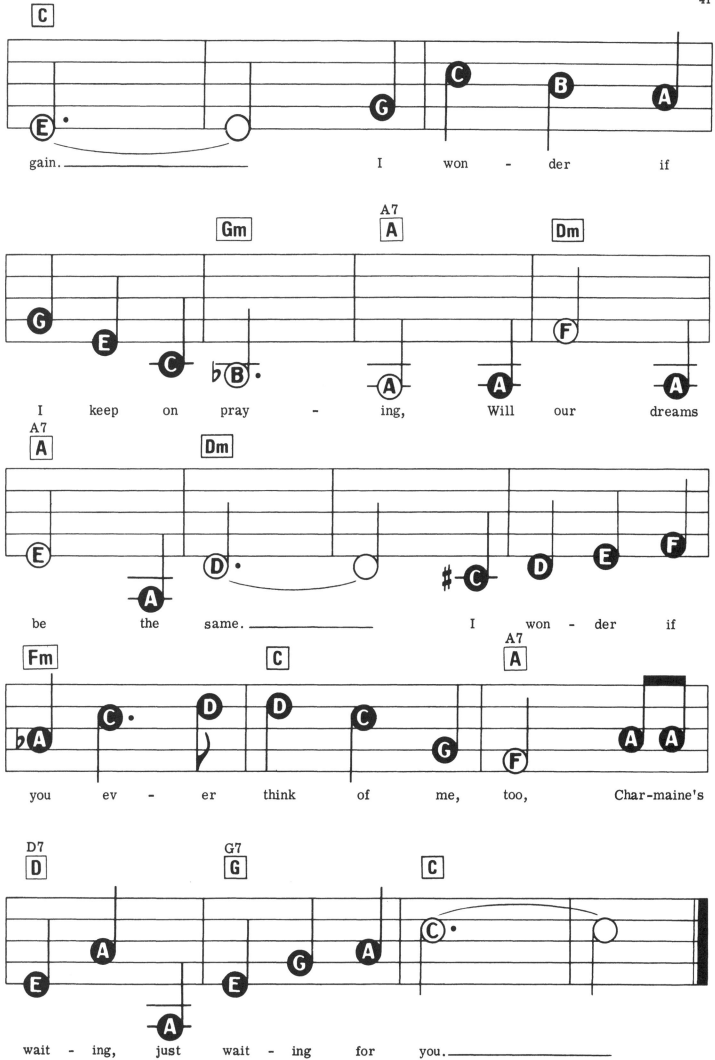

Crazy Rhythm
from THE COTTON CLUB

Registration 7
Rhythm: Swing or Jazz

Words by Irving Caesar
Music by Joseph Meyer and Roger Wolfe Kahn

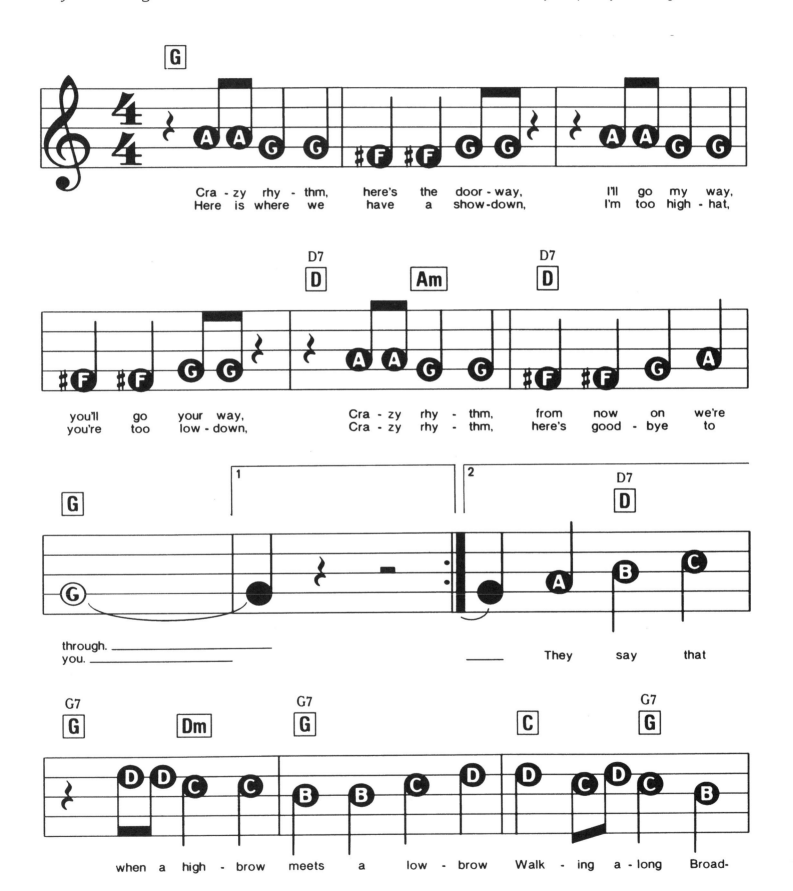

Copyright © 1928 (Renewed) Larry Spier Music LLC, Irving Caesar Music and WB Music Corp.
All Rights on behalf of Irving Caesar Music Administered by WB Music Corp.
International Copyright Secured   All Rights Reserved

43

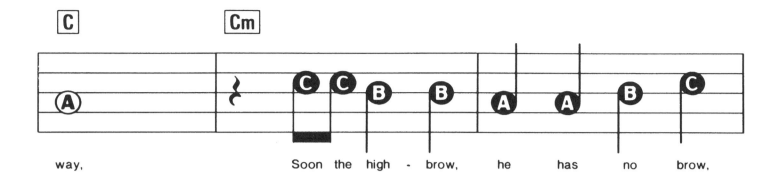

way, Soon the high - brow, he has no brow,

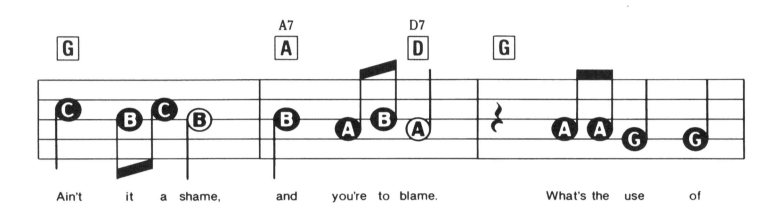

Ain't it a shame, and you're to blame. What's the use of

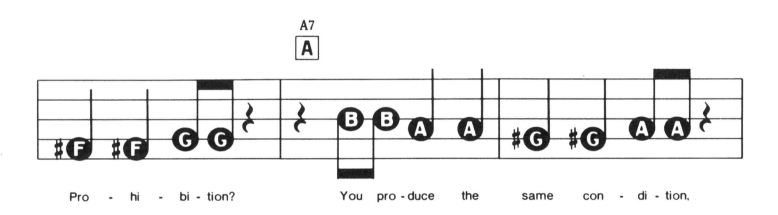

Pro - hi - bi - tion? You pro - duce the same con - di - tion,

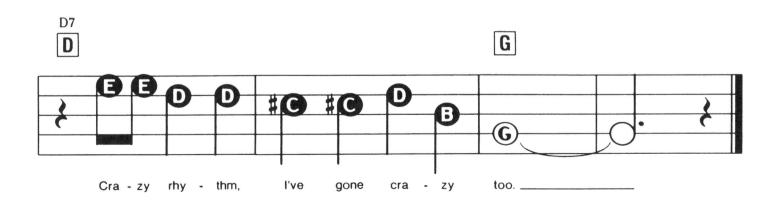

Cra - zy rhy - thm, I've gone cra - zy too. _____

'Deed I Do

Registration 3
Rhythm: Ballad

Words and Music by Walter Hirsch
and Fred Rose

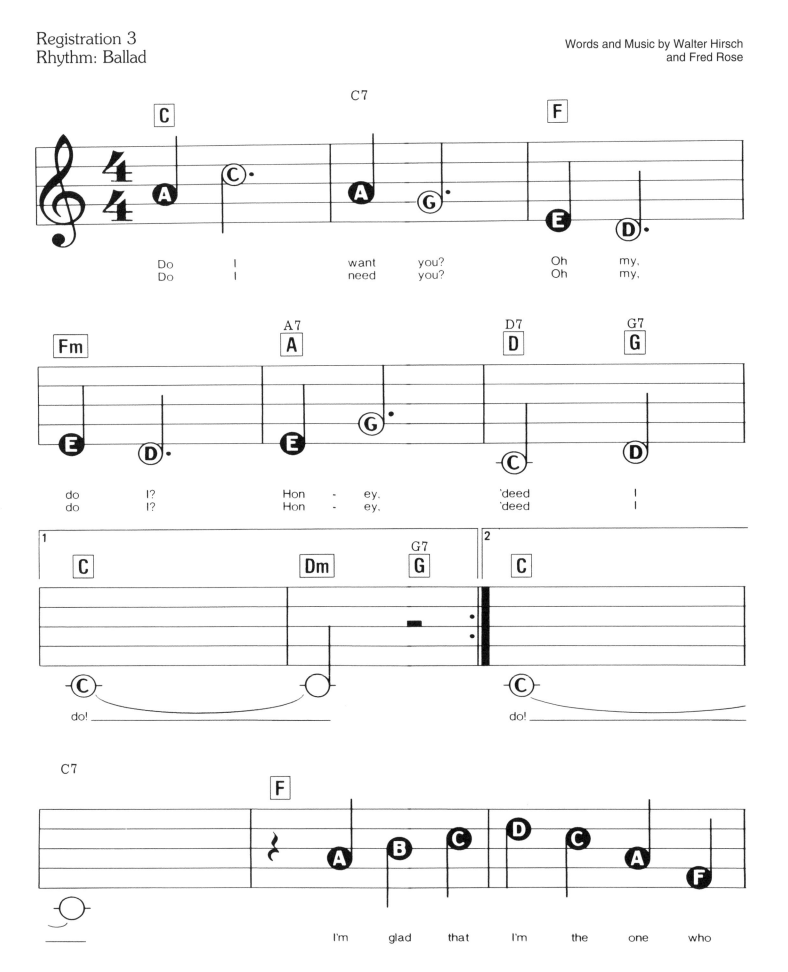

Copyright © 1926 by Range Road Music Inc. and Quartet Music
Copyright Renewed
All Rights for Quartet Music Administered by BMG Rights Management (US) LLC
International Copyright Secured   All Rights Reserved
Used by Permission

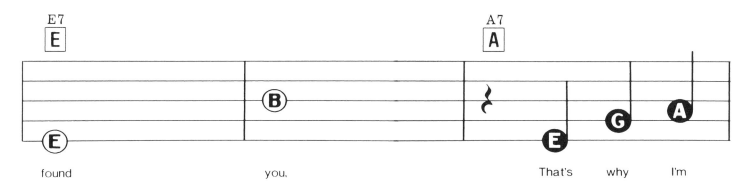

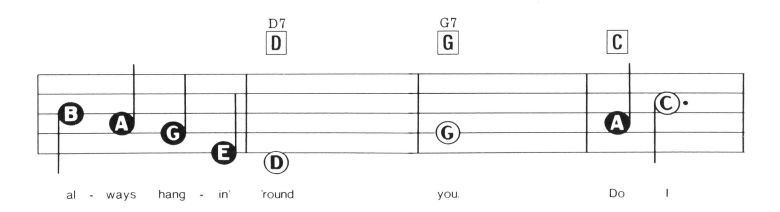

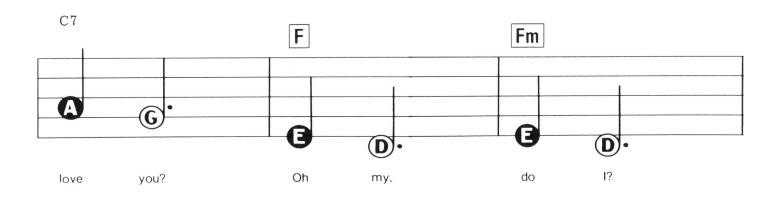

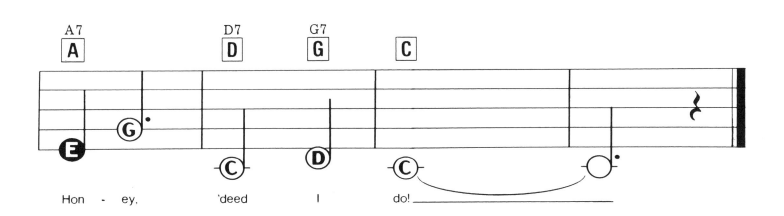

Everybody Loves My Baby
(But My Baby Don't Love Nobody but Me)

Registration 5
Rhythm: Swing or Fox Trot

Words and Music by Jack Palmer
and Spencer Williams

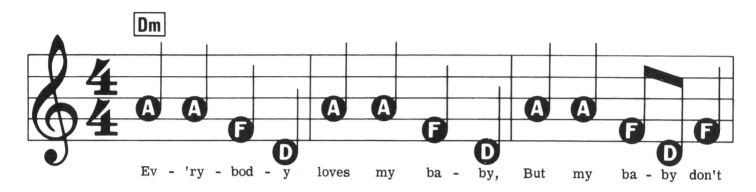

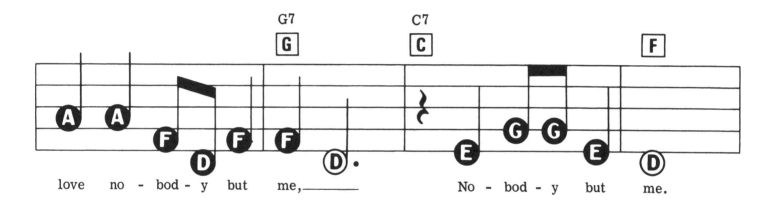

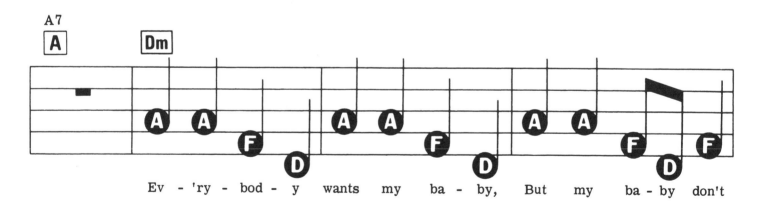

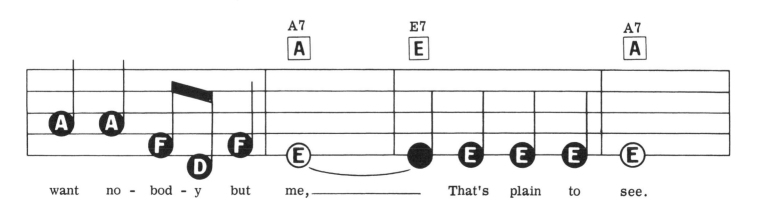

Copyright © 1924 UNIVERSAL MUSIC CORP.
Copyright Renewed
All Rights for the Jack Palmer share in Canada Administered by REDWOOD MUSIC LTD.
All Rights Reserved   Used by Permission

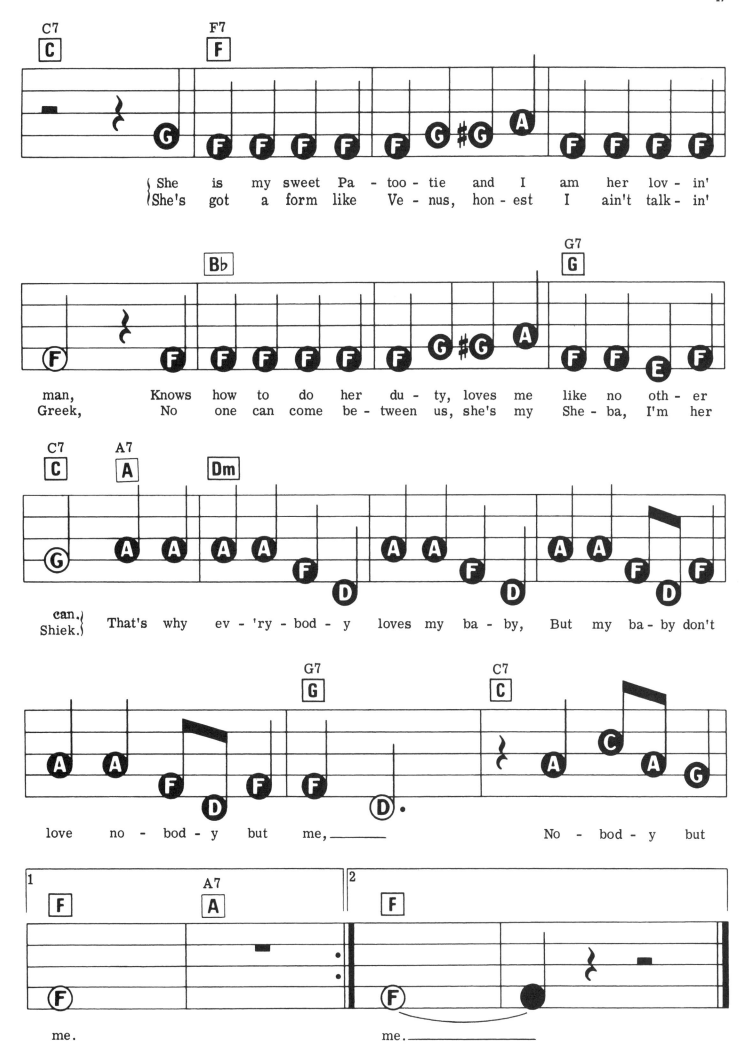

Fascinating Rhythm
from RHAPSODY IN BLUE
from the Broadway Musical LADY, BE GOOD

Registration 7
Rhythm: Fox Trot or Swing

Music and Lyrics by George Gershwin
and Ira Gershwin

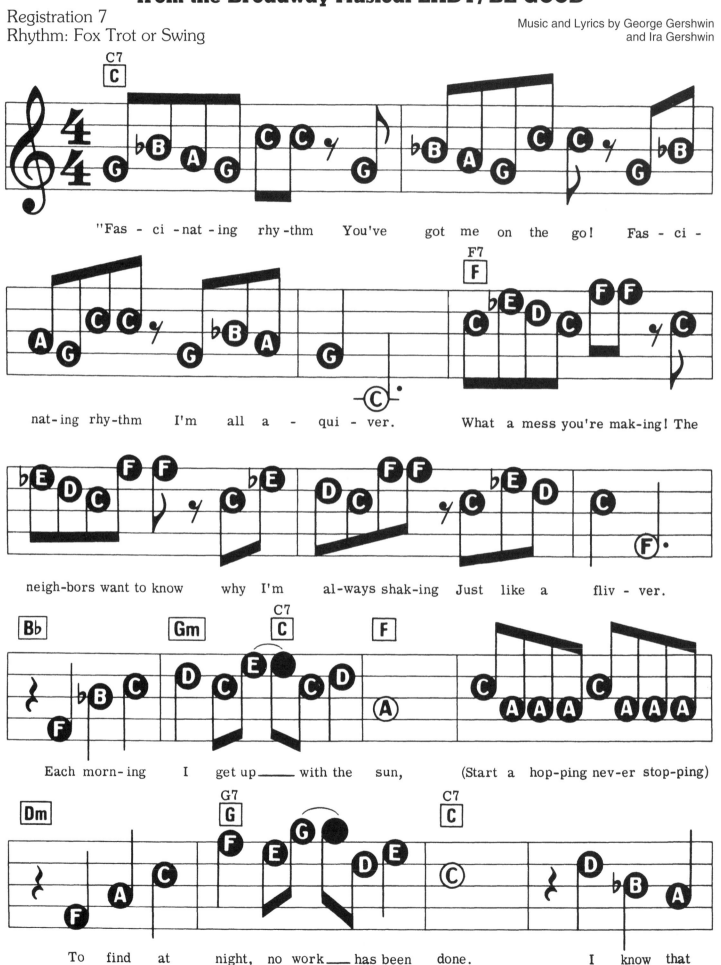

"Fas - ci -nat -ing rhy -thm You've got me on the go! Fas - ci -

nat-ing rhy-thm I'm all a - qui - ver. What a mess you're mak-ing! The

neigh-bors want to know why I'm al-ways shak-ing Just like a fliv - ver.

Each morn-ing I get up___ with the sun, (Start a hop-ping nev-er stop-ping)

To find at night, no work___has been done. I know that

© 1924 (Renewed) WB MUSIC CORP.
All Rights Reserved Used by Permission

49

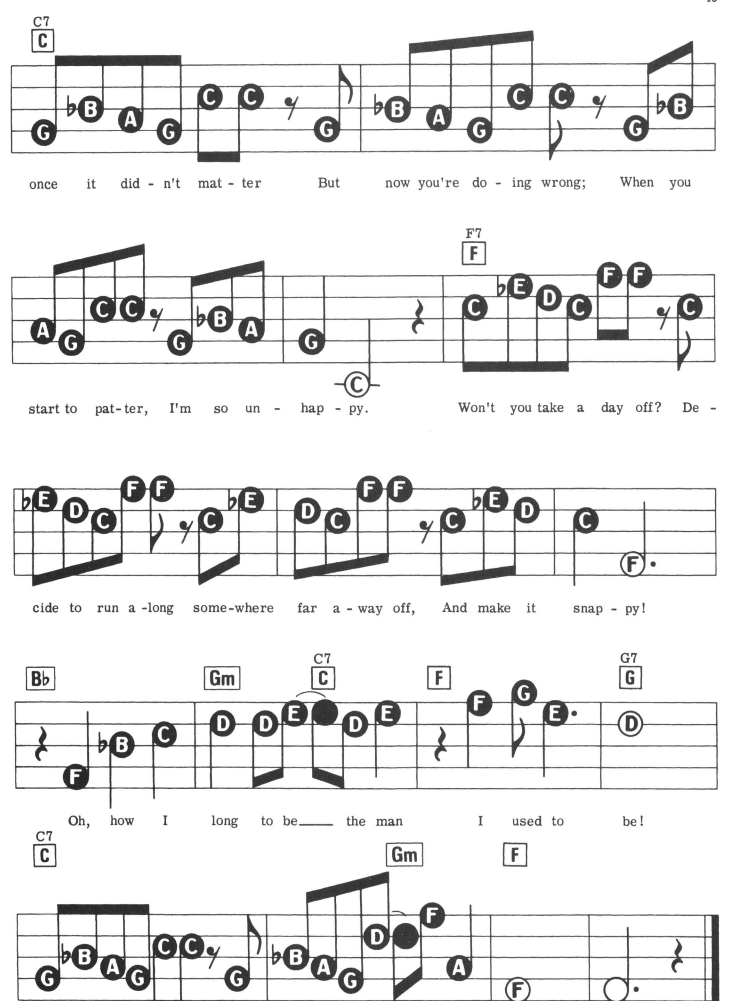

Five Foot Two, Eyes of Blue
(Has Anybody Seen My Girl?)

Registration 9
Rhythm: Fox Trot

Words by Joe Young and Sam Lewis
Music by Ray Henderson

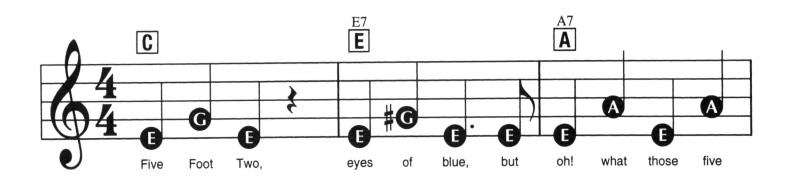

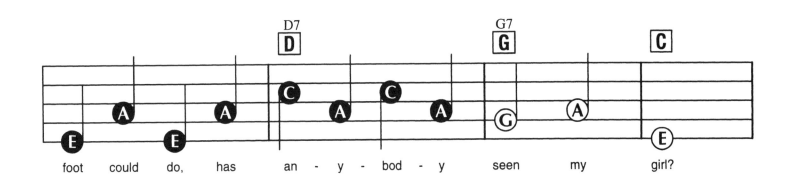

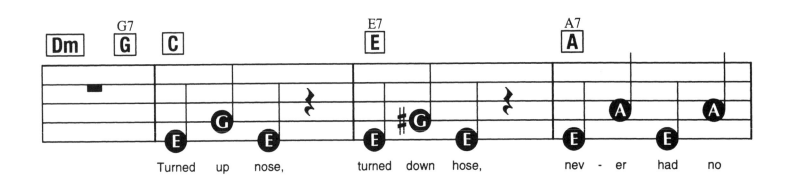

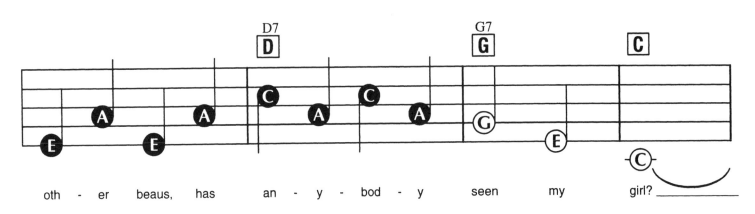

© 1925 LEO FEIST, INC.
© Renewed 1953 WAROCK CORP., EMI FEIST CATALOG INC. and RAY HENDERSON MUSIC CO. in the United States
All Rights for EMI FEIST CATALOG INC. Administered by EMI FEIST CATALOG INC. (Publishing) and ALFRED MUSIC (Print)
All Rights for the Sam Lewis and Ray Henderson shares in the British Reversionary Territories Administered by REDWOOD MUSIC LTD.
All Rights Reserved

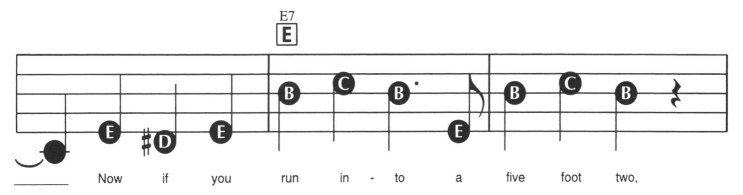

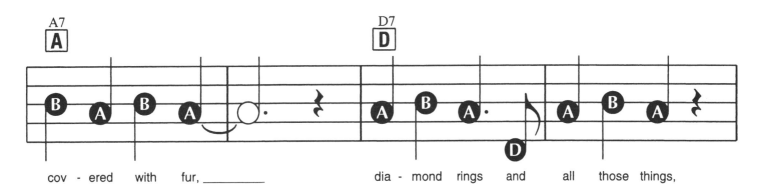

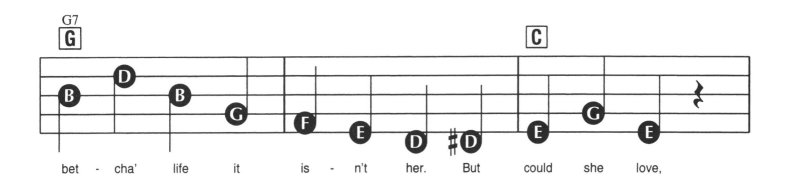

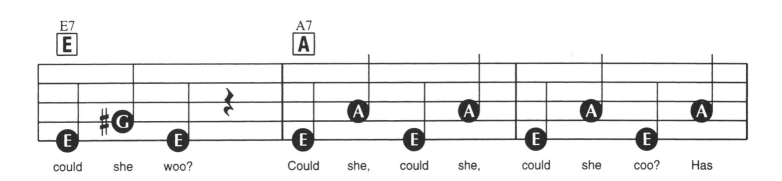

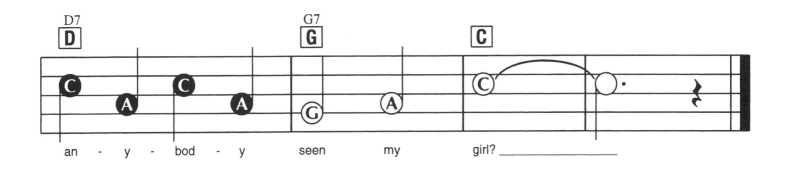

51

Honeysuckle Rose
from AIN'T MISBEHAVIN'

Registration 4
Rhythm: Fox Trot or Swing

Words by Andy Razaf
Music by Thomas "Fats" Waller

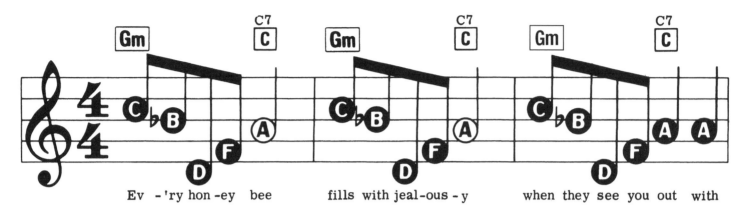

Ev - 'ry hon-ey bee   fills with jeal-ous - y   when they see you out with

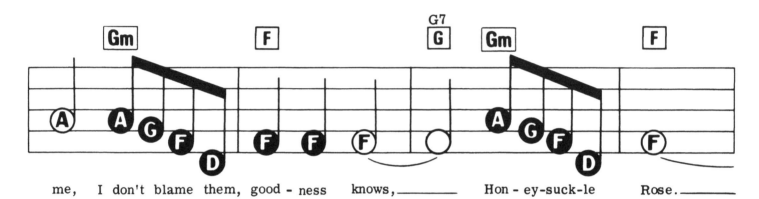

me, I don't blame them, good - ness   knows,_____   Hon - ey-suck-le   Rose._____

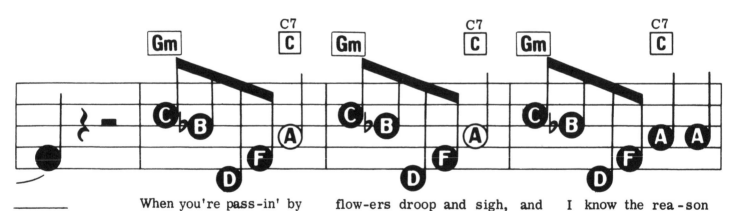

When you're pass-in' by   flow-ers droop and sigh, and   I know the rea-son

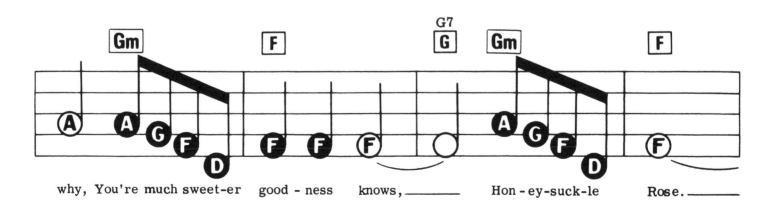

why, You're much sweet-er good - ness   knows,_____   Hon - ey-suck-le   Rose._____

Copyright © 1929 by Chappell & Co., Inc. and Razaf Music
Copyright Renewed
All Rights for Razaf Music Administered by BMG Rights Management (US) LLC
International Copyright Secured All Rights Reserved

53

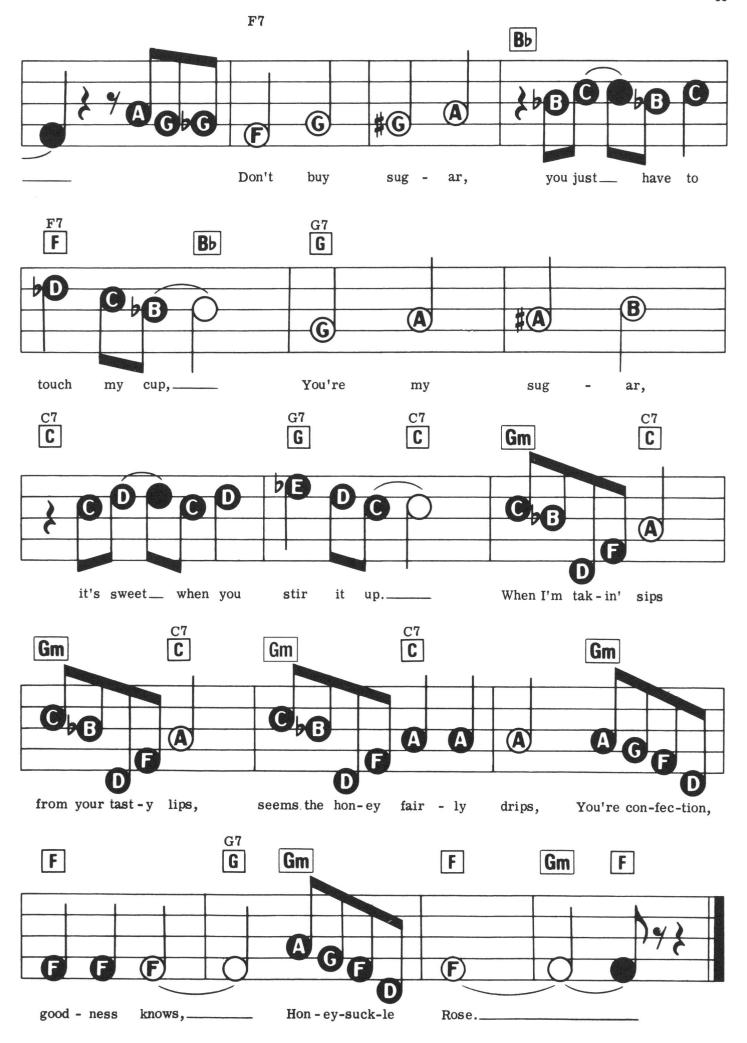

How Long Has This Been Going On?

from ROSALIE

Registration 2
Rhythm: Swing or Jazz

Music and Lyrics by George Gershwin
and Ira Gershwin

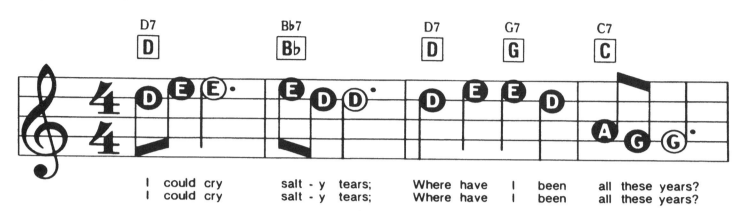

I could cry salt-y tears; Where have I been all these years?
I could cry salt-y tears; Where have I been all these years?

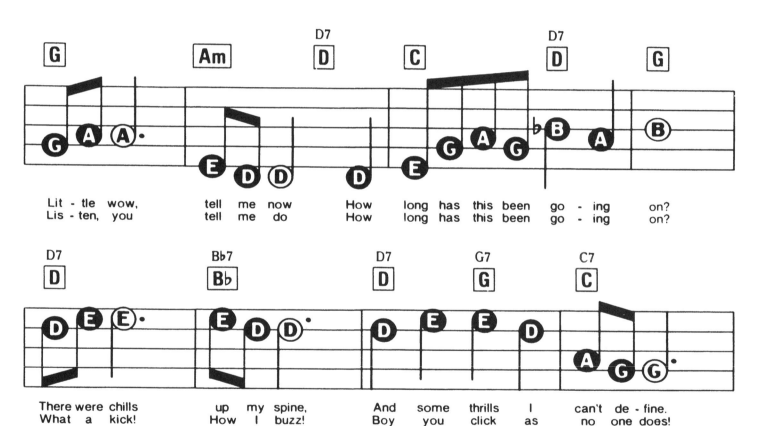

Lit-tle wow, tell me now How long has this been go-ing on?
Lis-ten, you tell me do How long has this been go-ing on?

There were chills up my spine, And some thrills I can't de-fine.
What a kick! How I buzz! Boy you click as no one does!

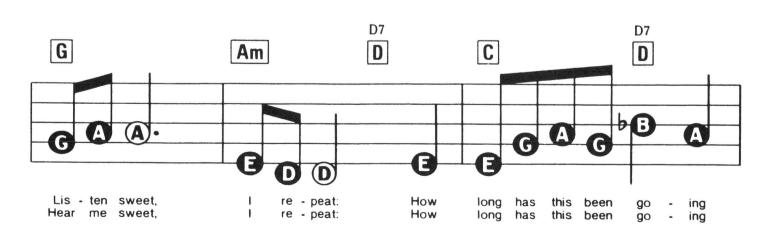

Lis-ten sweet, I re-peat: How long has this been go-ing
Hear me sweet, I re-peat: How long has this been go-ing

© 1927 (Renewed) WB MUSIC CORP.
All Rights Reserved Used by Permission

55

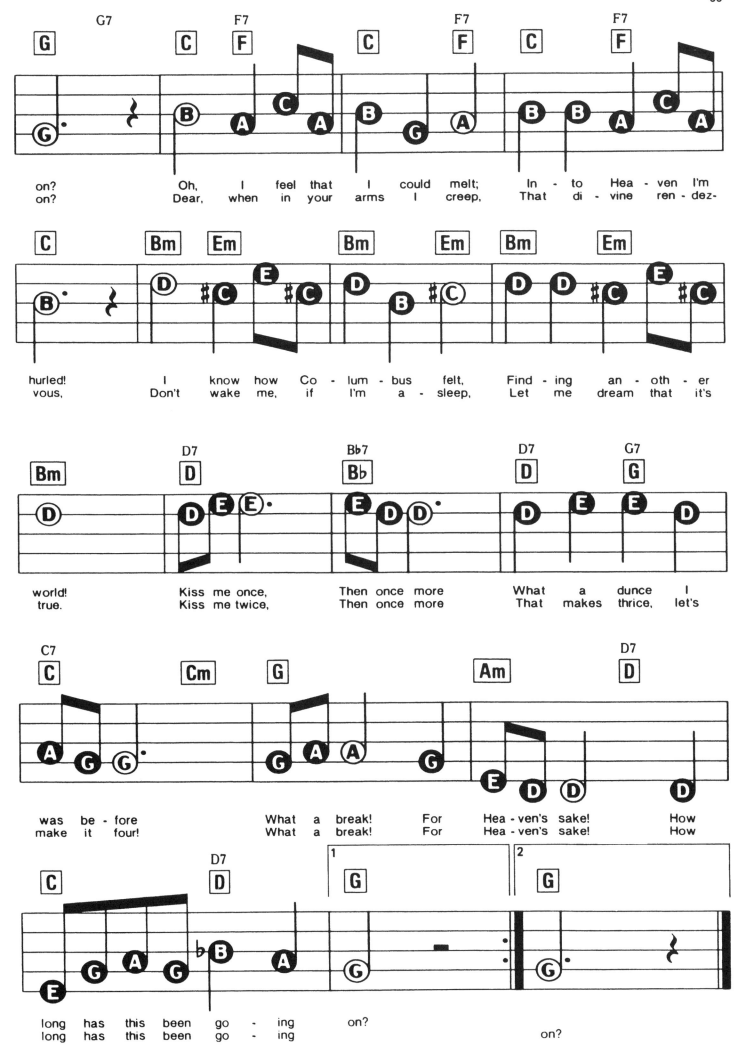

I Can't Believe That You're in Love with Me

Registration 9
Rhythm: Swing

Words and Music by Jimmy McHugh
and Clarence Gaskill

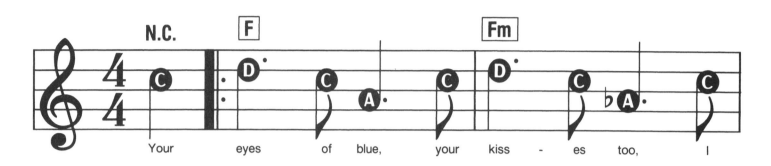

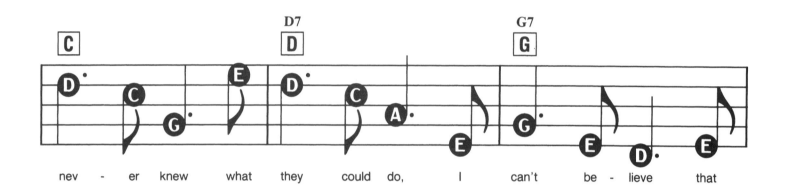

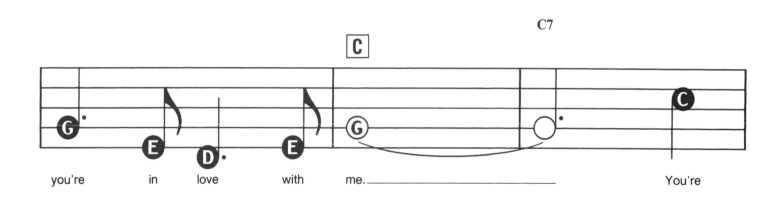

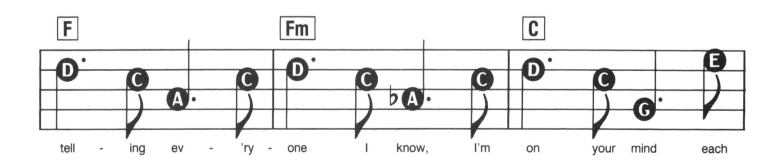

Copyright © 1926 EMI Mills Music Inc. and Cotton Club Publishing
Copyright Renewed
All Rights on behalf of Cotton Club Publishing Administered by Sony/ATV Music Publishing LLC, 424 Church Street, Suite 1200, Nashville, TN 37219
International Copyright Secured   All Rights Reserved

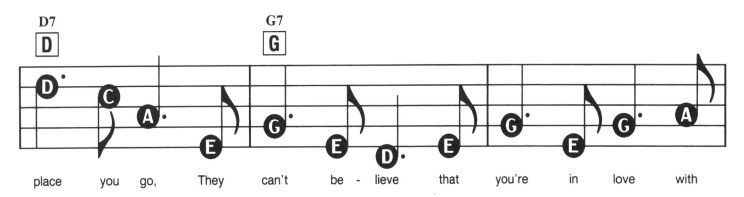

place you go, They can't be - lieve that you're in love with

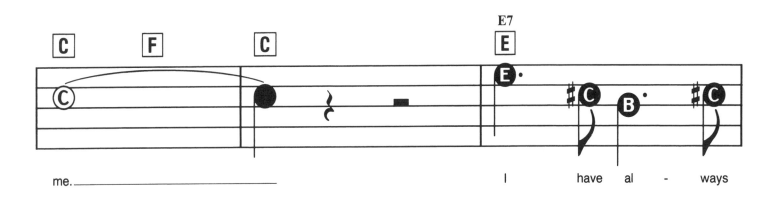

me. I have al - ways

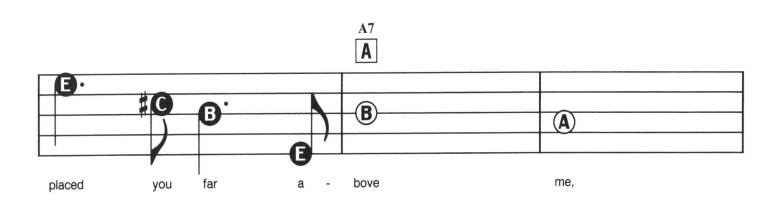

placed you far a - bove me,

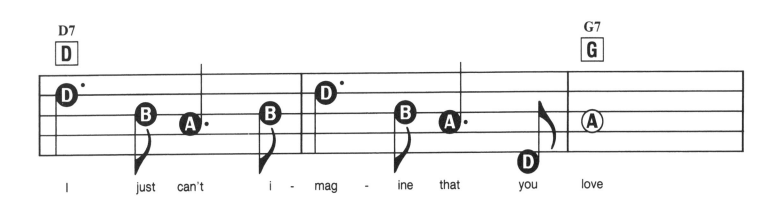

I just can't i - mag - ine that you love

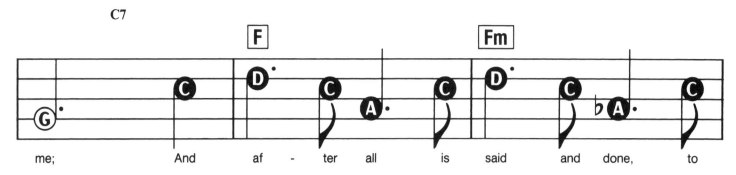

me; And af - ter all is said and done, to

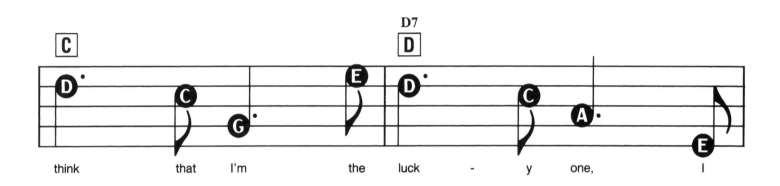

think that I'm the luck - y one, I

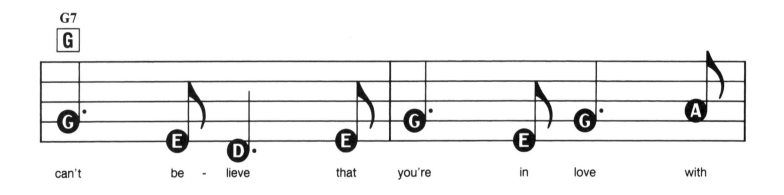

can't be - lieve that you're in love with

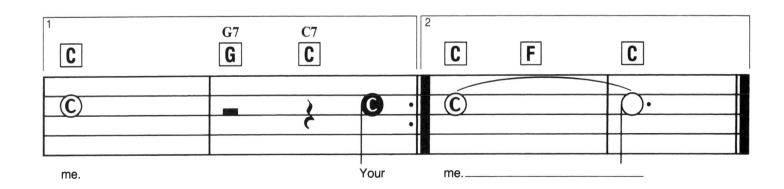

me. Your me.

It Had to Be You

Registration 9
Rhythm: Swing

Words by Gus Kahn
Music by Isham Jones

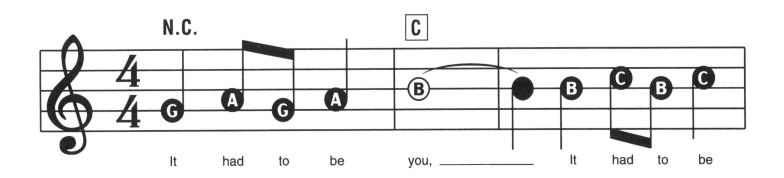

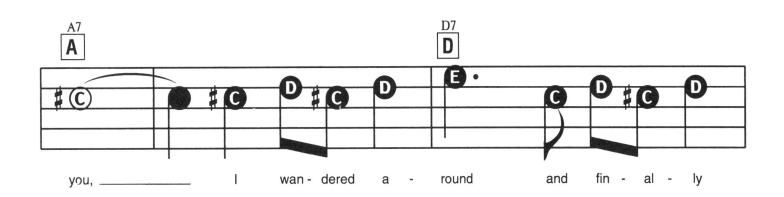

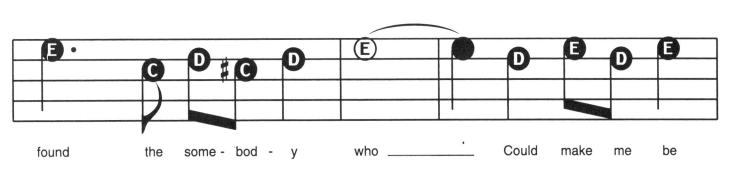

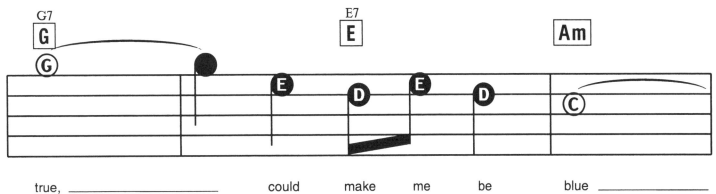

© 1924 (Renewed) GILBERT KEYES MUSIC and THE BANTAM MUSIC PUBLISHING CO.
All Rights Administered by WB MUSIC CORP.
All Rights Reserved   Used by Permission

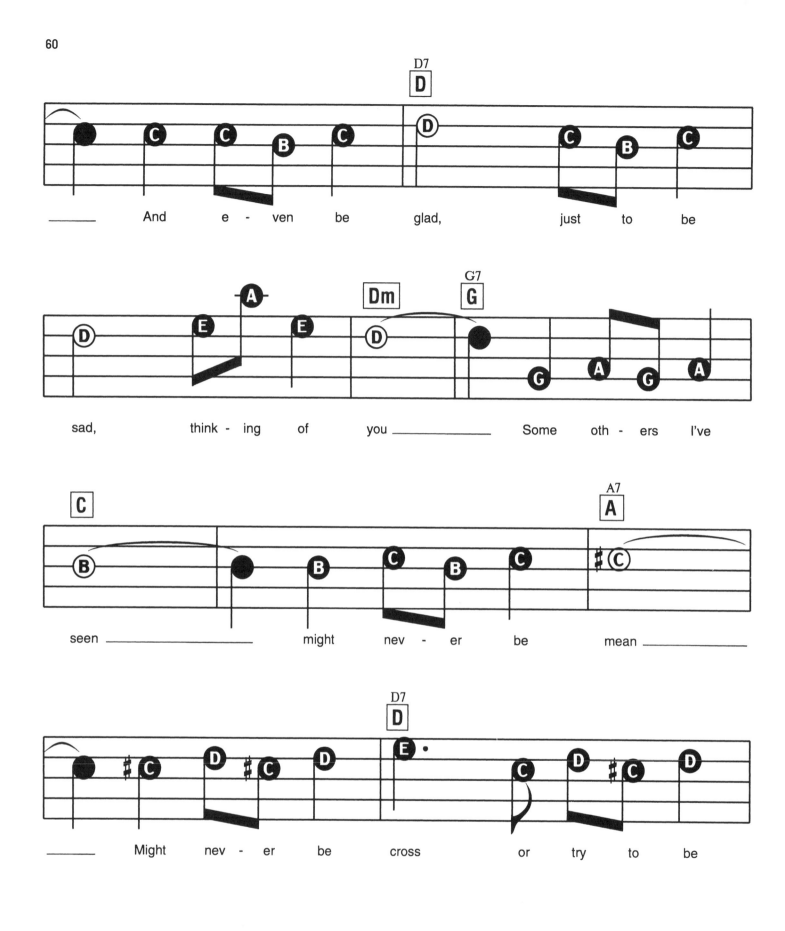

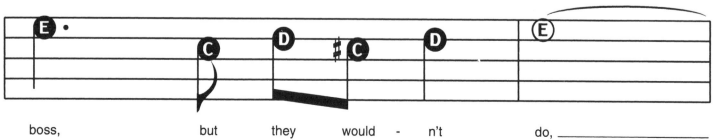

61

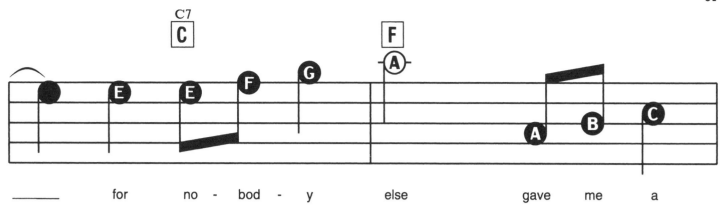

_____ for no - bod - y else gave me a

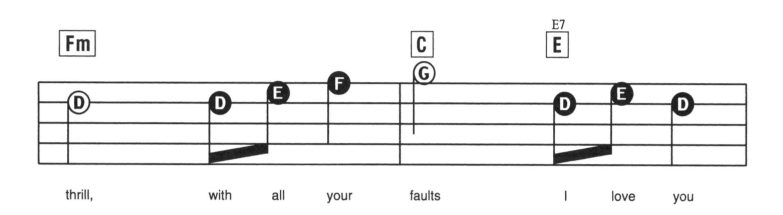

thrill, with all your faults I love you

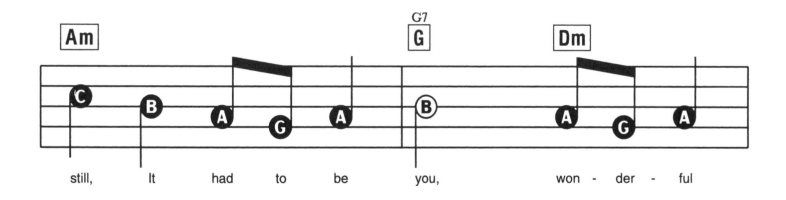

still, It had to be you, won - der - ful

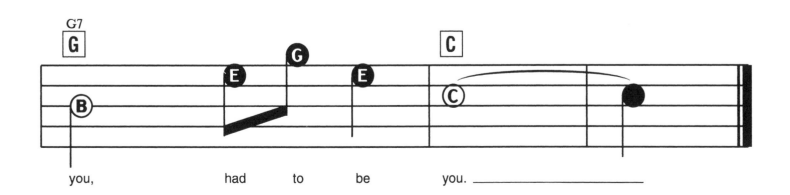

you, had to be you. _____

I Can't Give You Anything but Love
from BLACKBIRDS OF 1928

Registration 5
Rhythm: Swing or Jazz

Words and Music by Jimmy McHugh
and Dorothy Fields

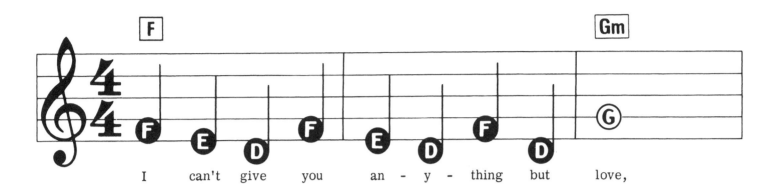

I can't give you an - y - thing but love,

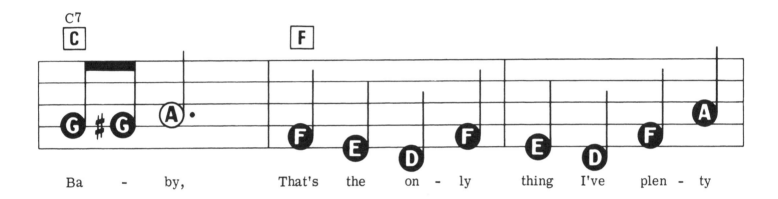

Ba - by, That's the on - ly thing I've plen - ty

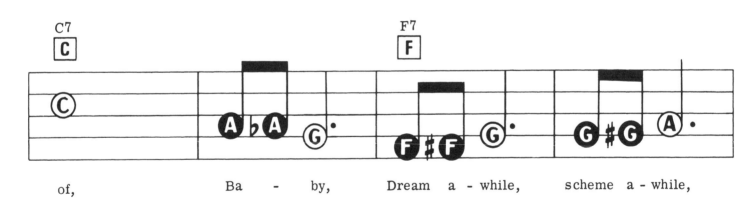

of, Ba - by, Dream a - while, scheme a - while,

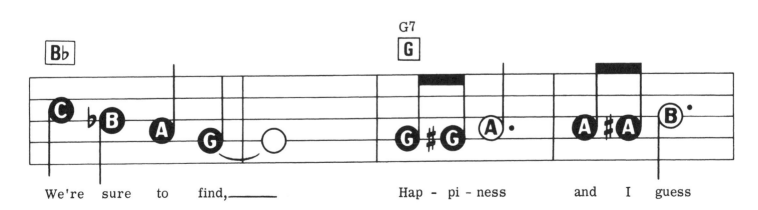

We're sure to find,_____ Hap - pi - ness and I guess

© 1928 (Renewed 1956) COTTON CLUB PUBLISHING and ALDI MUSIC
All Rights for COTTON CLUB PUBLISHING Controlled and Administered by EMI APRIL MUSIC INC.
Print Rights for ALDI MUSIC in the U.S. Controlled and Administered by HAPPY ASPEN MUSIC LLC c/o SHAPIRO, BERNSTEIN & CO., INC.
All Rights Reserved   International Copyright Secured   Used by Permission

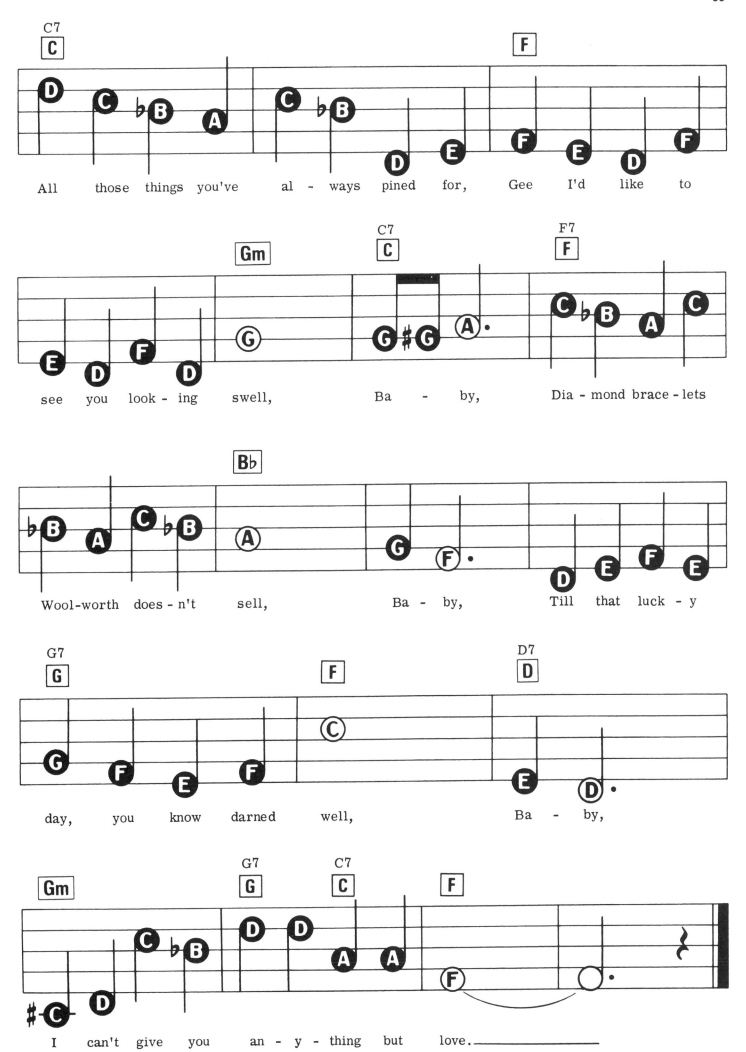

I Cried for You

Registration 2
Rhythm: Swing or Jazz

Words and Music by Arthur Freed,
Gus Arnheim and Abe Lyman

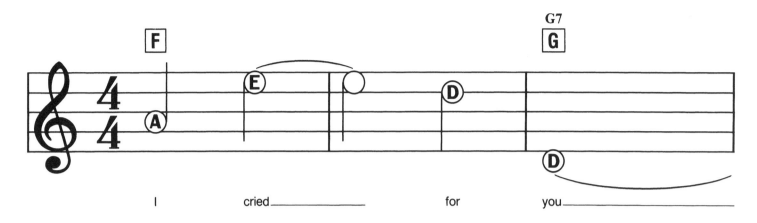

I cried_____ for you_____

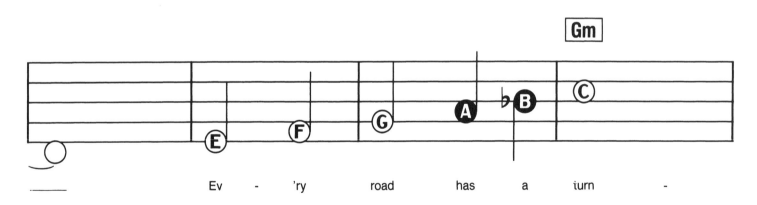

_____ Now it's your turn to cry o - ver me._____

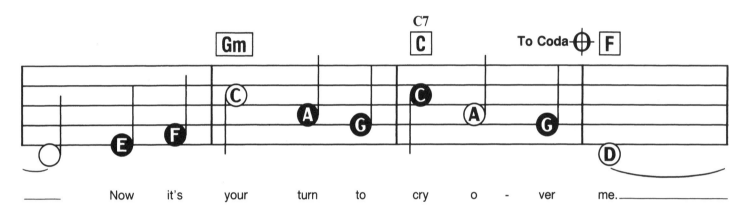

_____ Ev - 'ry road has a turn -

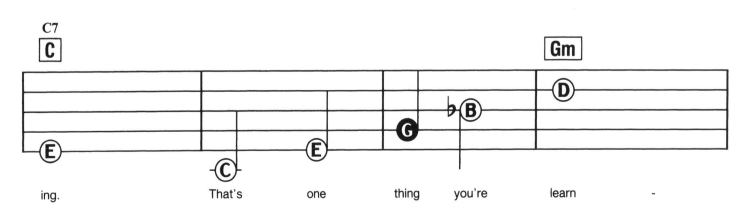

ing. That's one thing you're learn -

© 1923 (Renewed) EMI MILLER CATALOG INC.
All Rights Administered by EMI MILLER CATALOG INC. (Publishing) and ALFRED MUSIC (Print)
All Rights Reserved   Used by Permission

65

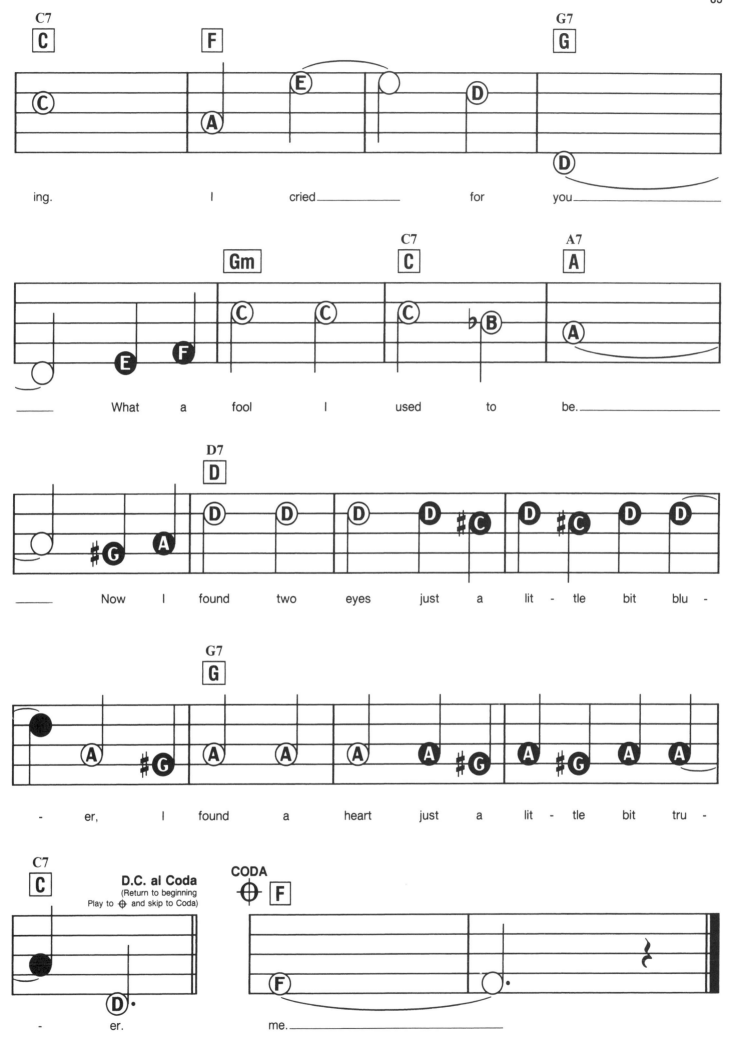

I Wanna Be Loved by You

from GOOD BOY

Lyric by Bert Kalmar
Music by Herbert Stothart and Harry Ruby

Registration 4
Rhythm: Fox Trot or Swing

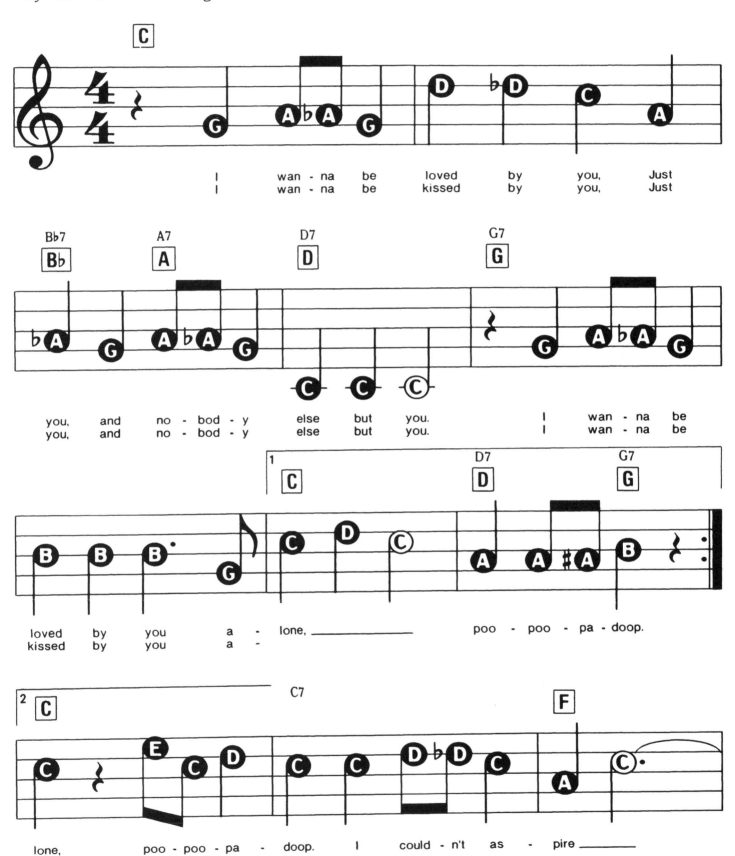

© 1928 (Renewed) WARNER BROS. INC.
Rights for the Extended Renewal Term in the United States Controlled by EDWIN H. MORRIS & COMPANY,
A Division of MPL Music Publishing, Inc., WARNER BROS. INC., BMG FIREFLY and HARRY RUBY MUSIC
All Rights for BMG FIREFLY Administered by BMG RIGHTS MANAGEMENT (US) LLC
All Rights for HARRY RUBY MUSIC in the United States Administered by THE SONGWRITERS GUILD OF AMERICA
All Rights for HARRY RUBY MUSIC in Canada and the British Reversionary Territories Administered by MEMORY LANE MUSIC GROUP LIMITED
All Rights Reserved   Used by Permission

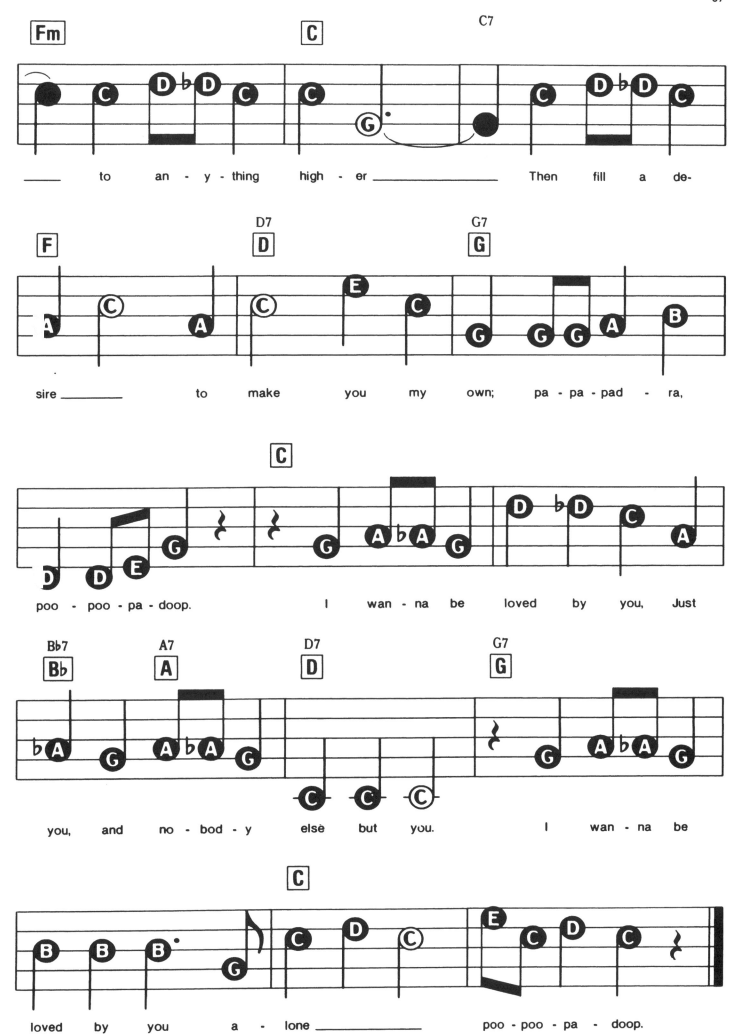

I Want to Be Happy

Registration 1
Rhythm: Fox Trot or Ballad

Words by Irving Caesar
Music by Vincent Youmans

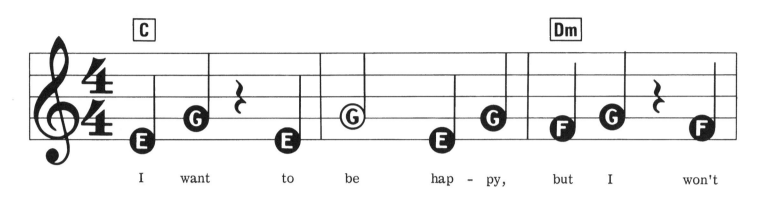

I want to be hap - py, but I won't

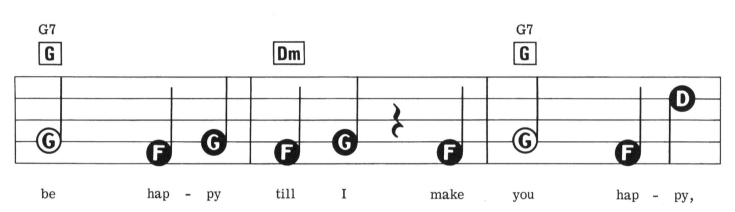

be hap - py till I make you hap - py,

too; _____ Life's real - ly worth liv - ing,

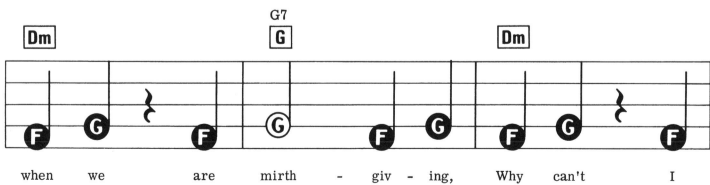

when we are mirth - giv - ing, Why can't I

© 1924 (Renewed) WB MUSIC CORP. and IRVING CAESAR MUSIC CORP.
All Rights Administered by WB MUSIC CORP.
All Rights Reserved   Used by Permission

69

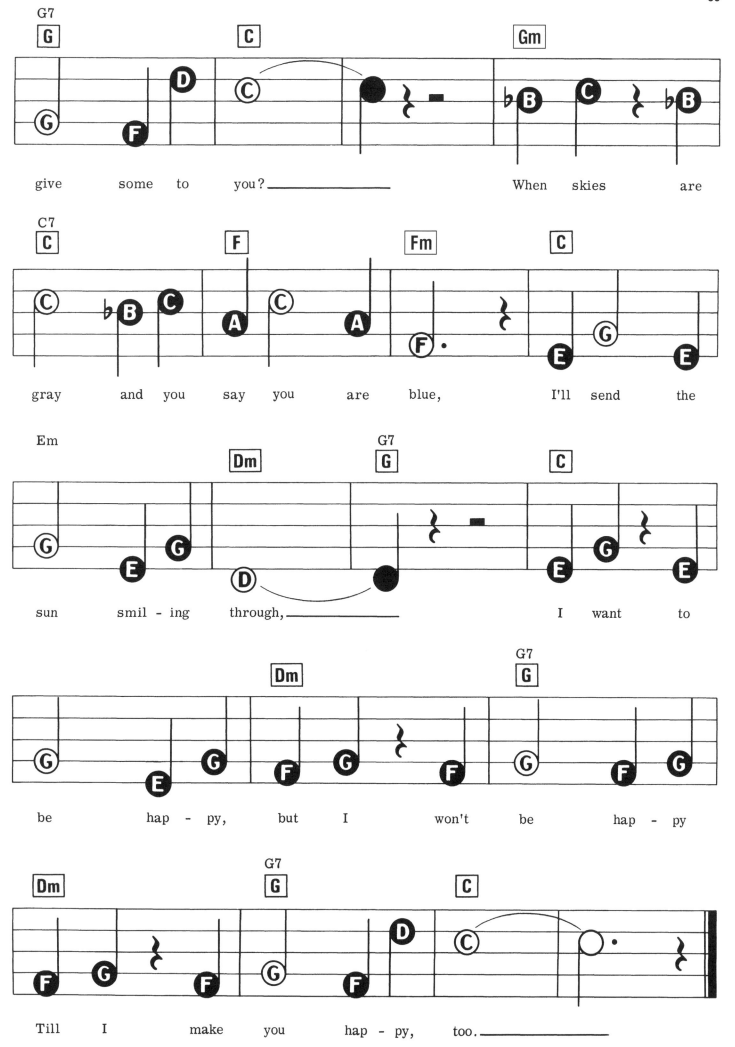

I'll Get By
(As Long as I Have You)

Registration 2
Rhythm: Fox Trot or Swing

Lyric by Roy Turk
Music by Fred E. Ahlert

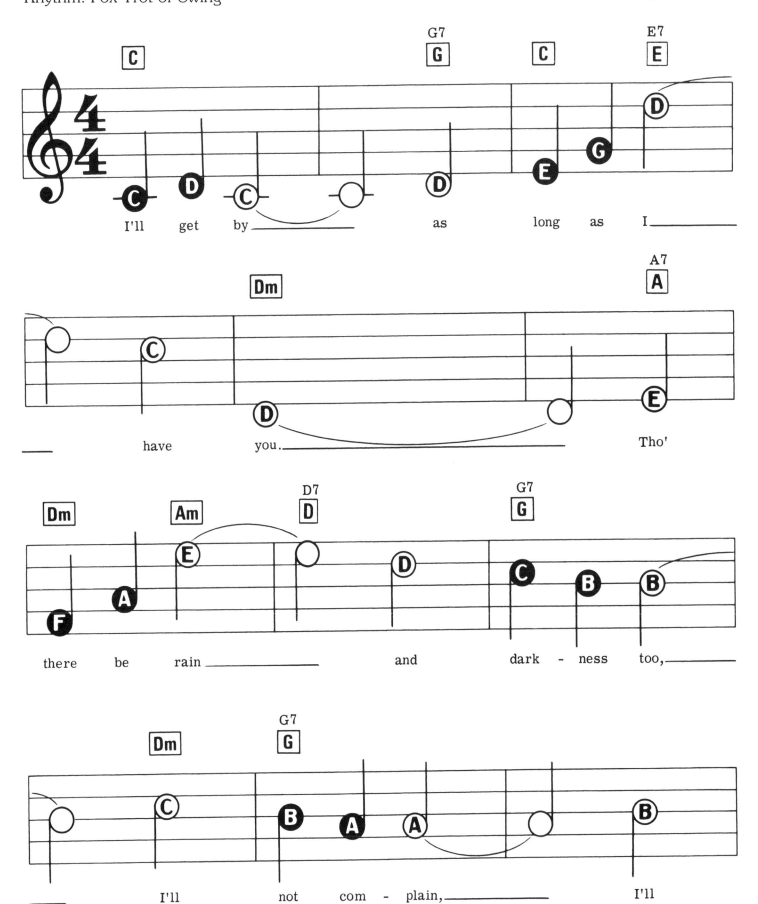

TRO - © Copyright 1928 (Renewed) Cromwell Music, Inc., New York, NY, Pencil Mark Music, Inc., Bronxville, NY, Azure Pearl Music, Beeping Good Music and David Ahlert Music
All Rights for Azure Pearl Music, Beeping Good Music and David Ahlert Music Administered by Bluewater Music Services Corp.
International Copyright Secured
All Rights Reserved Including Public Performance For Profit
Used by Permission

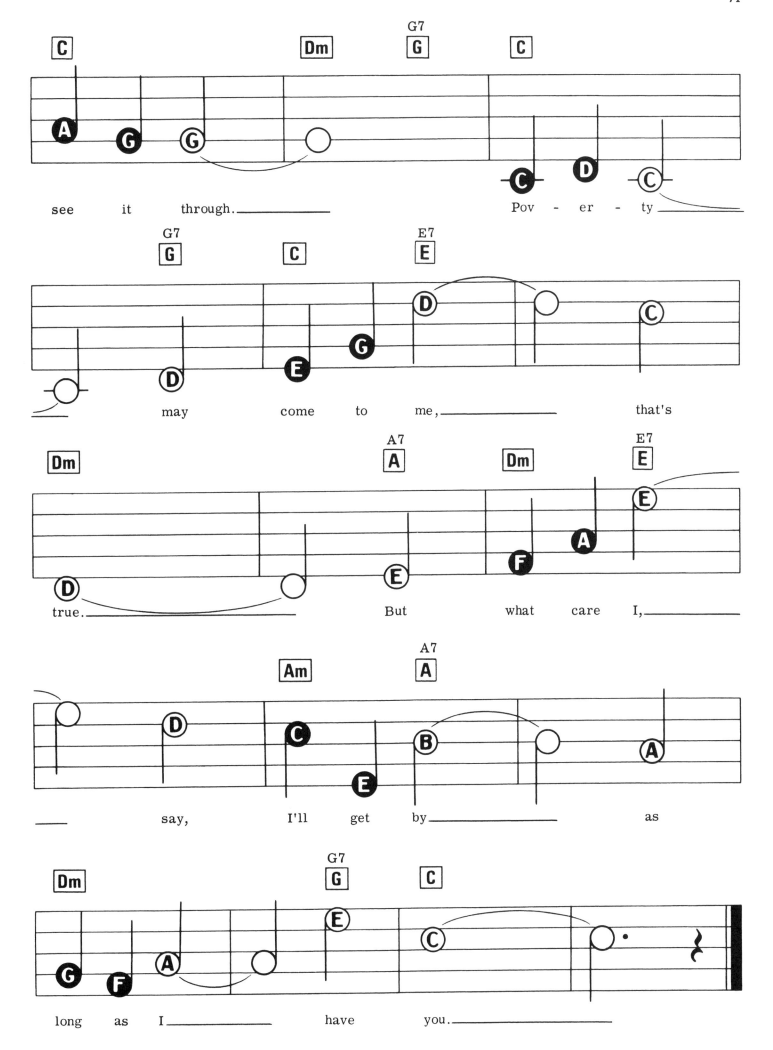

71

I'll See You in My Dreams

Registration 2
Rhythm: Swing

Words by Gus Kahn
Music by Isham Jones

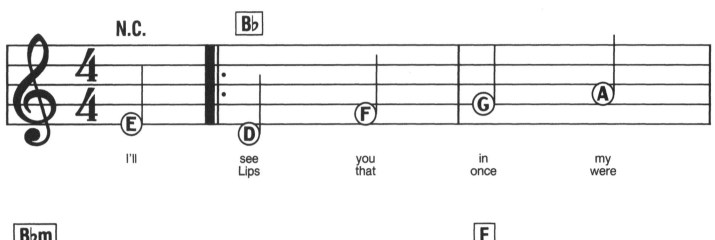

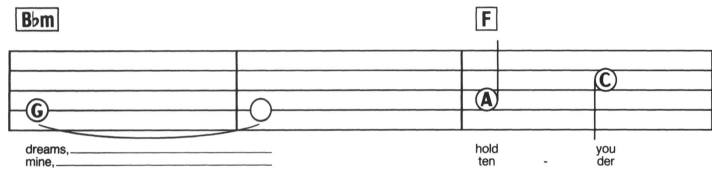

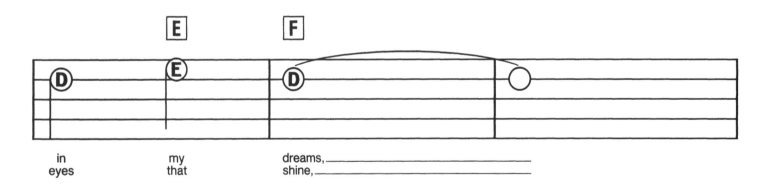

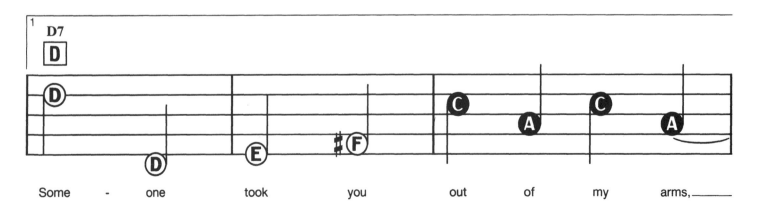

© 1924 (Renewed) GILBERT KEYES MUSIC COMPANY and BANTAM MUSIC PUBLISHING CO.
All Rights Administered by WB MUSIC CORP.
All Rights Reserved   Used by Permission

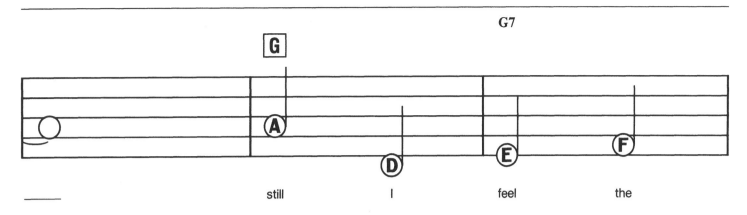

still I feel the

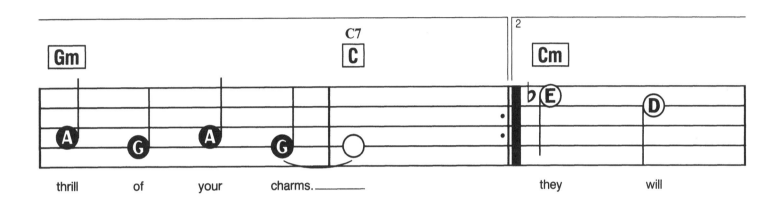

thrill of your charms._____ they will

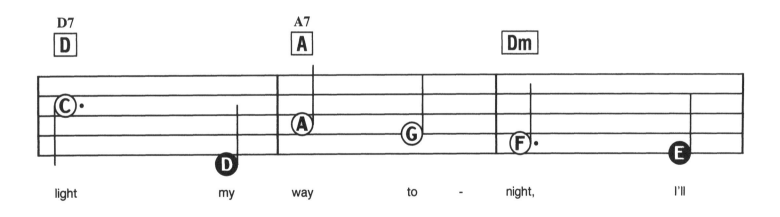

light my way to - night, I'll

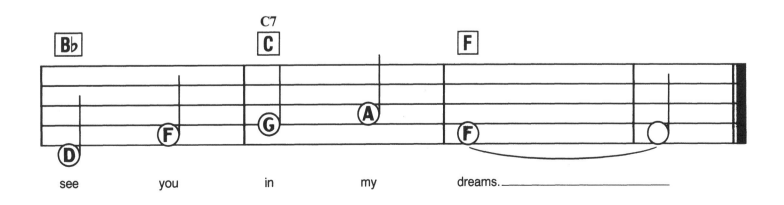

see you in my dreams._____

I'm Sitting on Top of the World
from THE JOLSON STORY

Registration 3
Rhythm: Fox Trot

Words by Sam M. Lewis and Joe Young
Music by Ray Henderson

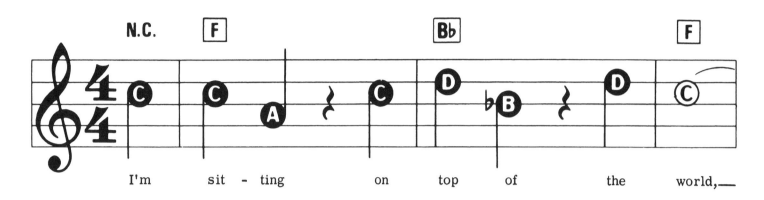

I'm sit - ting on top of the world,—

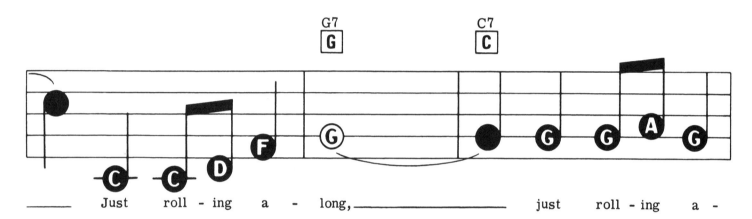

_____ Just roll - ing a - long,_____ just roll - ing a -

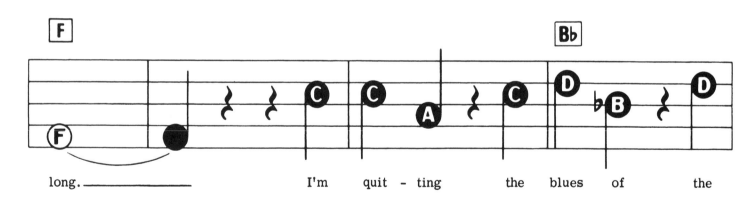

long._____ I'm quit - ting the blues of the

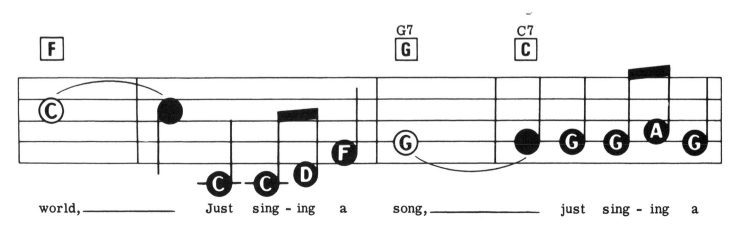

world,_____ Just sing - ing a song,_____ just sing - ing a

© 1925 LEO FEIST, INC.
© Renewed 1953 WAROCK CORP., LEO FEIST, INC. and HENDERSON MUSIC CO.
All Rights Reserved

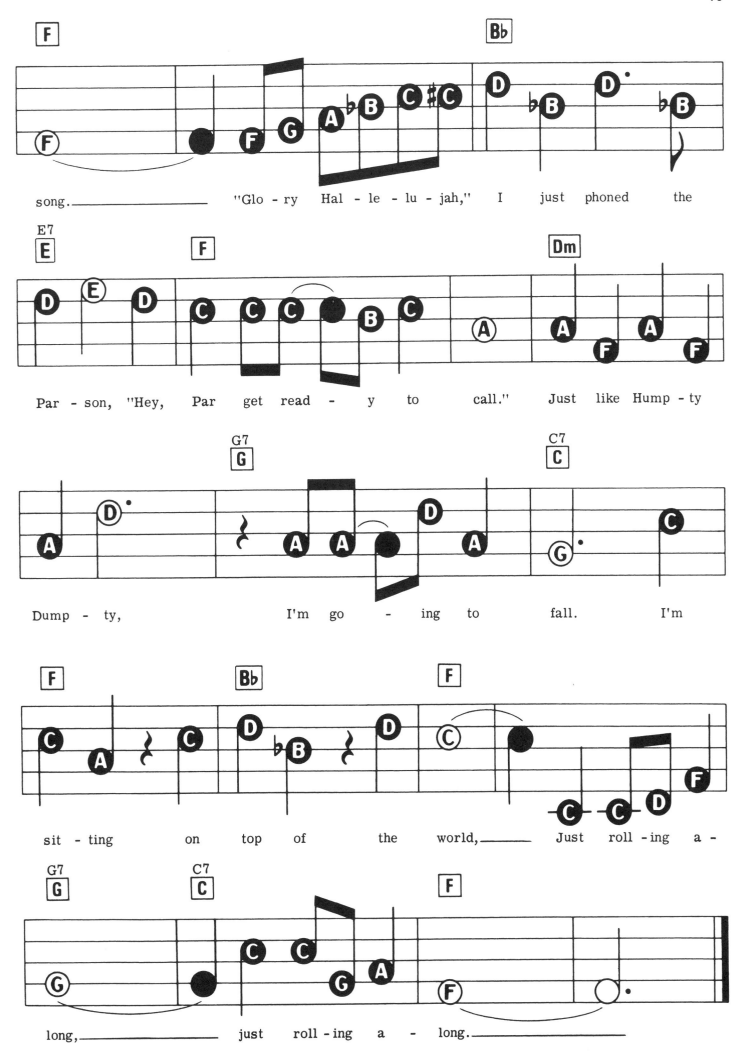

If I Could be with You
(One Hour Tonight)

Registration 2
Rhythm: Swing

Words and Music by Henry Creamer
and Jimmy Johnson

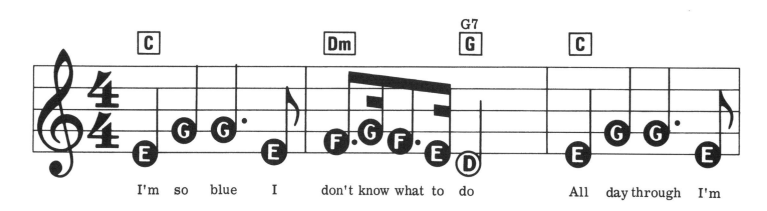

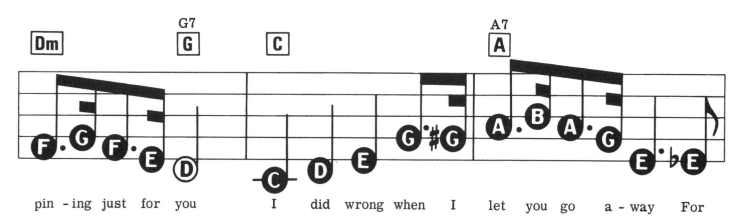

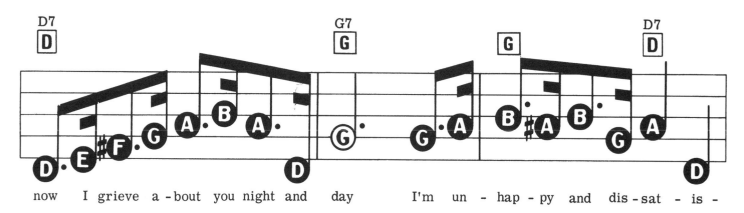

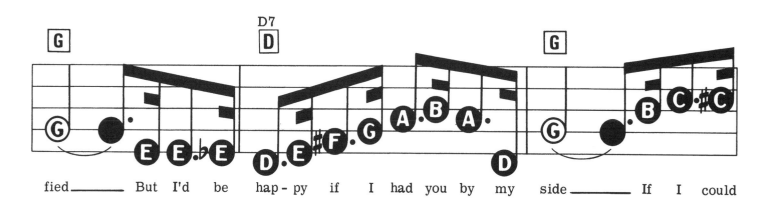

© 1926 (Renewed) WB MUSIC CORP.
All Rights Reserved   Used by Permission

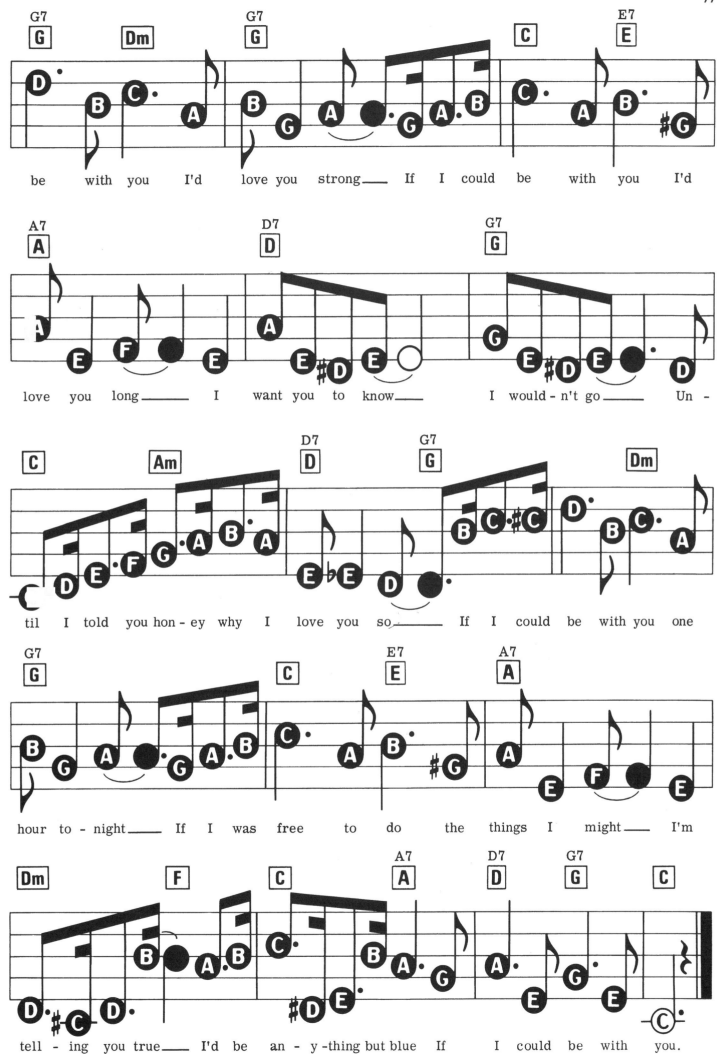

If I Had You

Registration 8
Rhythm: Fox Trot or Swing

Words and Music by Ted Shapiro,
Jimmy Campbell and Reg Connelly

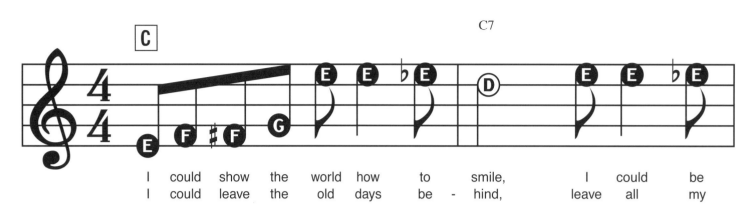

I could show the world how to smile, I could be
I could leave the old days be - hind, leave all my

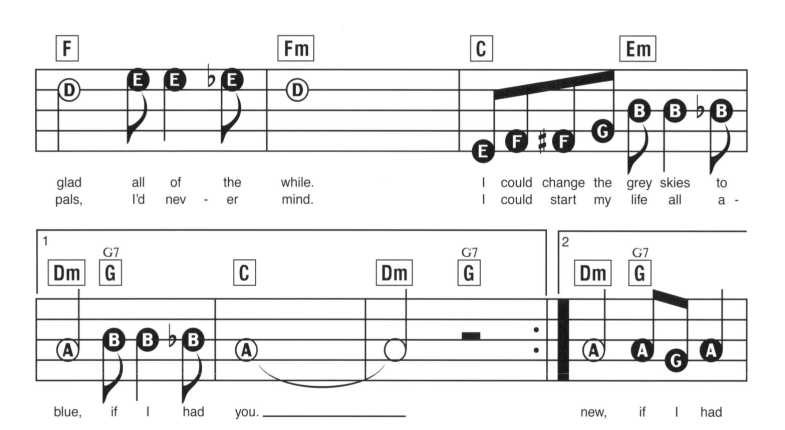

glad all of the while. I could change the grey skies to
pals, I'd nev - er mind. I could start my life all a -

blue, if I had you. _____
new, if I had

you. _____ I could climb the snow - capped

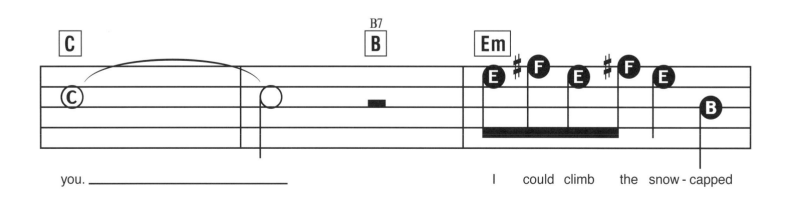

© 1928 (Renewed) CAMPBELL, CONNELLY & CO., LTD.
All Rights for the U.S. and Canada Administered by EMI ROBBINS CATALOG INC. (Publishing) and ALFRED MUSIC (Print)
All Rights Reserved   Used by Permission

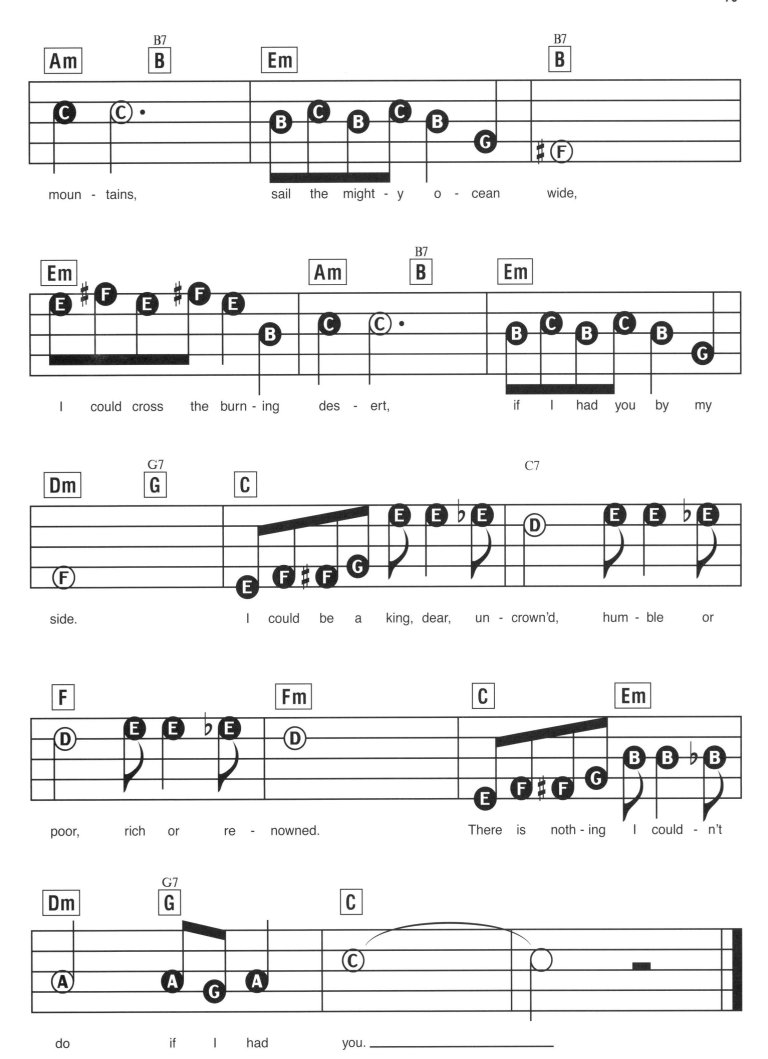

If You Knew Susie
(Like I Know Susie)

Registration 7
Rhythm: Fox Trot

Words and Music by B.G. DeSylva
and Joseph Meyer

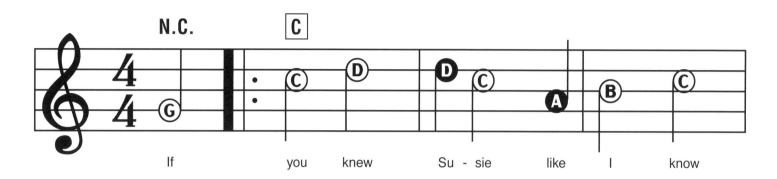

If you knew Su - sie like I know

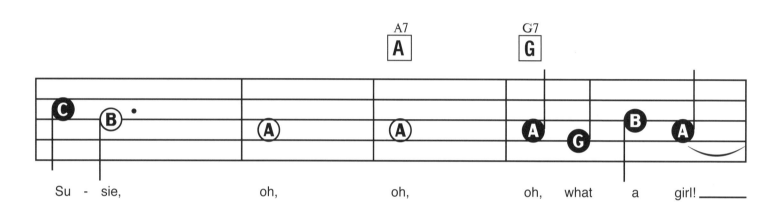

Su - sie, oh, oh, oh, what a girl! _____

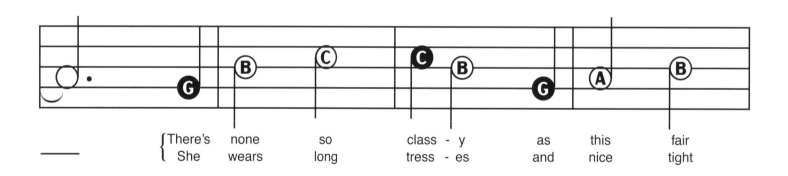

_____ { There's none so class - y as this fair
She wears long tress - es and nice tight

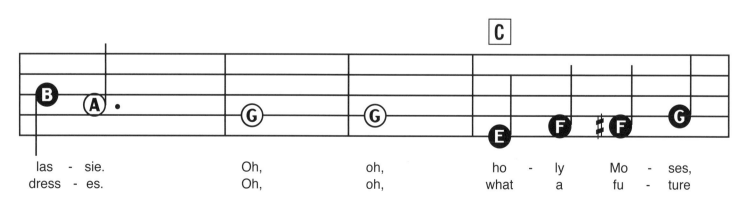

las - sie. Oh, oh, ho - ly Mo - ses,
dress - es. Oh, oh, what a fu - ture

Copyright © 1925 Shapiro, Bernstein & Co., Inc., New York, JoRo Music Corp., New York,
and Stephen Ballentine Music Publishing Co., New York for the U.S.A.
Copyright Renewed
All Rights for JoRo Music Corp. Administered by Larry Spier, Inc., New York
All Rights for Canada Controlled by Shapiro, Bernstein & Co., Inc., New York
International Copyright Secured   All Rights Reserved
Used by Permission

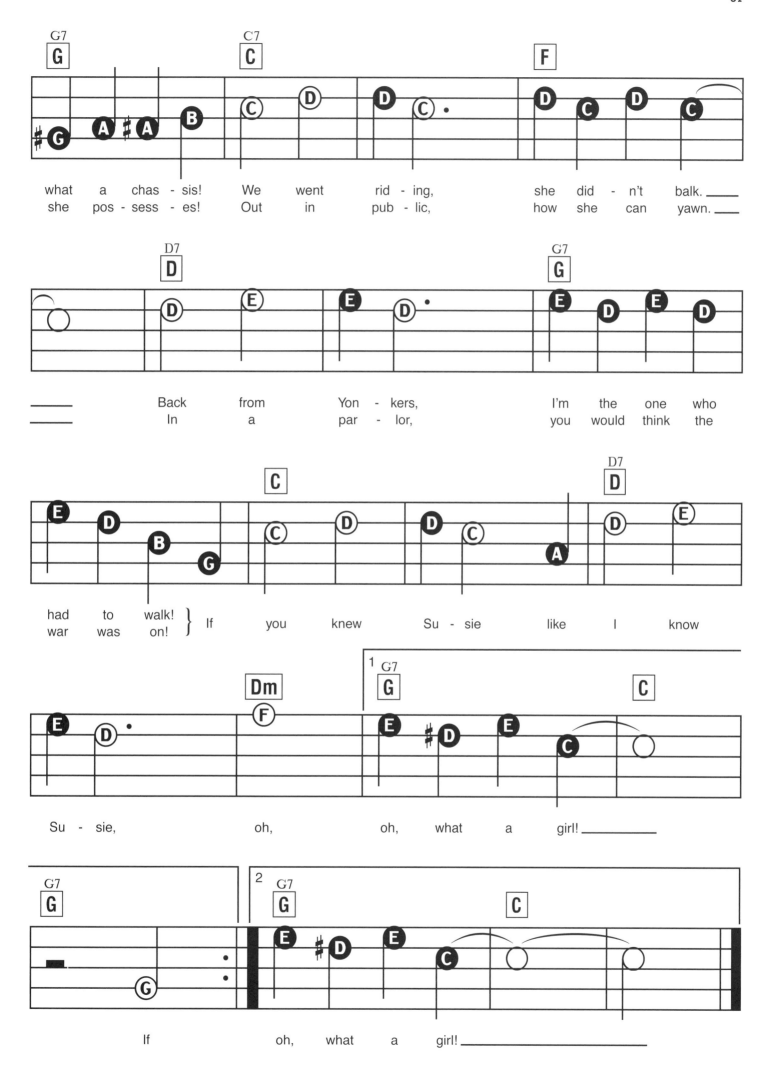

In a Little Spanish Town
('Twas on a Night Like This)

Registration 3
Rhythm: Waltz

Words by Sam M. Lewis and Joe Young
Music by Mabel Wayne

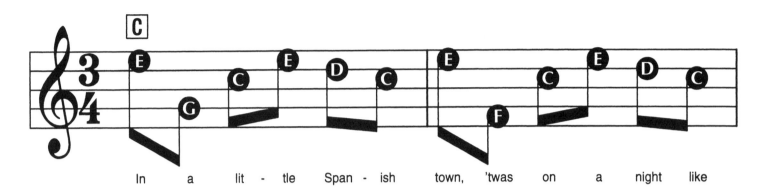

In a lit - tle Span - ish town, 'twas on a night like

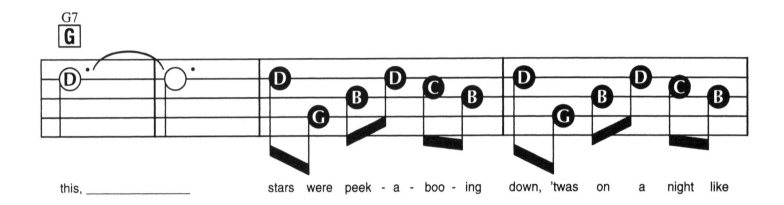

this, _____ stars were peek - a - boo - ing down, 'twas on a night like

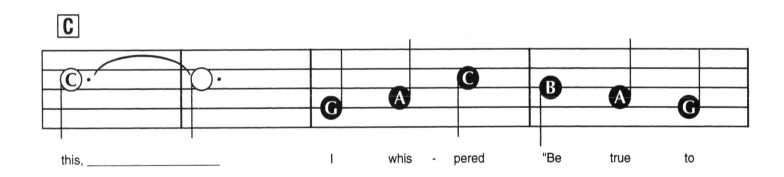

this, _____ I whis - pered "Be true to

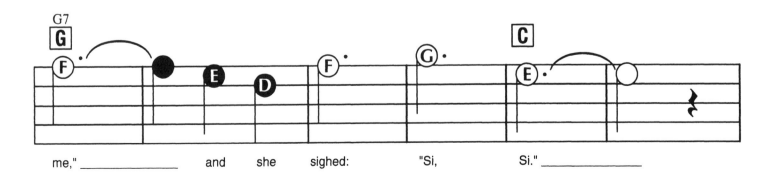

me," _____ and she sighed: "Si, Si." _____

© 1926 LEO FEIST, INC.
© Renewed 1954 WAROCK CORP. and LEO FEIST, INC.
All Rights Reserved

83

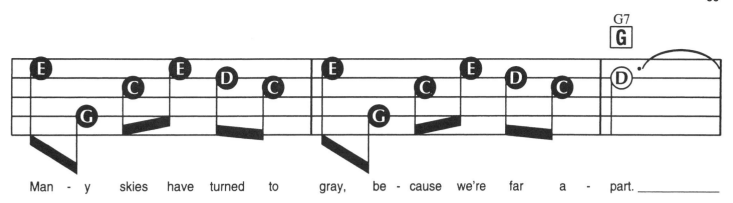

Man - y skies have turned to gray, be - cause we're far a - part. _____

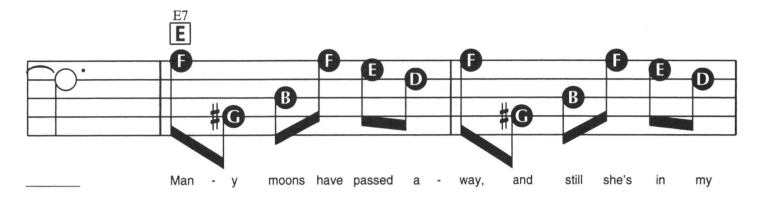

_____ Man - y moons have passed a - way, and still she's in my

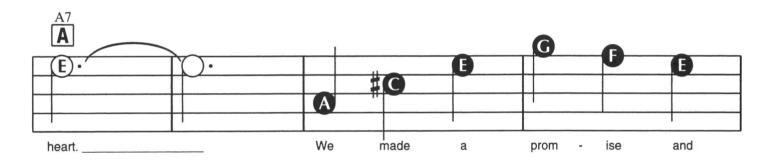

heart. _____ We made a prom - ise and

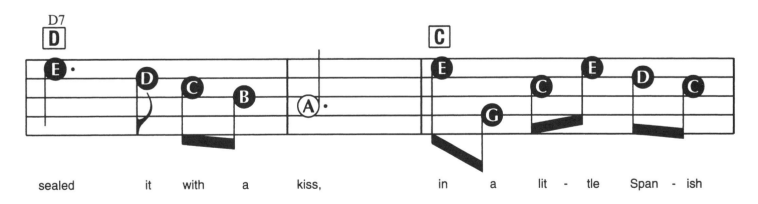

sealed it with a kiss, in a lit - tle Span - ish

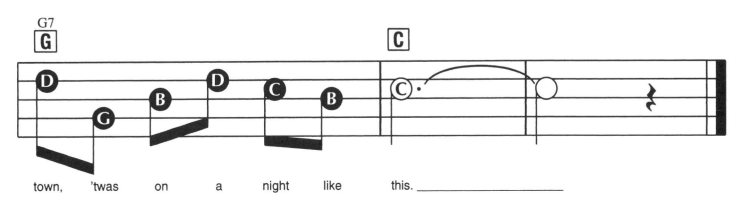

town, 'twas on a night like this. _____

It All Depends on You
from THE SINGING FOOL

Registration 7
Rhythm: Fox Trot or Swing

Words and Music by B.G. DeSylva,
Lew Brown and Ray Henderson

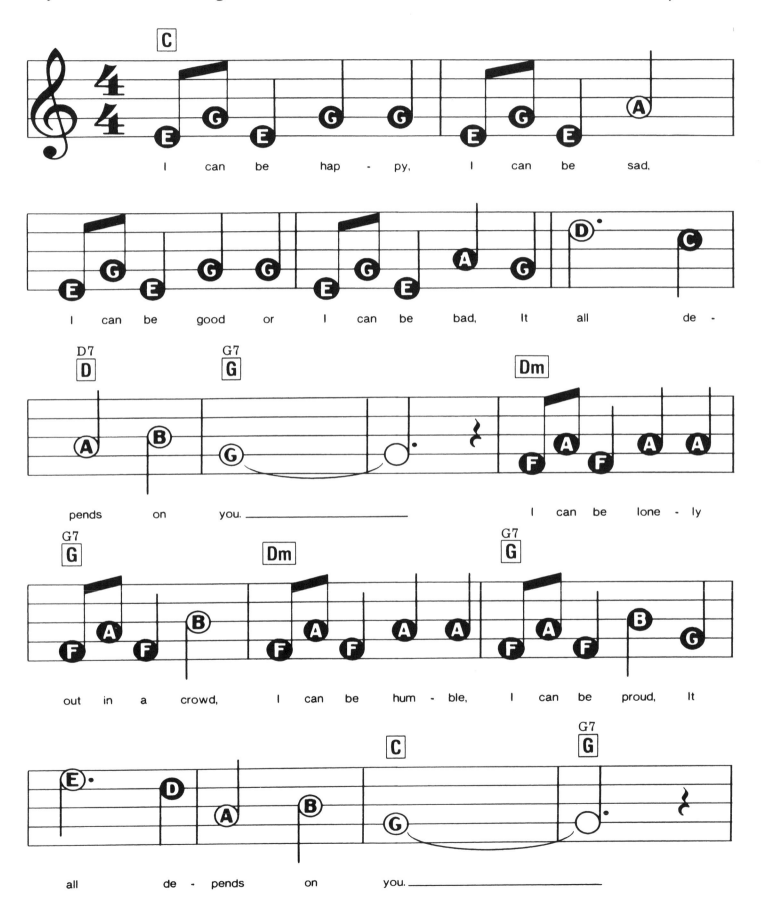

© 1926 (Renewed) CHAPPELL & CO., INC., STEPHEN BALLENTINE MUSIC PUBLISHING CO. and RAY HENDERSON MUSIC CO.
International Copyright Secured   All Rights Reserved

85

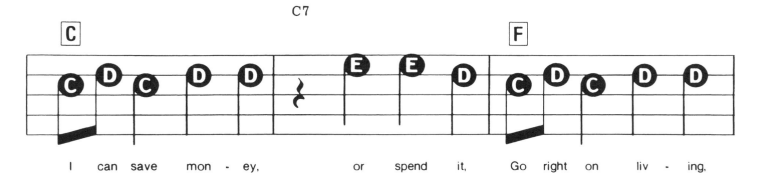

I can save mon - ey, or spend it, Go right on liv - ing,

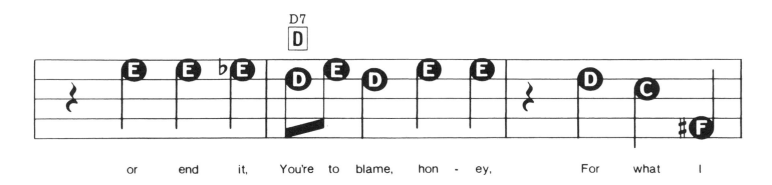

or end it, You're to blame, hon - ey, For what I

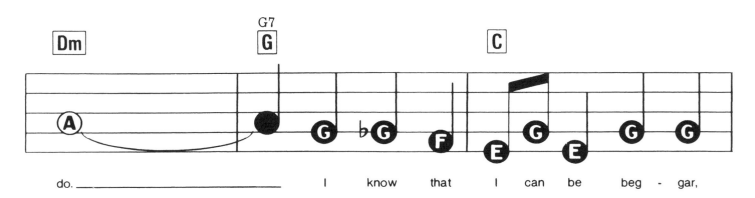

do. _____ I know that I can be beg - gar,

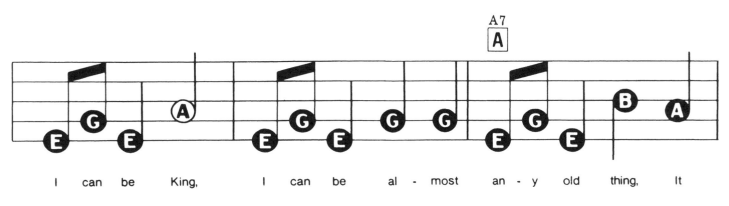

I can be King, I can be al - most an - y old thing, It

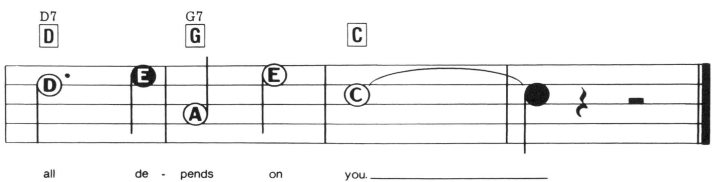

all de - pends on you. _____

Just You, Just Me

Registration 2
Rhythm: Swing or Fox Trot

Music by Jesse Greer
Lyrics by Raymond Klages

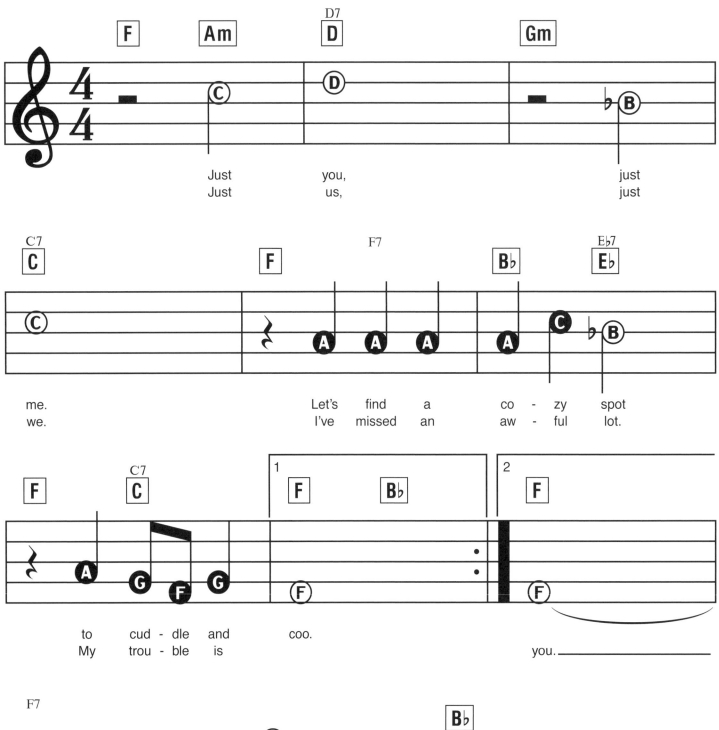

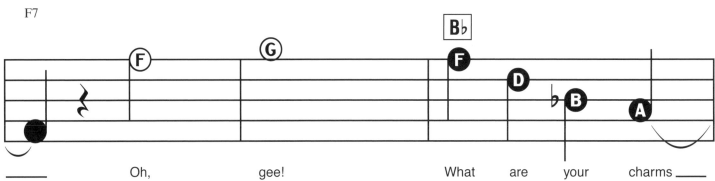

© 1929 (Renewed) METRO-GOLDWYN-MAYER INC.
All Rights Administered by EMI ROBBINS CATALOG INC. (Publishing) and ALFRED MUSIC (Print)
All Rights Reserved   Used by Permission

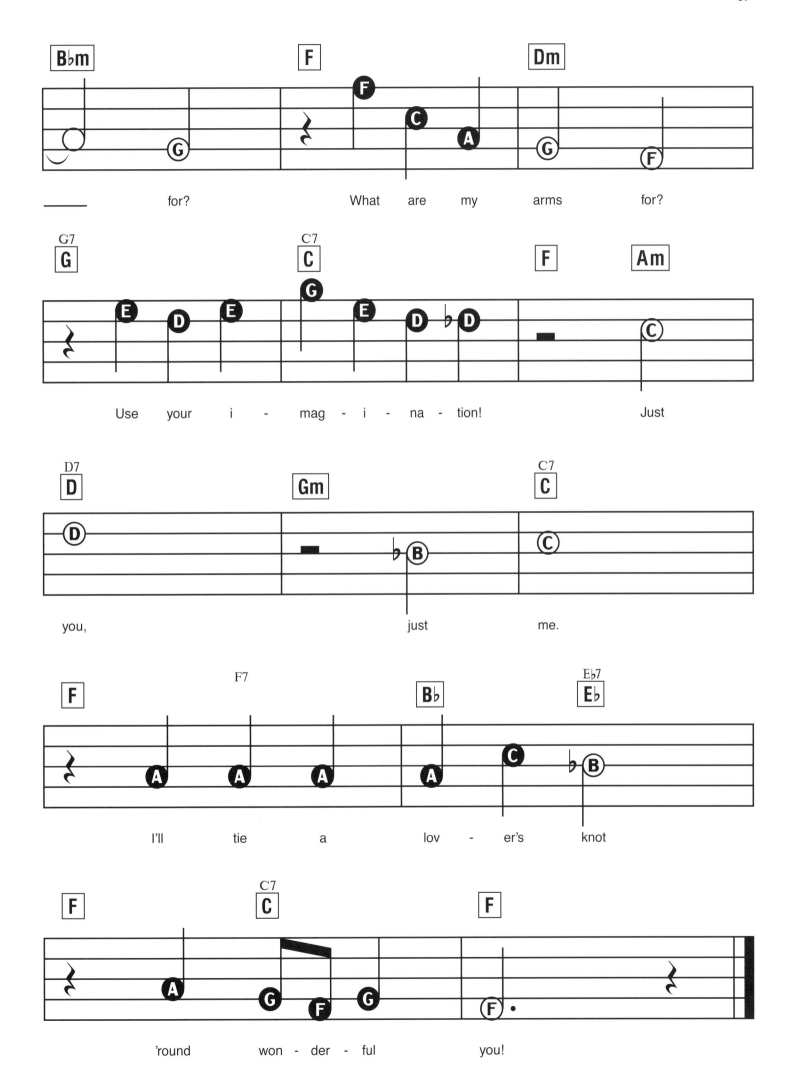

Let a Smile Be Your Umbrella

Registration 5
Rhythm: Fox Trot

Words by Irving Kahal and Francis Wheeler
Music by Sammy Fain

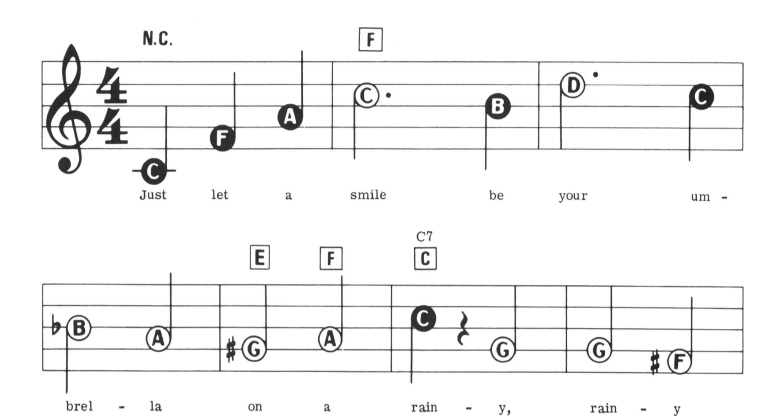

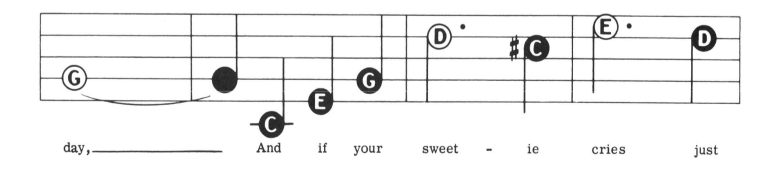

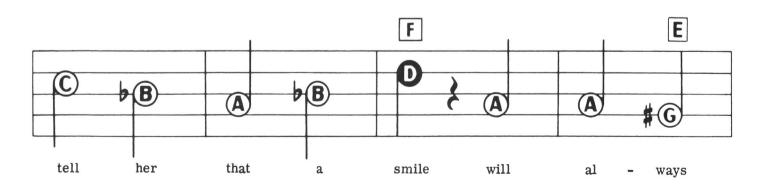

© 1927 MILLS MUSIC, INC.
© Renewed 1985 RYTVOC, INC., MILLS MUSIC, INC. and FAIN MUSIC CO.
All Rights Reserved

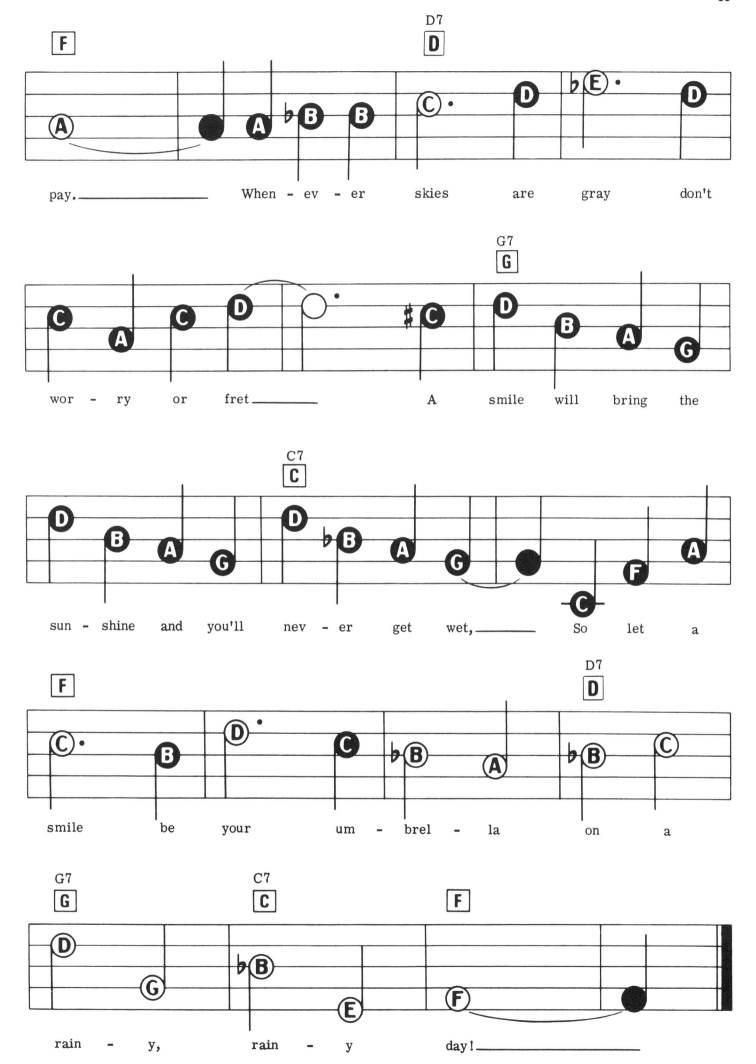

Liza
(All the Clouds'll Roll Away)

Registration 3
Rhythm: Fox Trot

Music by George Gershwin
Lyrics by Ira Gershwin and Gus Kahn

© 1929 (Renewed) WB MUSIC CORP. and GILBERT KEYES MUSIC
All Rights Administered by WB MUSIC CORP.
All Rights Reserved   Used by Permission

91

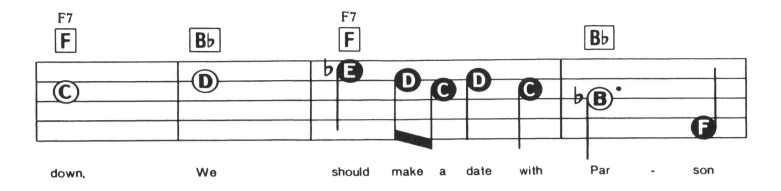

down,   We   should make a date with   Par - son

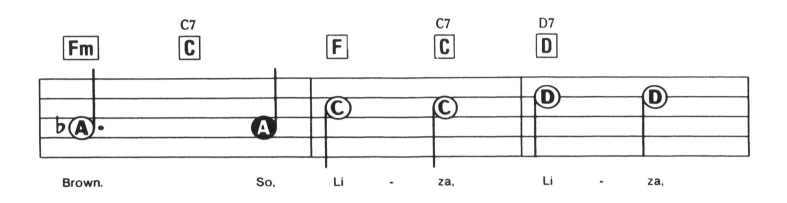

Brown.   So,   Li - za,   Li - za,

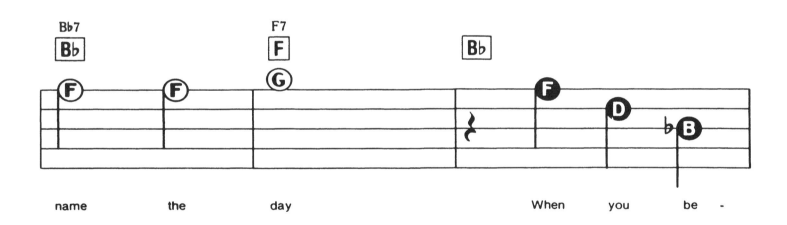

name   the   day   When you be -

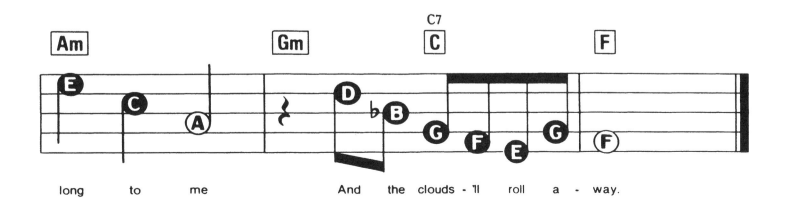

long   to   me   And   the clouds - 'll roll a - way.

Look for the Silver Lining
from SALLY

Registration 2
Rhythm: Fox Trot or Swing

Words by Buddy DeSylva
Music by Jerome Kern

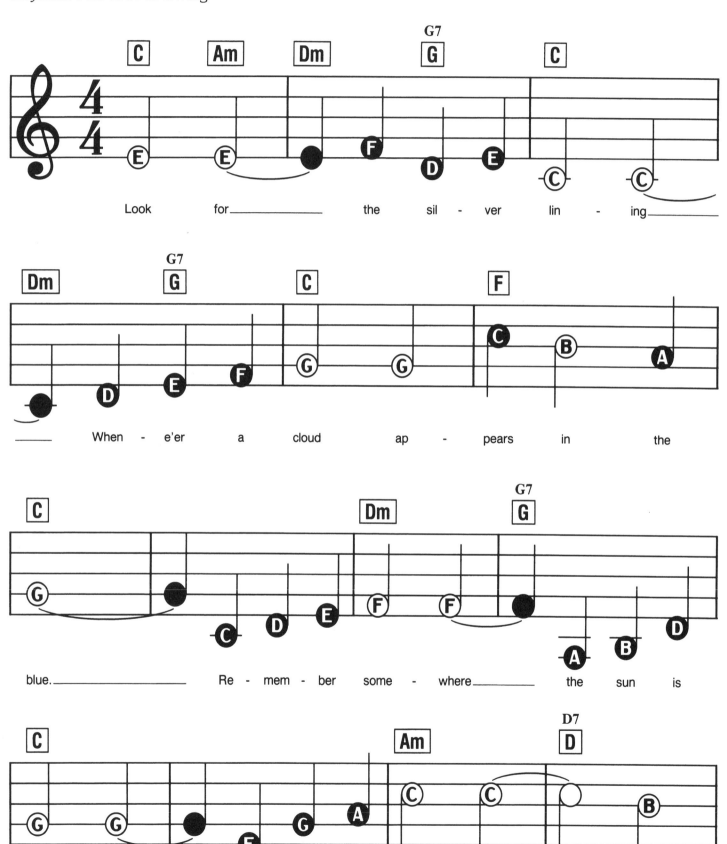

Copyright © 2004 by HAL LEONARD CORPORATION
International Copyright Secured   All Rights Reserved

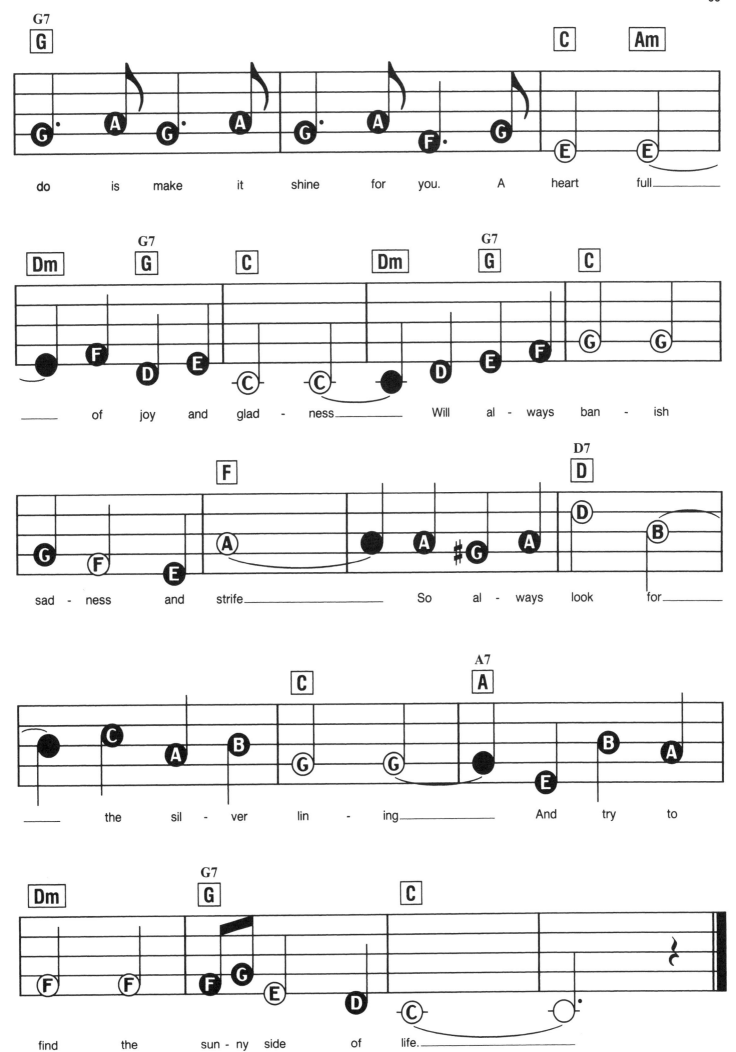

Louise
from the Paramount Picture INNOCENTS OF PARIS

Registration 7
Rhythm: Swing or Shuffle

Words by Leo Robin
Music by Richard A. Whiting

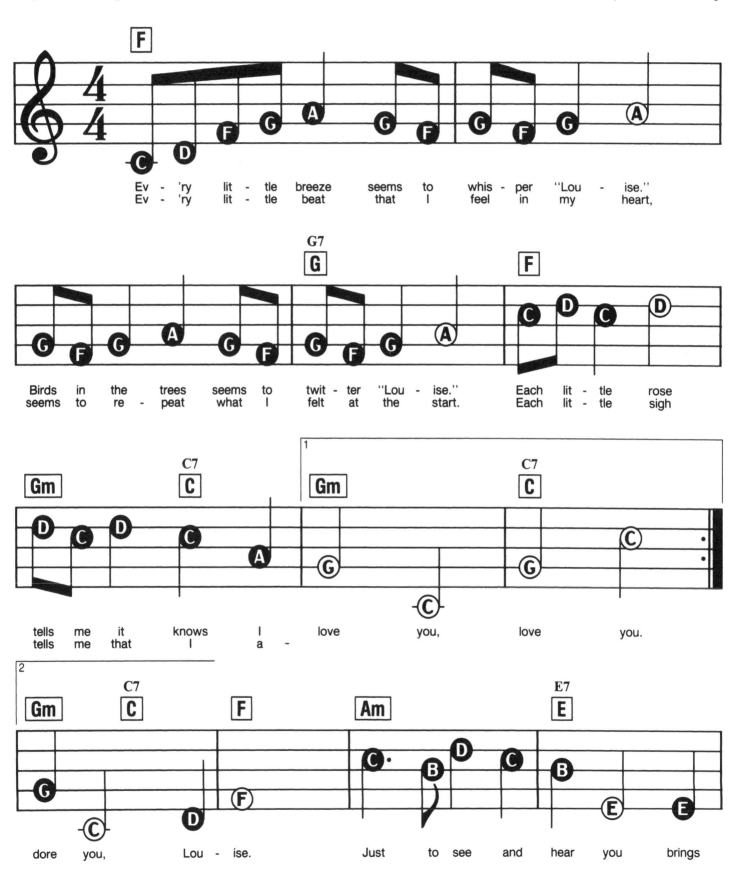

Copyright © 1929 Sony/ATV Music Publishing LLC
Copyright Renewed
All Rights Administered by Sony/ATV Music Publishing LLC, 424 Church Street, Suite 1200, Nashville, TN 37219
International Copyright Secured All Rights Reserved

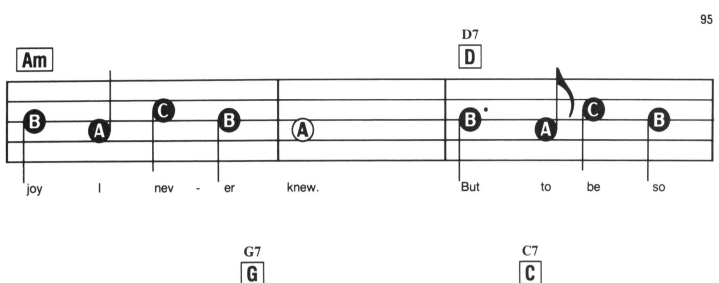

joy I nev - er knew. But to be so

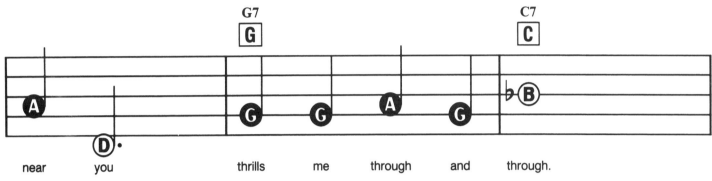

near you thrills me through and through.

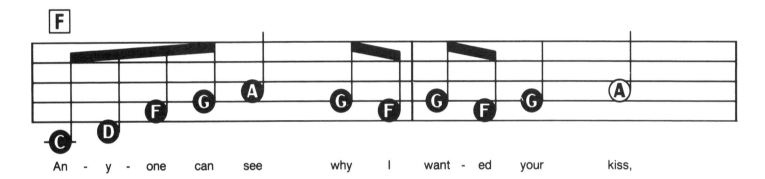

An - y - one can see why I want - ed your kiss,

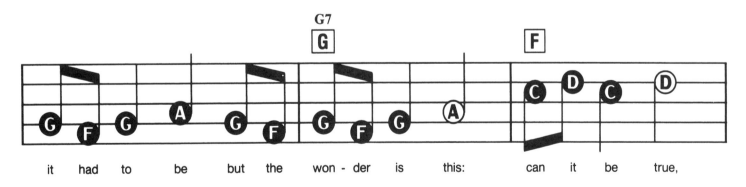

it had to be but the won - der is this: can it be true,

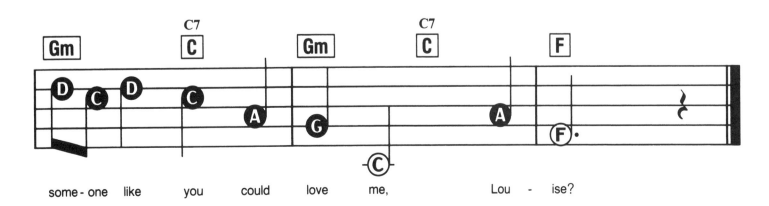

some - one like you could love me, Lou - ise?

Love Me or Leave Me

from LOVE ME OR LEAVE ME
from WHOOPEE!

Registration 4
Rhythm: Fox Trot or Swing

Lyrics by Gus Kahn
Music by Walter Donaldson

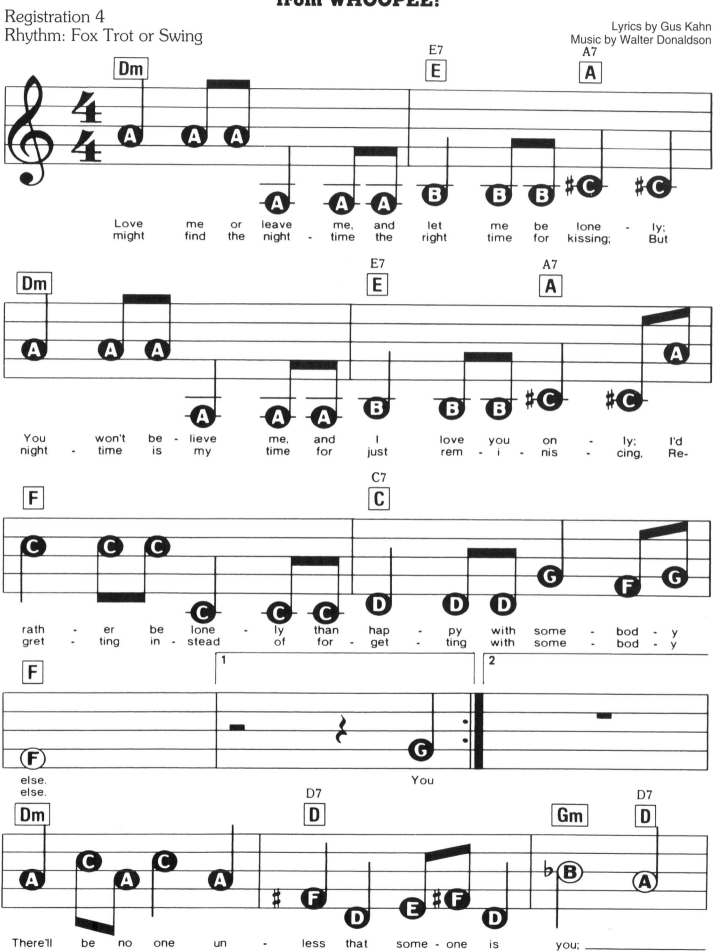

Copyright © 1928 (Renewed) by Donaldson Publishing Co., Dreyer Music Co. and Gilbert Keyes Music Co.
All Rights for Dreyer Music Co. Administered by Larry Spier, Inc., New York
All Rights for Gilbert Keyes Music Co. Administered by WB Music Corp.
International Copyright Secured   All Rights Reserved

97

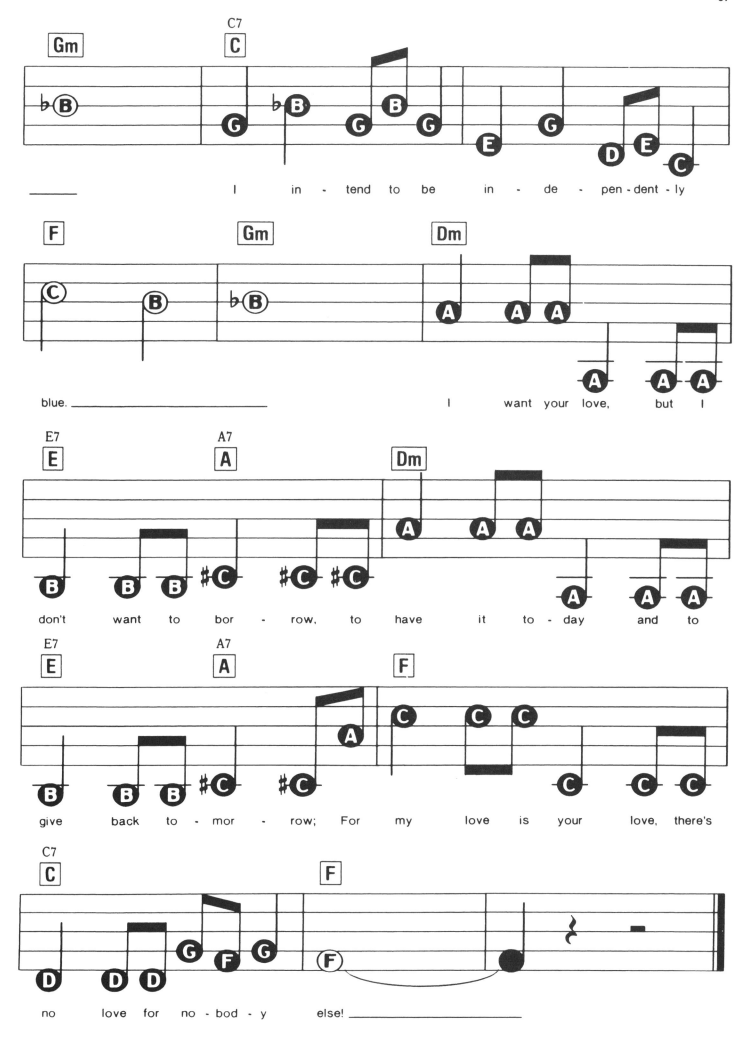

Lover, Come Back to Me
from THE NEW MOON

Registration 5
Rhythm: Fox Trot or Swing

Lyrics by Oscar Hammerstein II
Music by Sigmund Romberg

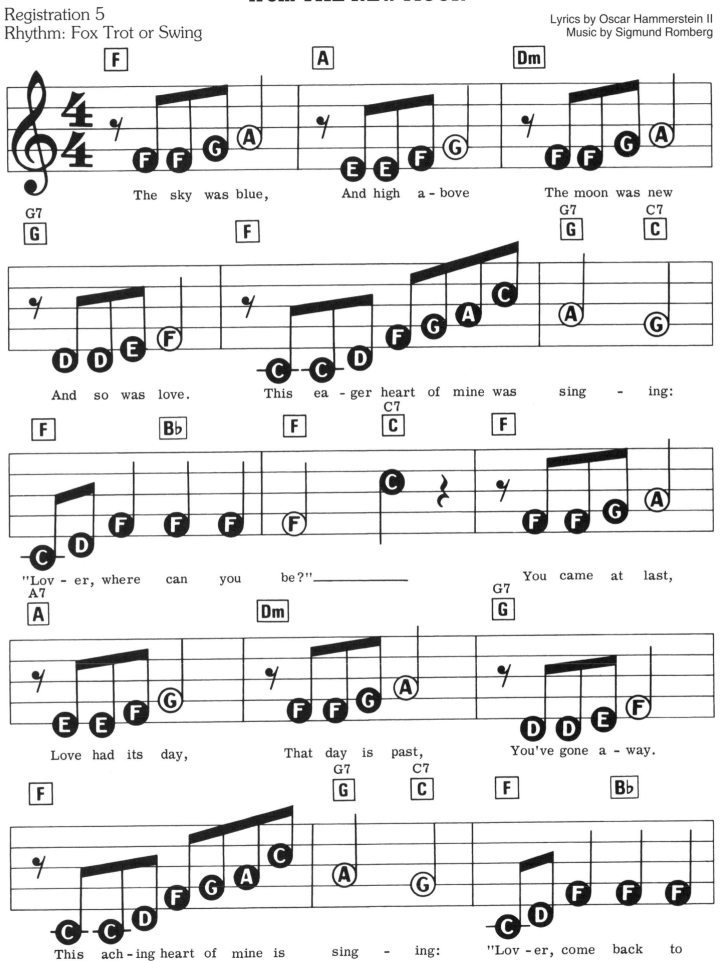

Copyright © 1928 by Bambalina Music Publishing Co. and WB Music Corp.
Copyright Renewed
All Rights on behalf of Bambalina Music Publishing Co. Administered by Williamson Music, a Division of Rodgers & Hammerstein: an Imagem Company
International Copyright Secured   All Rights Reserved

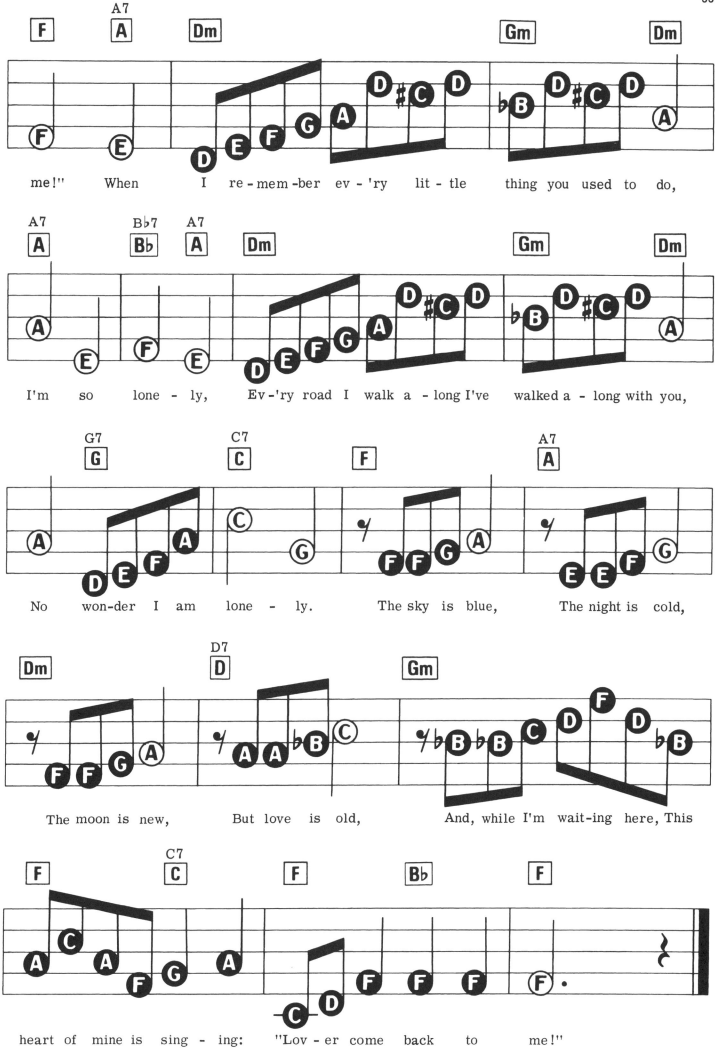

Mack the Knife
from THE THREEPENNY OPERA

English Words by Marc Blitzstein
Original German Words by Bert Brecht
Music by Kurt Weill

Registration 8
Rhythm: Swing

Oh, the shark has _____ pret - ty teeth, dear _____
side - walk _____ Sun - day morn - ing _____

_____ And he shows them _____ pearl - y
_____ Lies a bod - y _____ ooz - ing

white. _____ Just a jack - knife _____ has Mac -
life; _____ Some - one's sneak - ing _____ 'round the

heath, dear _____ And he keeps it _____ out of
cor - ner. _____ Is the some - one _____ Mack the

© 1928 (Renewed) UNIVERSAL EDITION
© 1955 (Renewed) WEILL-BRECHT-HARMS CO., INC.
Renewal Rights Assigned to the KURT WEILL FOUNDATION FOR MUSIC, BERT BRECHT and THE ESTATE OF MARC BLITZSTEIN
All Rights Administered by WB MUSIC CORP.
All Rights Reserved   Used by Permission

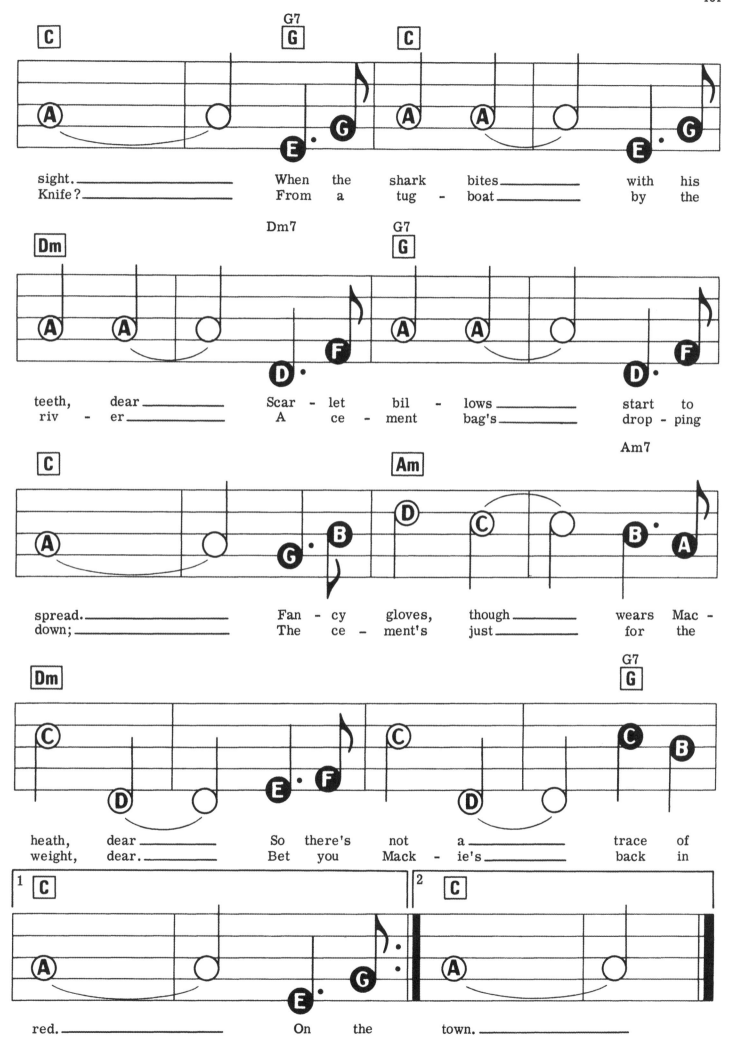

Make Believe
from SHOW BOAT

Registration 10
Rhythm: Ballad or Fox Trot

Lyrics by Oscar Hammerstein II
Music by Jerome Kern

Copyright © 1927 UNIVERSAL - POLYGRAM INTERNATIONAL PUBLISHING, INC.
Copyright Renewed
All Rights Reserved   Used by Permission

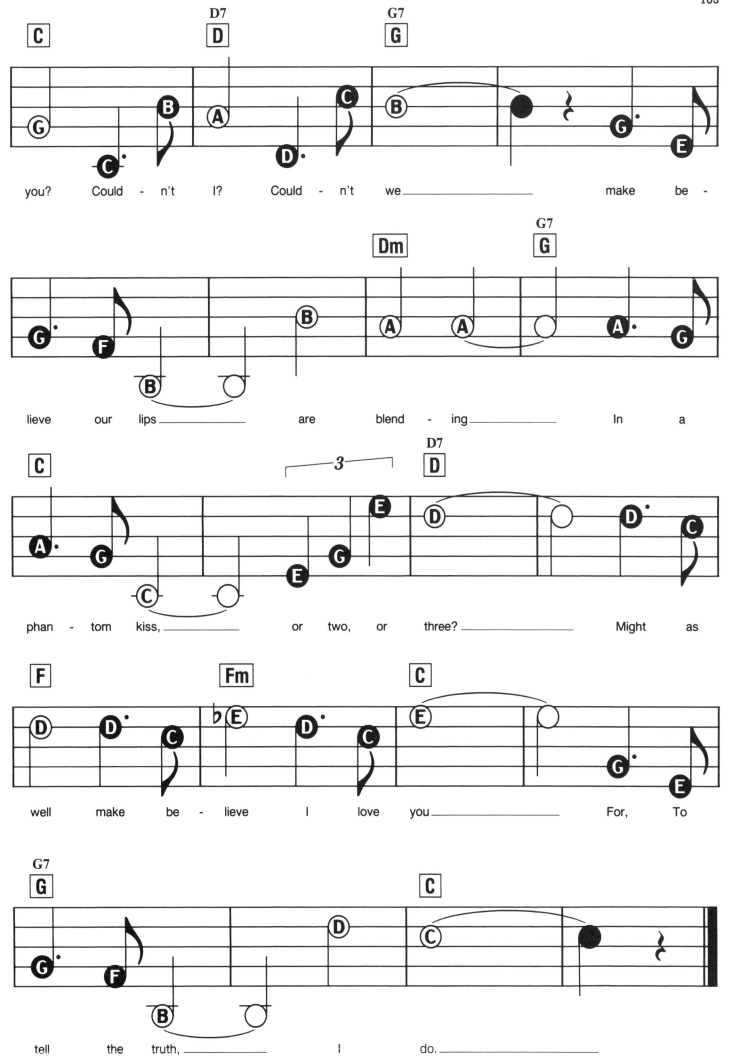

Makin' Whoopee!
from WHOOPEE!

Registration 9
Rhythm: Fox Trot or Swing

Lyrics by Gus Kahn
Music by Walter Donaldson

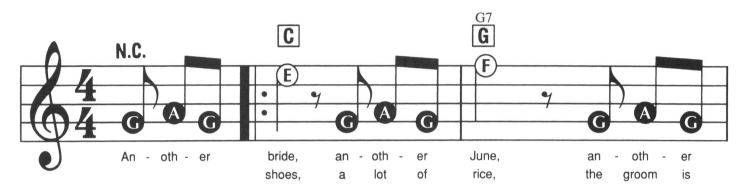

An - oth - er bride, an - oth - er June, an - oth - er
shoes, a lot of rice, the groom is

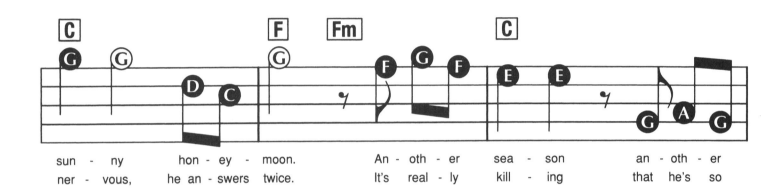

sun - ny hon - ey - moon. An - oth - er sea - son an - oth - er
ner - vous, he an - swers twice. It's real - ly kill - ing that he's so

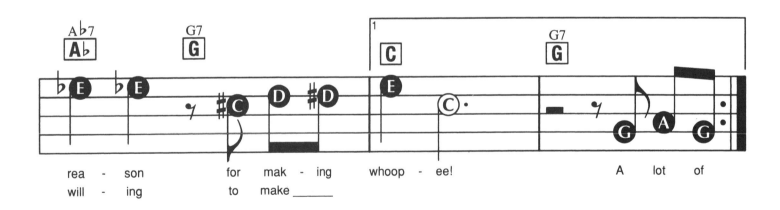

rea - son for mak - ing whoop - ee! A lot of
will - ing to make _____

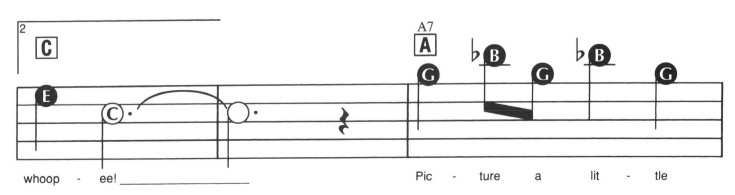

whoop - ee! _____ Pic - ture a lit - tle

Copyright © 1928 (Renewed) by Donaldson Publishing Co., Dreyer Music Co. and Gilbert Keyes Music Company
All Rights for Dreyer Music Co. Administered by Larry Spier, Inc., New York
All Rights for Gilbert Keyes Music Company Administered by WB Music Corp.
International Copyright Secured All Rights Reserved

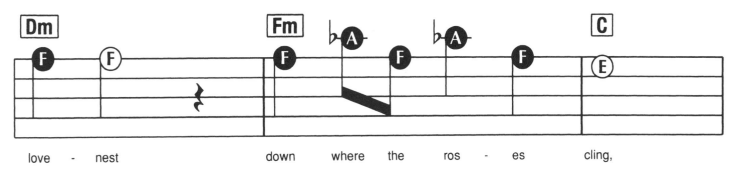

love - nest   down where the ros - es cling,

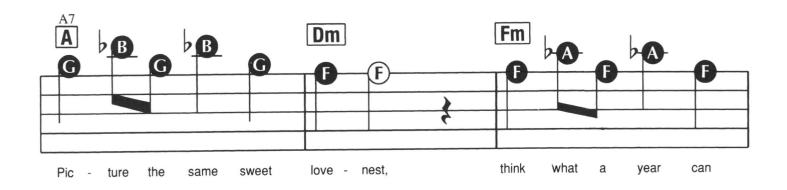

Pic - ture the same sweet love - nest,   think what a year can

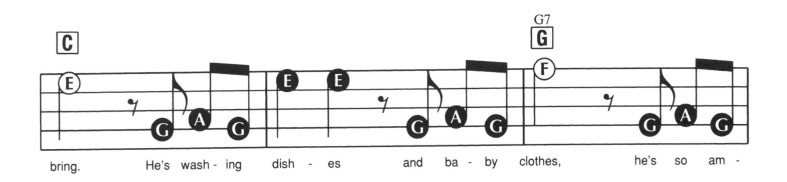

bring. He's wash - ing dish - es and ba - by clothes, he's so am -

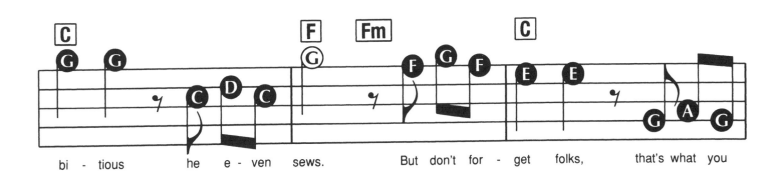

bi - tious he e - ven sews. But don't for - get folks, that's what you

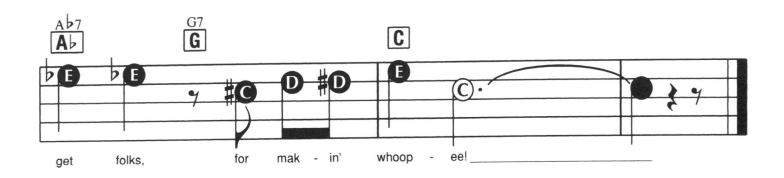

get folks, for mak - in' whoop - ee! _____

The Man I Love
from LADY BE GOOD

Registration 10
Rhythm: Swing or Jazz

Music and Lyrics by George Gershwin
and Ira Gershwin

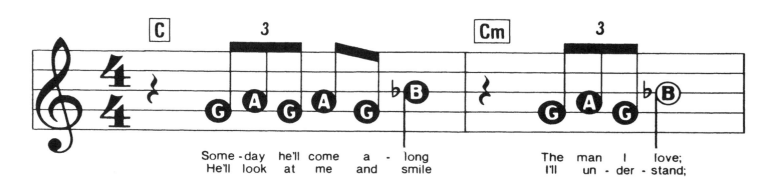

Some-day he'll come a - long
He'll look at me and smile

The man I love;
I'll un - der - stand;

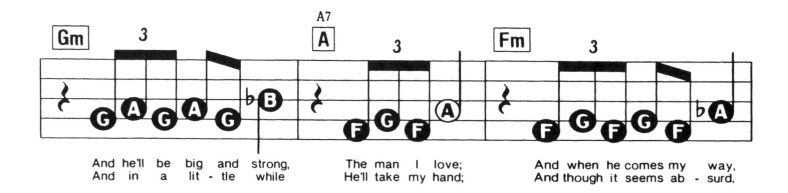

And he'll be big and strong,
And in a lit - tle while

The man I love;
He'll take my hand;

And when he comes my way,
And though it seems ab - surd,

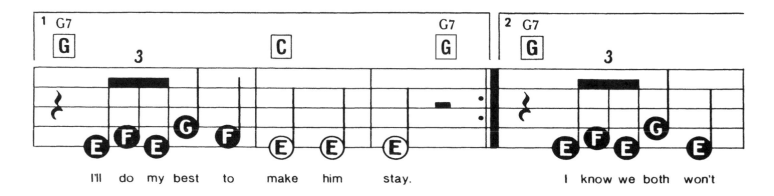

I'll do my best to make him stay.

I know we both won't

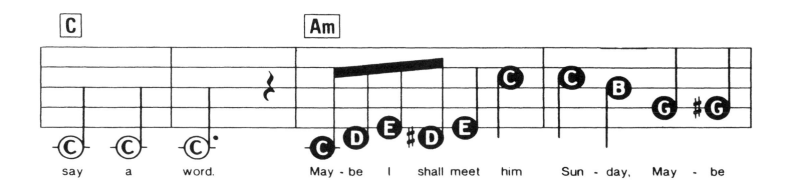

say a word.

May - be I shall meet him Sun - day, May - be

© 1924 (Renewed) WB MUSIC CORP.
All Rights Reserved   Used by Permission

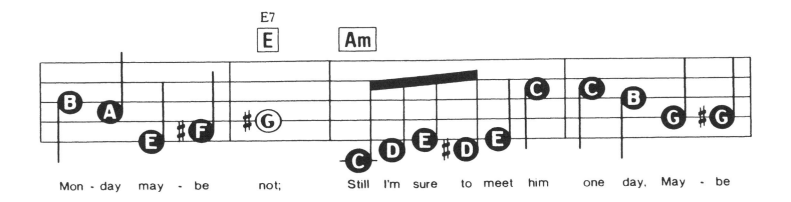

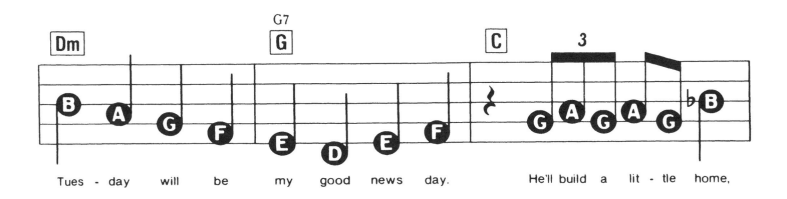

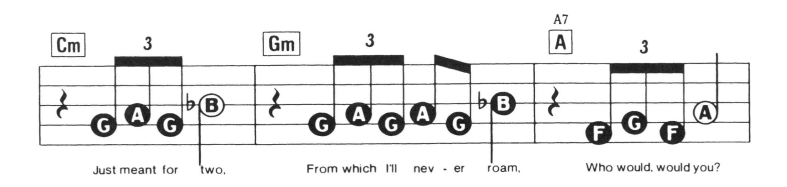

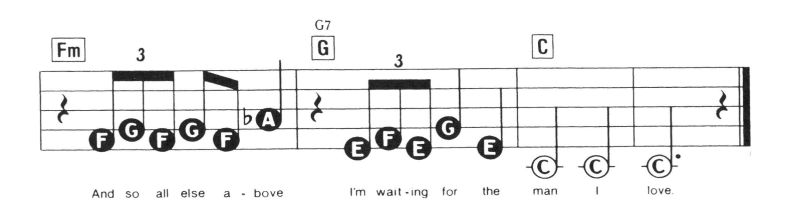

Manhattan
from the Broadway Musical THE GARRICK GAIETIES

Registration 7
Rhythm: Fox Trot

Words by Lorenz Hart
Music by Richard Rodgers

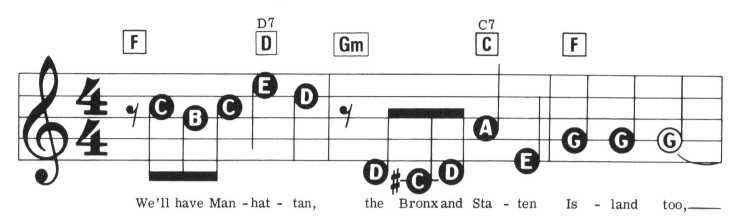

We'll have Man - hat - tan, the Bronx and Sta - ten Is - land too,—

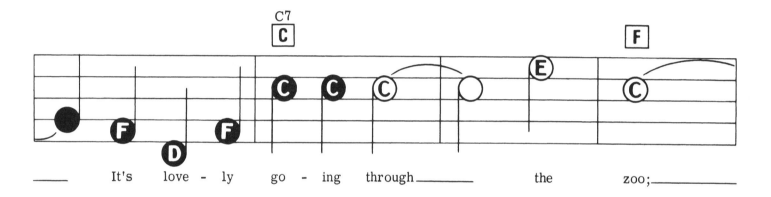

— It's love - ly go - ing through the zoo;—

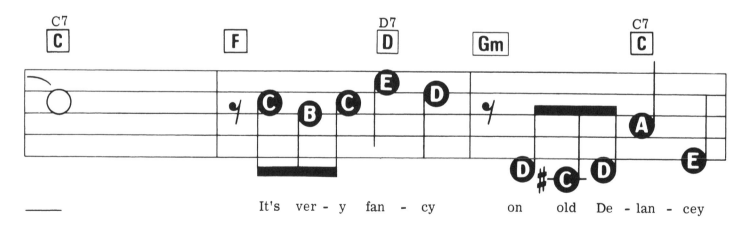

— It's ver - y fan - cy on old De - lan - cey

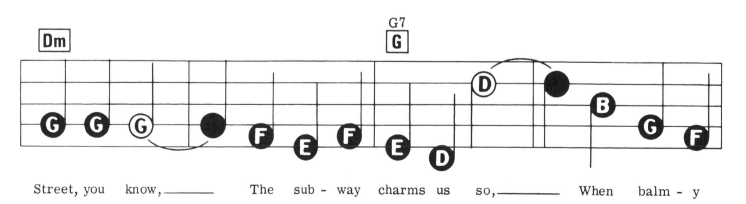

Street, you know,— The sub - way charms us so,— When balm - y

Copyright © 1925 by Edward B. Marks Music Company
Copyright Renewed
International Copyright Secured All Rights Reserved
Used by Permission

109

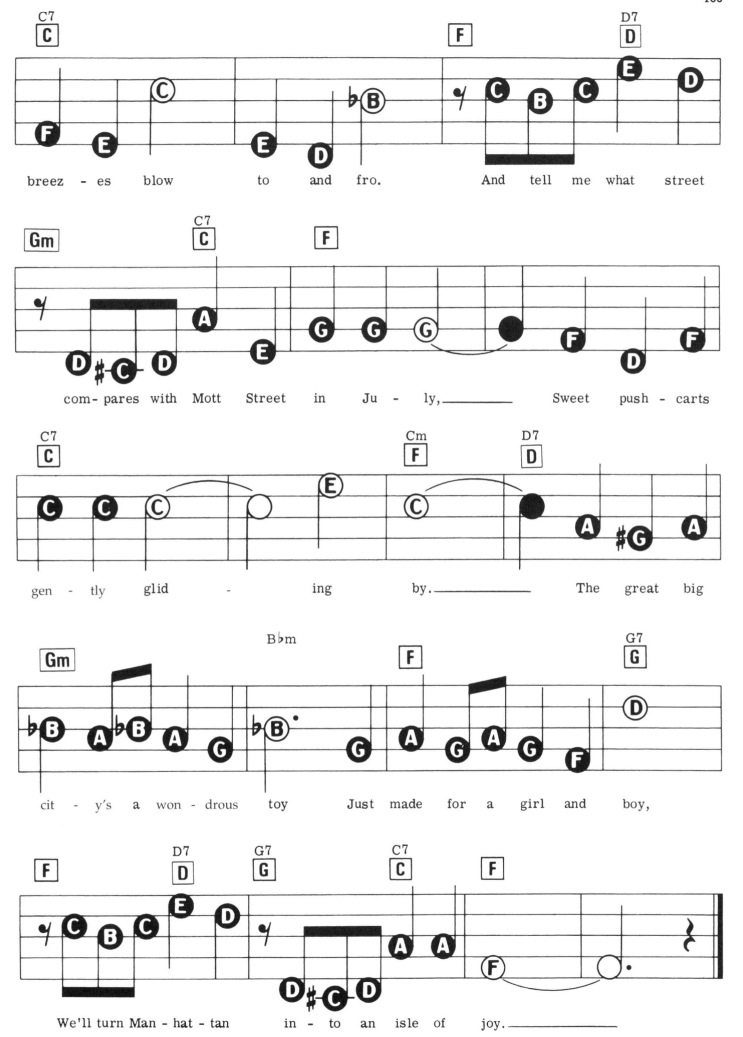

Me and My Shadow

Registration 1
Rhythm: Fox Trot

Words by Billy Rose
Music by Al Jolson and Dave Dreyer

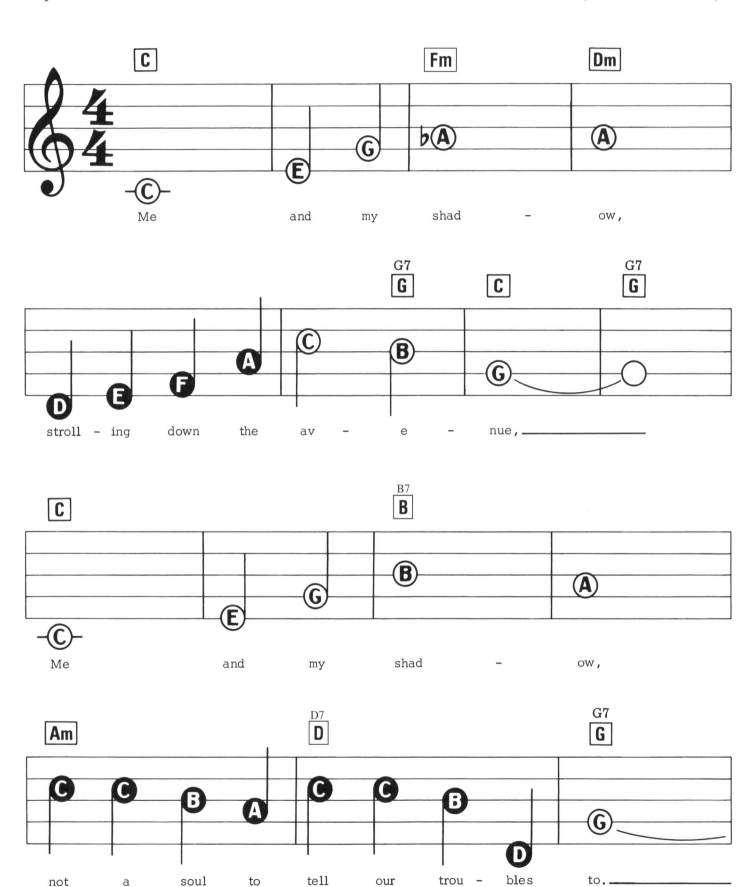

Copyright © 1927 by Bourne Co. (ASCAP) and Larry Spier, Inc.
Copyright Renewed
International Copyright Secured   All Rights Reserved

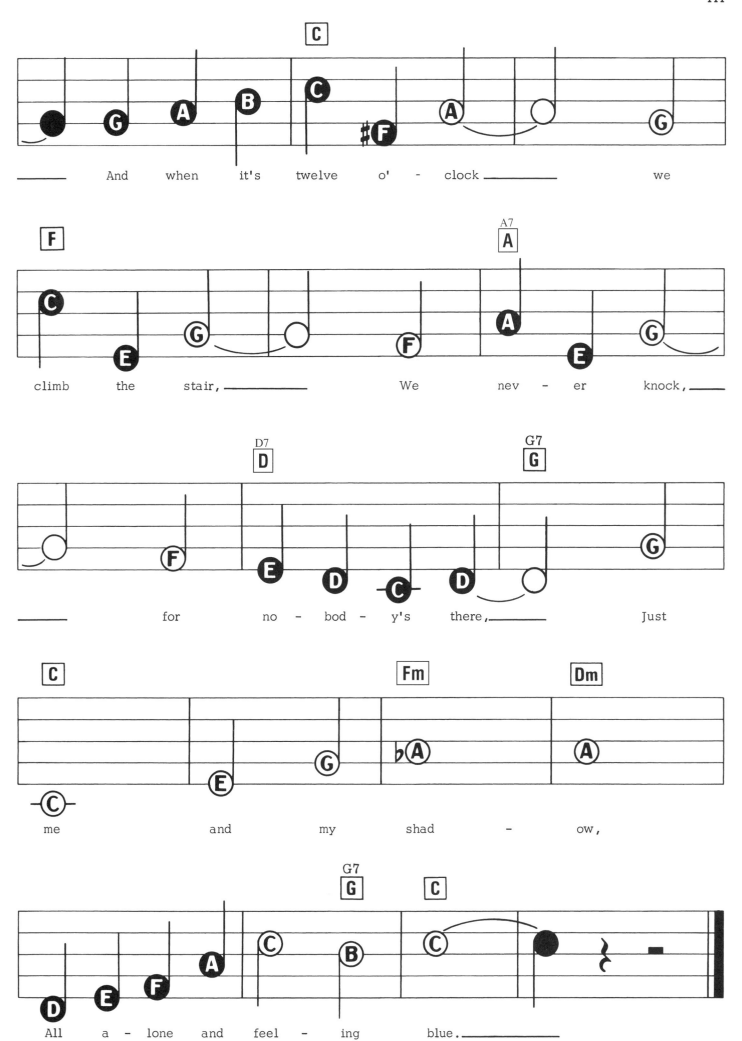

Mean to Me

Registration 4
Rhythm: Swing

Lyric by Roy Turk
Music by Fred E. Ahlert

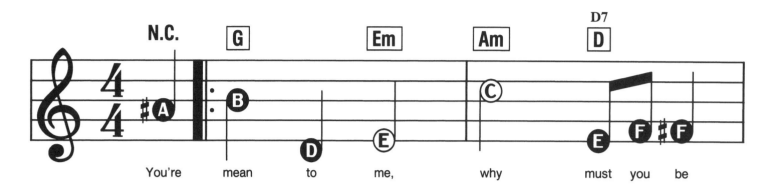

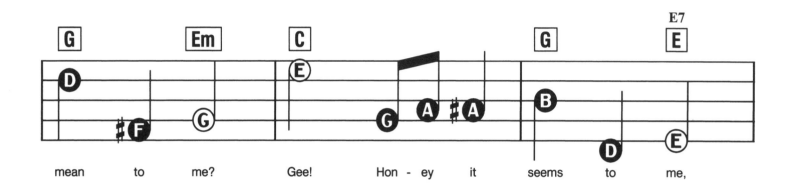

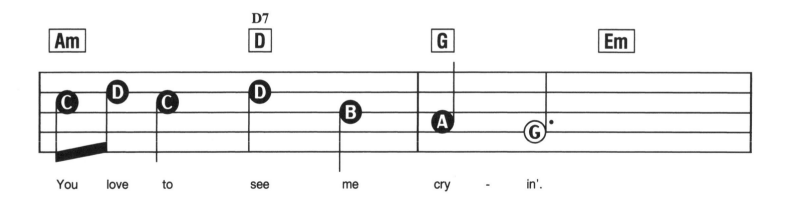

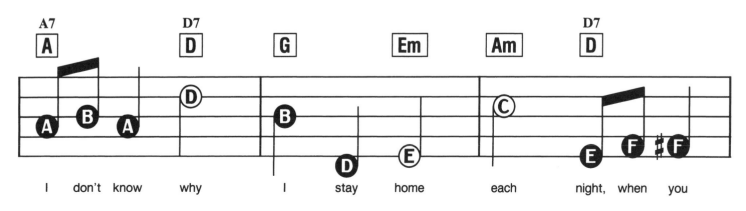

TRO - © Copyright 1929 (Renewed) Cromwell Music, Inc., New York, NY, Pencil Mark Music, Inc., Bronxville, NY, Azure Pearl Music, Beeping Good Music and David Ahlert Music
All Rights for Pencil Mark Music Administered by BMG Rights Management (US) LLC
All Rights for Azure Pearl Music, Beeping Good Music and David Ahlert Music Administered by Bluewater Music Services Corp.
International Copyright Secured
All Rights Reserved Including Public Performance For Profit
Used by Permission

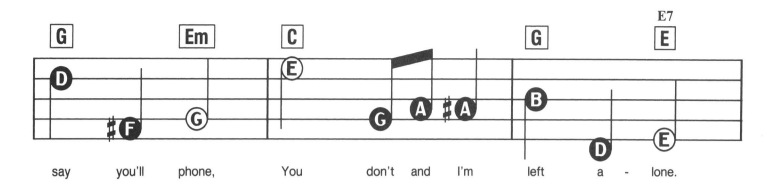

say you'll phone, You don't and I'm left a - lone.

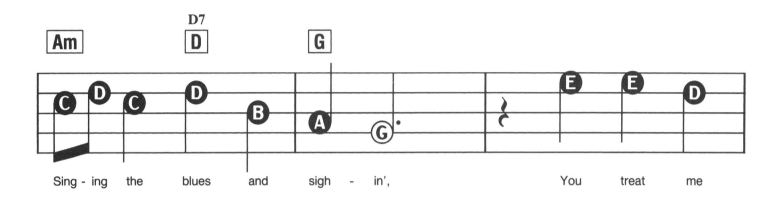

Sing - ing the blues and sigh - in', You treat me

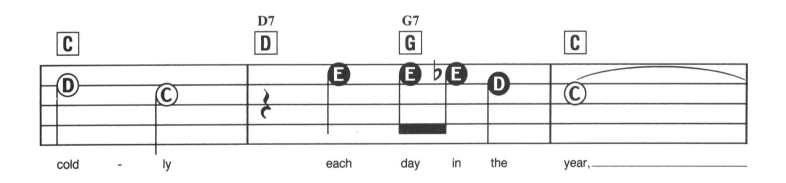

cold - ly each day in the year,

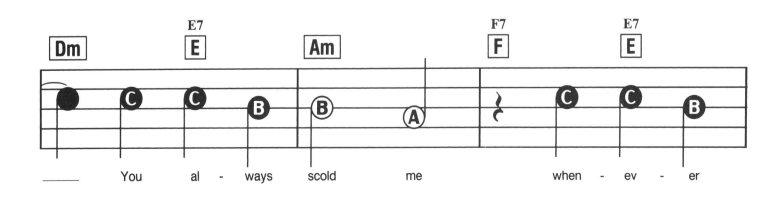

You al - ways scold me when - ev - er

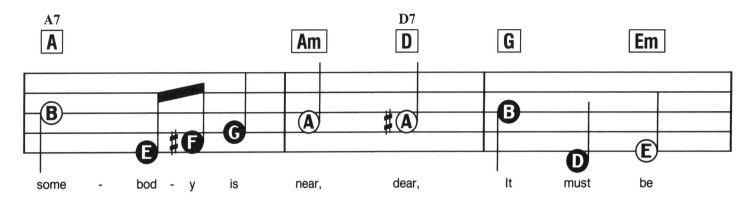

some - bod - y is near, dear, It must be

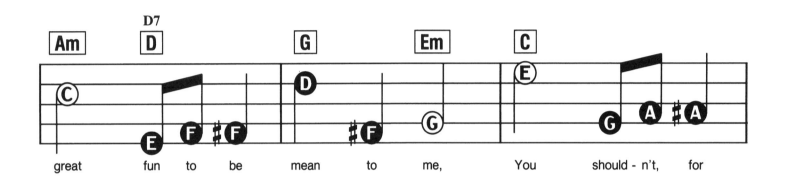

great fun to be mean to me, You should - n't, for

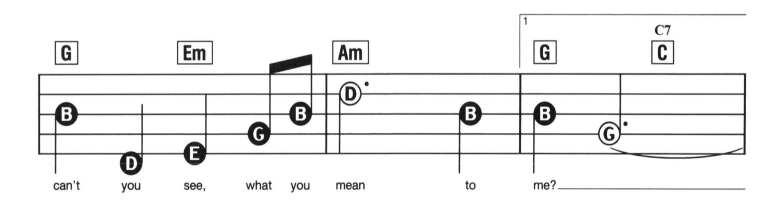

can't you see, what you mean to me?

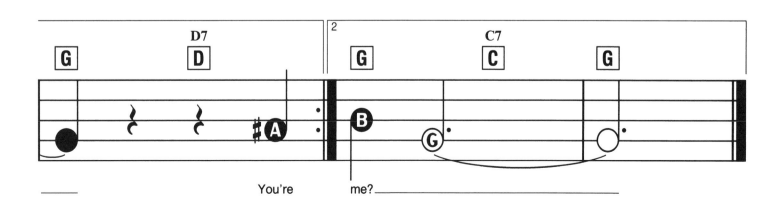

You're me?

Mississippi Mud

Registration 4
Rhythm: Swing

Words and Music by James Cavanaugh
and Harry Barris

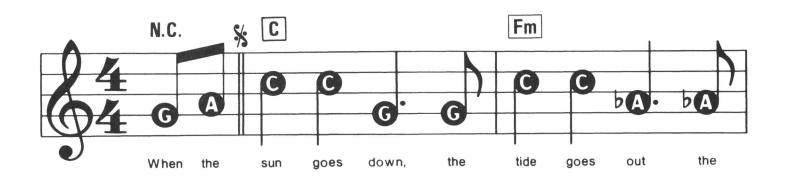

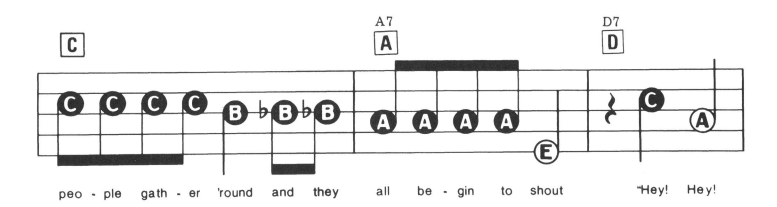

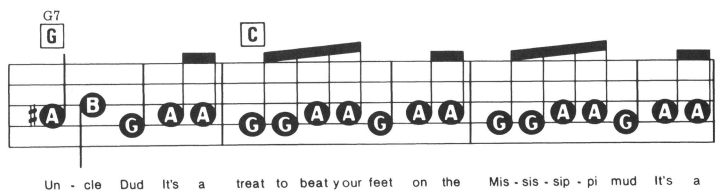

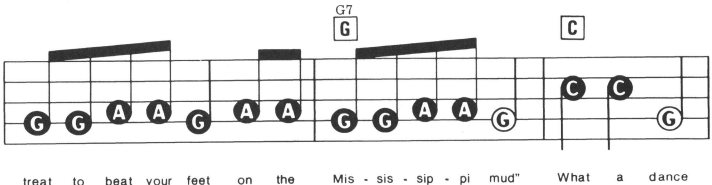

Copyright © 1927 Shapiro, Bernstein & Co., Inc., New York
Copyright Renewed
International Copyright Secured All Rights Reserved
Used by Permission

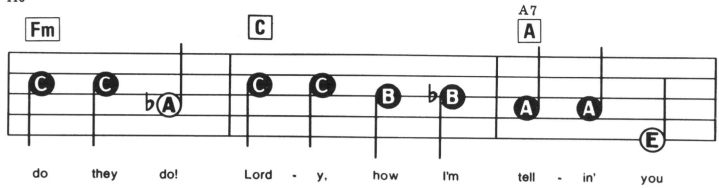

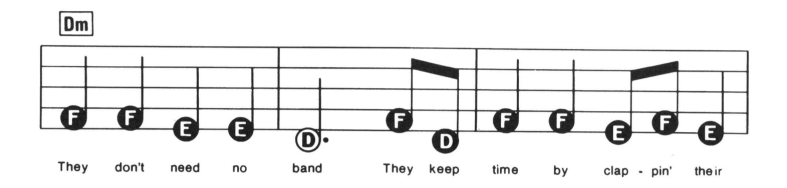

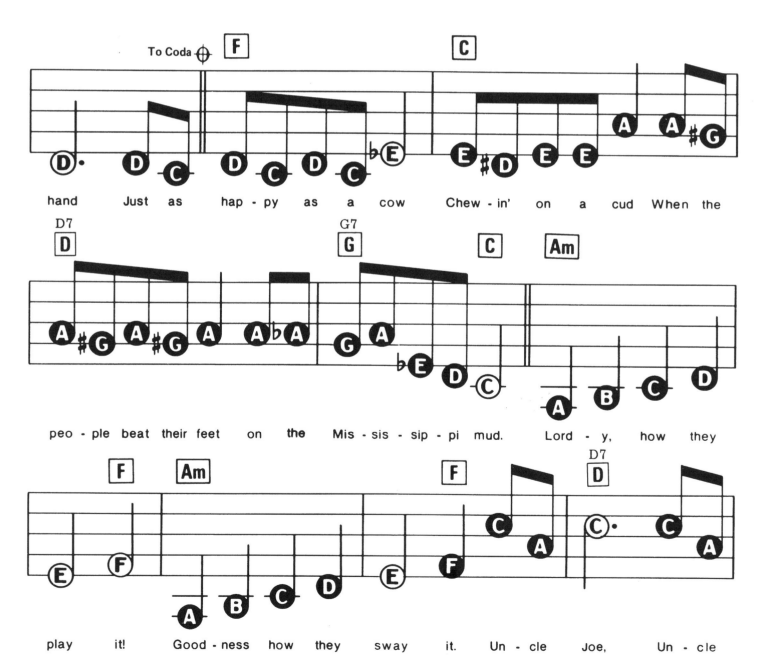

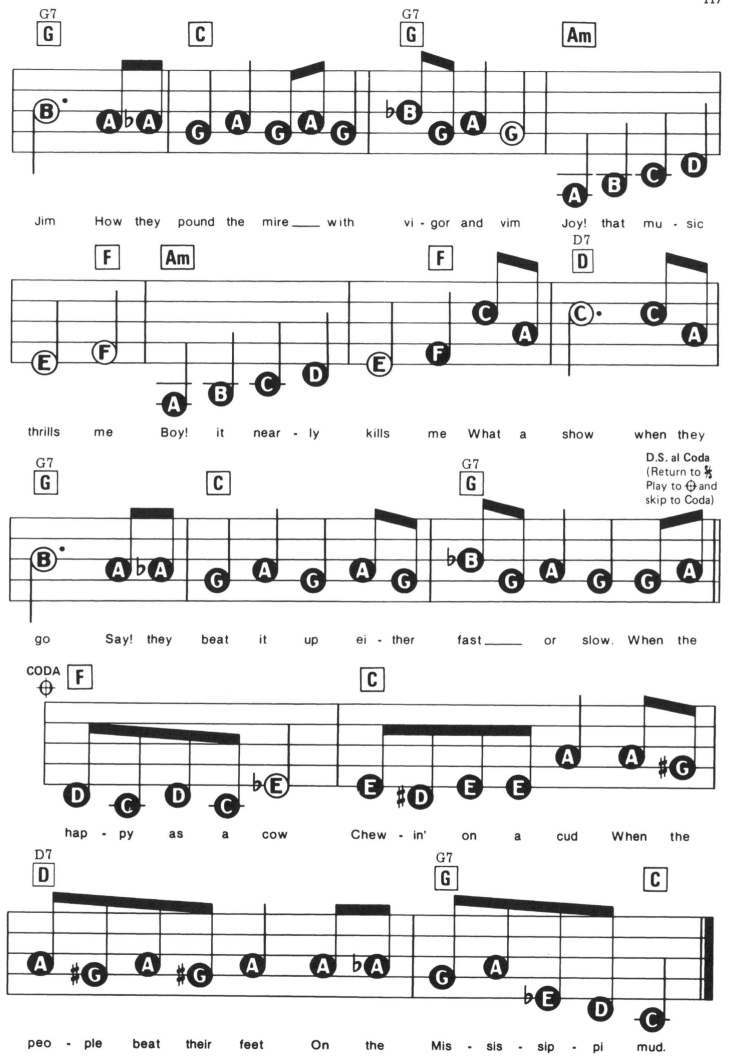

Moonlight and Roses
(Bring Mem'ries of You)

Registration 9
Rhythm: Ballad or Fox Trot

Words and Music by Ben Black,
Edwin Lemare and Neil Moret

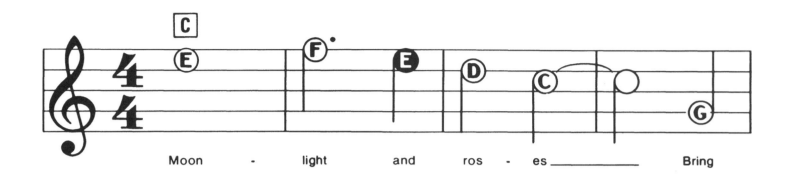

Moon - light and ros - es ___ Bring

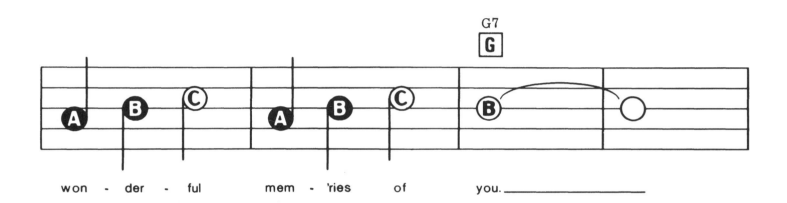

won - der - ful mem - 'ries of you. ___

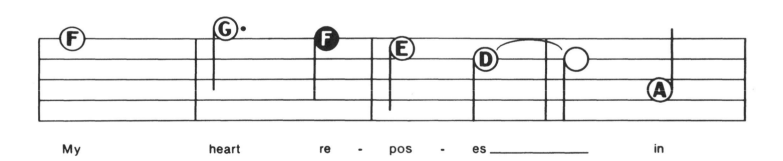

My heart re - pos - es ___ in

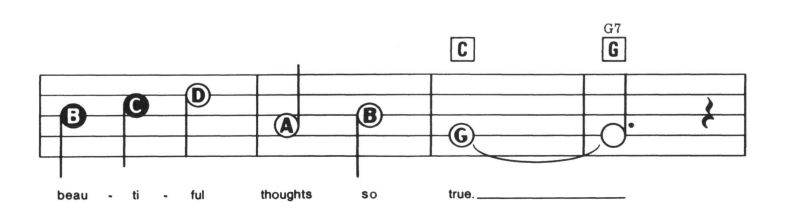

beau - ti - ful thoughts so true. ___

© 1925 (Renewed) CHAPPELL & CO., INC.
All Rights Reserved   Used by Permission

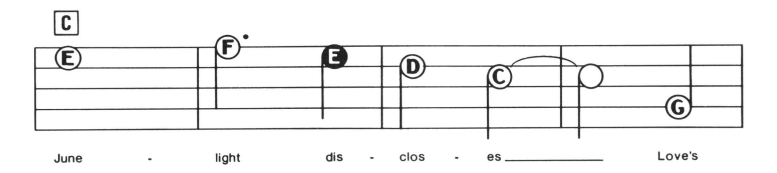

June - light dis - clos - es _____ Love's

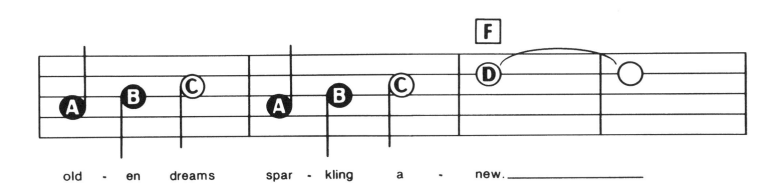

old - en dreams spar - kling a - new. _____

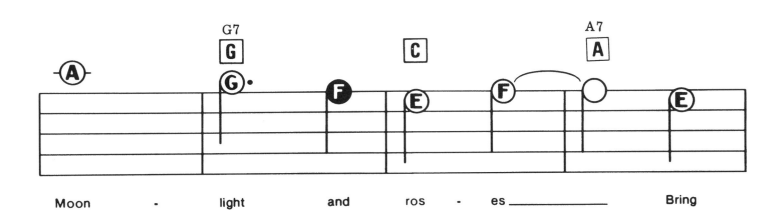

Moon - light and ros - es _____ Bring

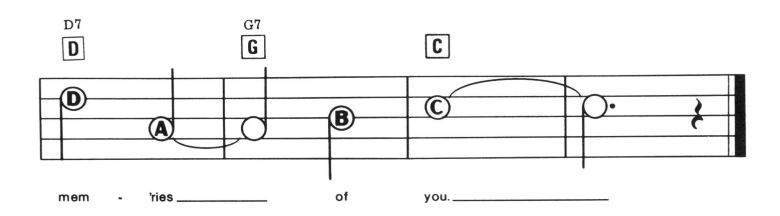

mem - 'ries _____ of you. _____

More Than You Know

Registration 8
Rhythm: Fox Trot

Words by William Rose and Edward Eliscu
Music by Vincent Youmans

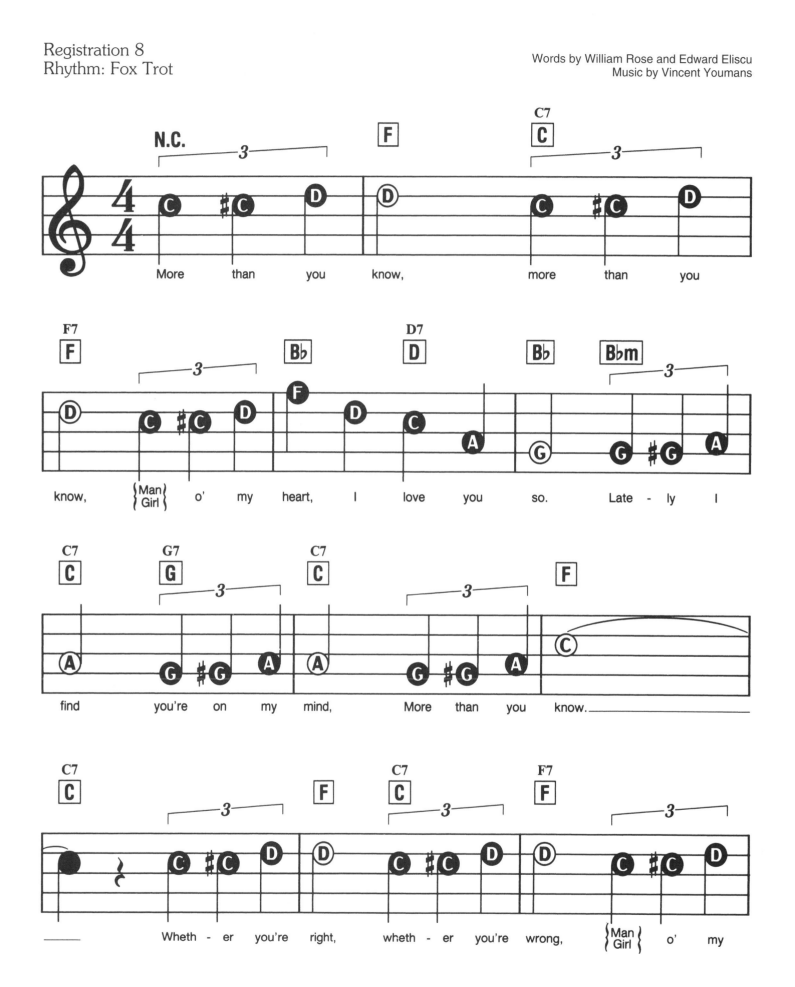

© 1929 (Renewed) WB MUSIC CORP., CHAPPELL & CO., INC. and LSQ MUSIC CO.
All Rights for LSQ MUSIC CO. Administered by THE SONGWRITERS GUILD OF AMERICA
All Rights in Canada Administered by EMI ROBBINS CATALOG INC. (Publishing) and ALFRED MUSIC (Print)
All Rights Reserved   Used by Permission

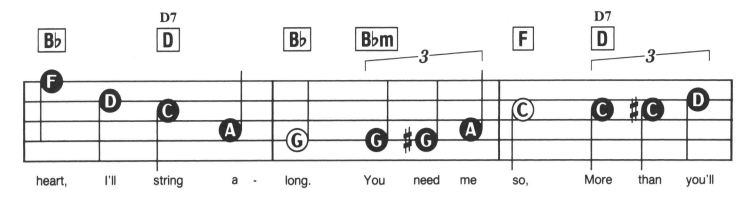

heart, I'll string a - long. You need me so, More than you'll

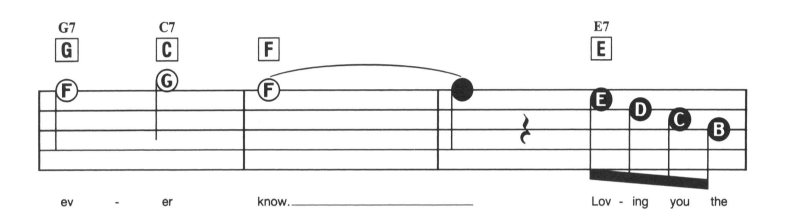

ev - er know._____ Lov - ing you the

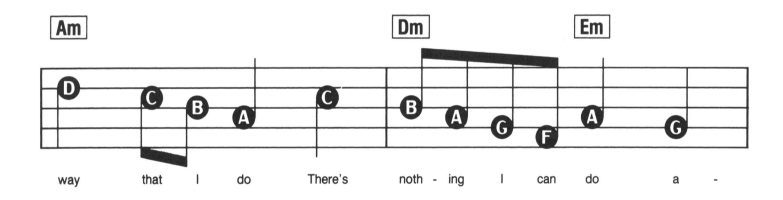

way that I do There's noth - ing I can do a -

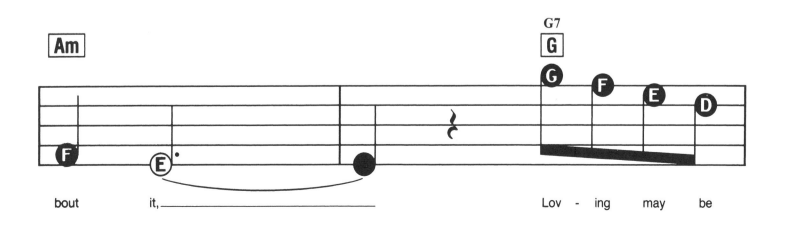

bout it,_____ Lov - ing may be

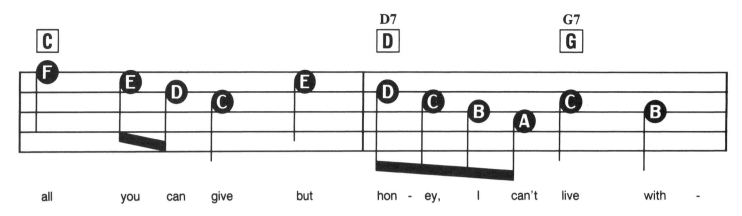

all you can give but hon - ey, I can't live with -

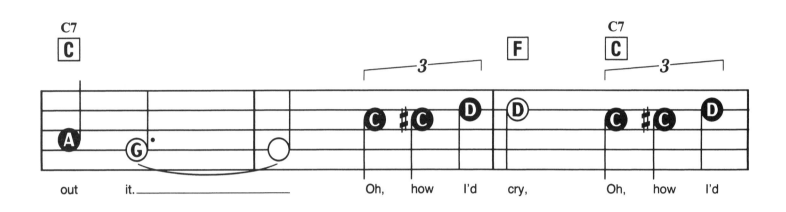

out it.＿＿＿ Oh, how I'd cry, Oh, how I'd

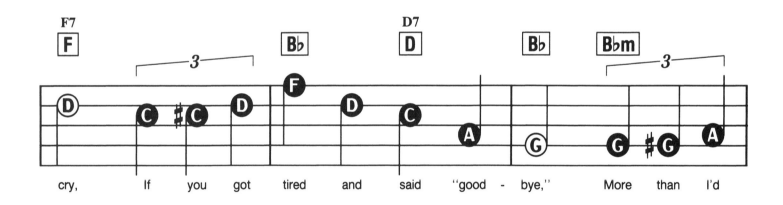

cry, If you got tired and said "good - bye," More than I'd

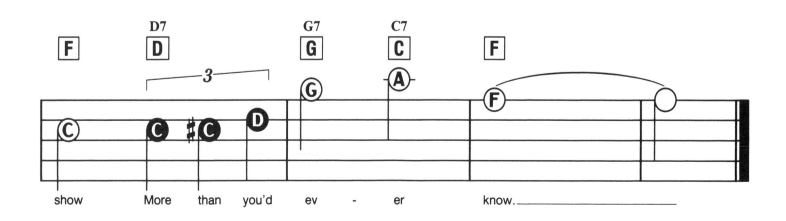

show More than you'd ev - er know.＿＿＿

Muskrat Ramble

Registration 2
Rhythm: Swing

Written by Edward Ory
and Ray Gilbert

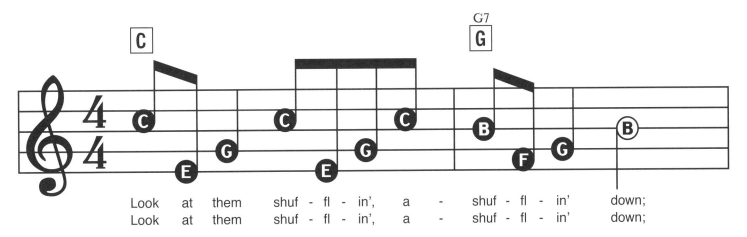

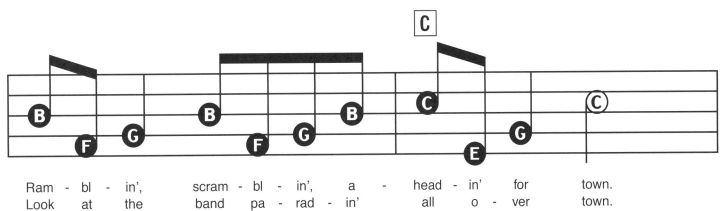

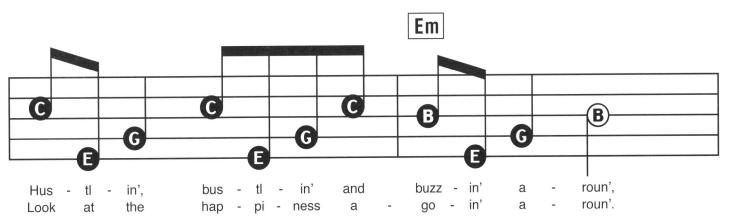

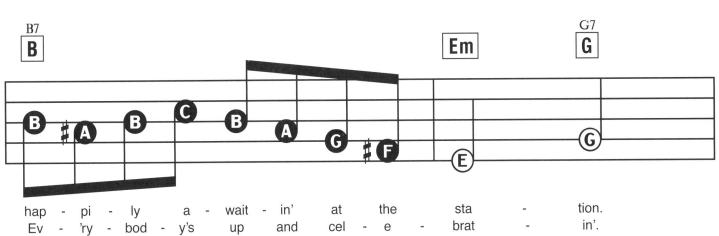

© 1926 (Renewed 2001) SLICK TONGUE ORY MUSIC (ASCAP) and IPANEMA MUSIC CORP. (ASCAP)
All Rights Administered by BMG RIGHTS MANAGEMENT (US) LLC
All Rights Reserved   Used by Permission

125

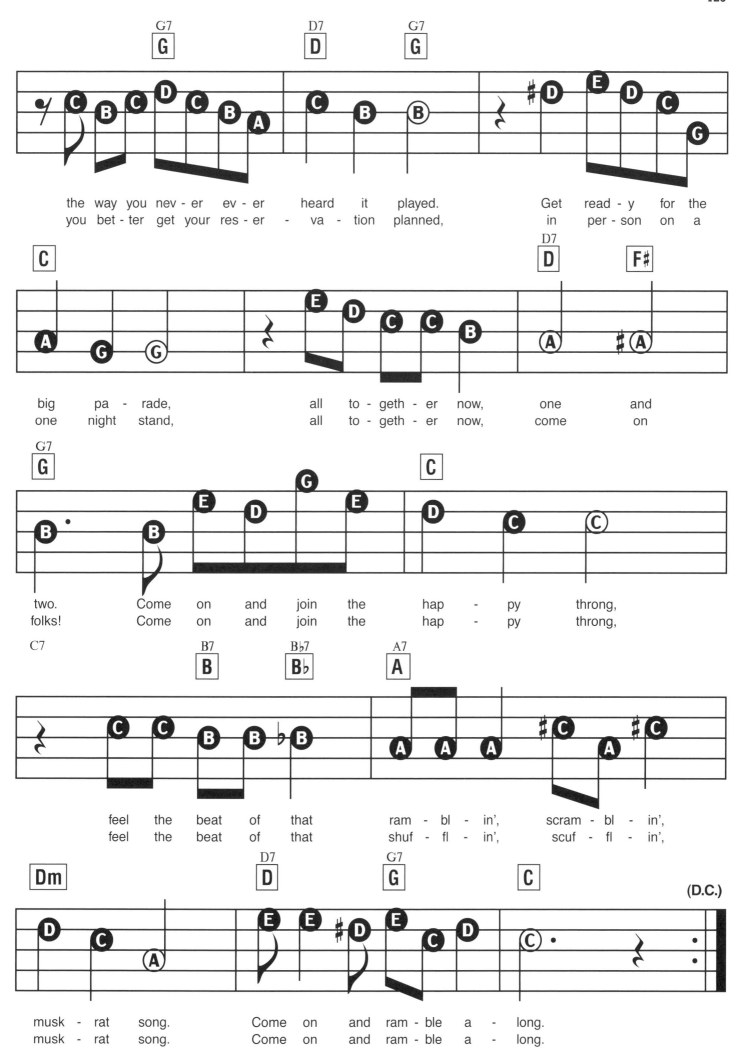

Mountain Greenery
from the Broadway Musical THE GARRICK GAIETIES

Registration 2
Rhythm: Fox Trot or Swing

Words by Lorenz Hart
Music by Richard Rodgers

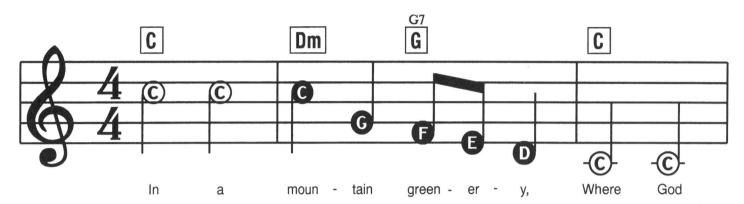

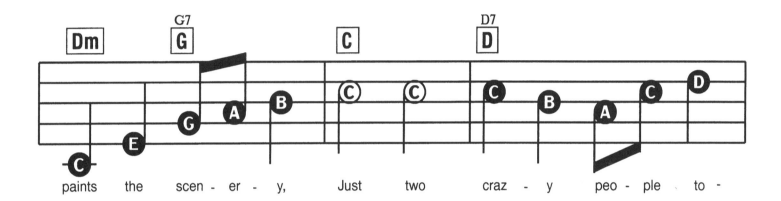

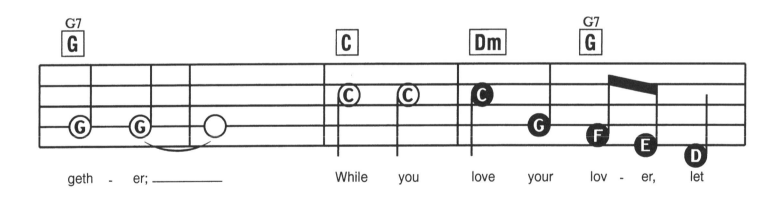

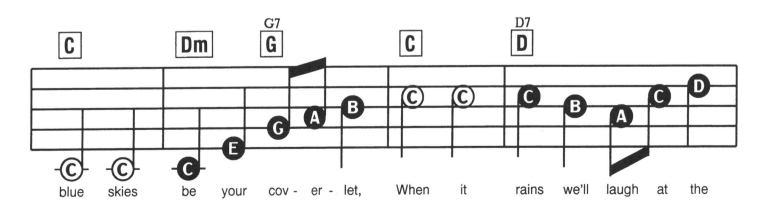

Copyright © 1926 (Renewed) by Chappell & Co.
Rights for the Extended Renewal Term in the U.S. Controlled by Williamson Music, a Division of Rodgers & Hammerstein: an Imagem Company and WB Music Corp.
International Copyright Secured   All Rights Reserved

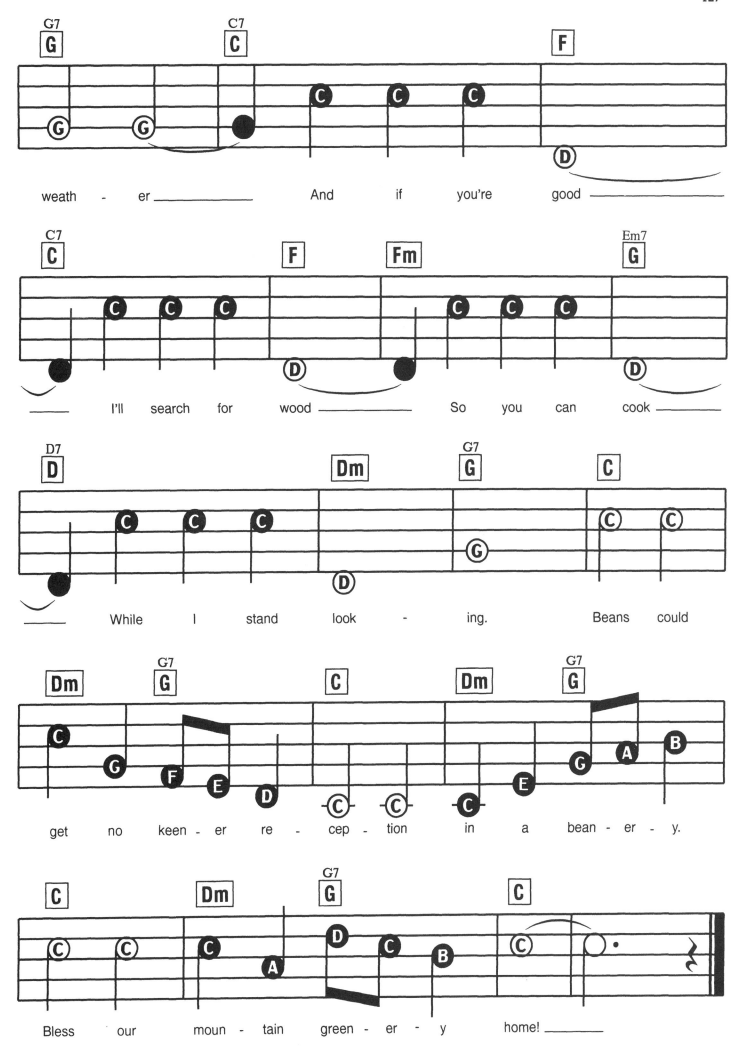

My Blue Heaven

Registration 9
Rhythm: Swing

Lyric by George Whiting
Music by Walter Donaldson

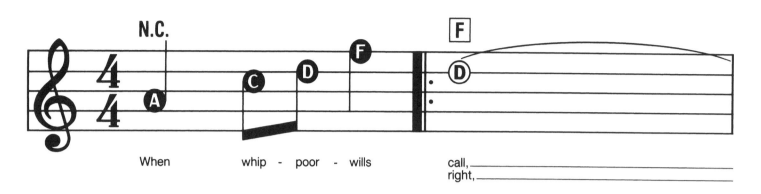

When whip - poor - wills call, ____
right, ____

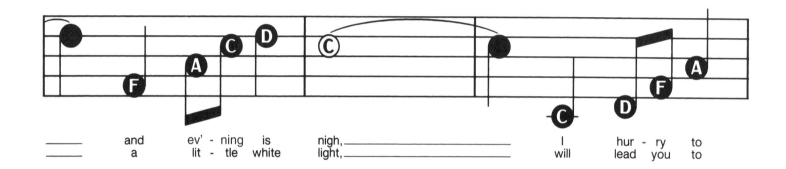

____ and ev' - ning is nigh, ____ I hur - ry to
a lit - tle white light, ____ will lead you to

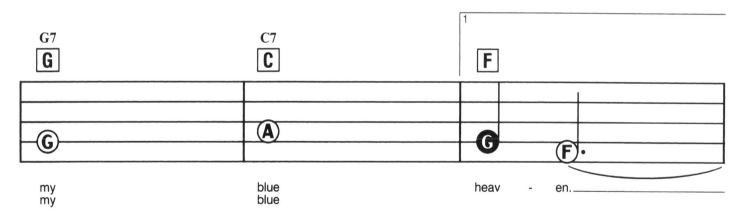

my blue heav - en. ____
my blue

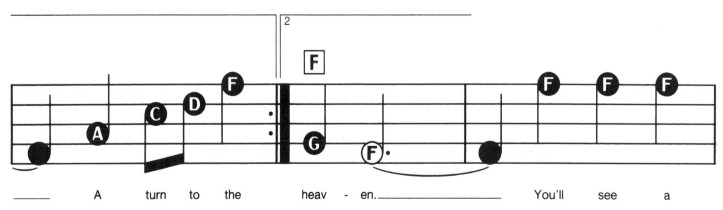

____ A turn to the heav - en. ____ You'll see a

Copyright © 1927 (Renewed) by Donaldson Publishing Co. and George Whiting Publishing
International Copyright Secured   All Rights Reserved

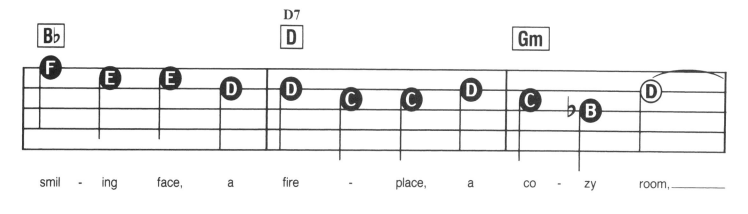

smil - ing face, a fire - place, a co - zy room, ____

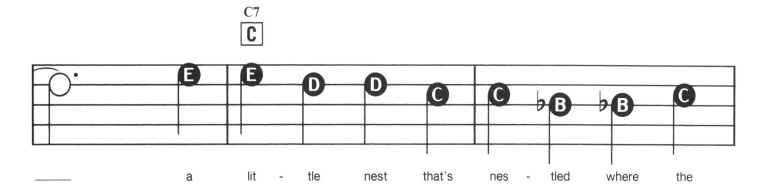

____ a lit - tle nest that's nes - tled where the

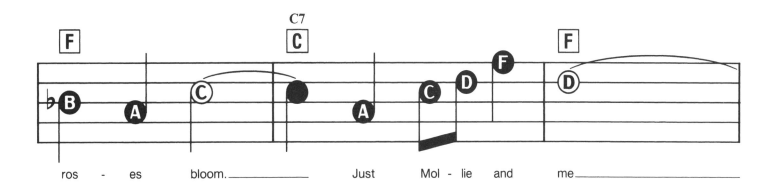

ros - es bloom. _____ Just Mol - lie and me _____

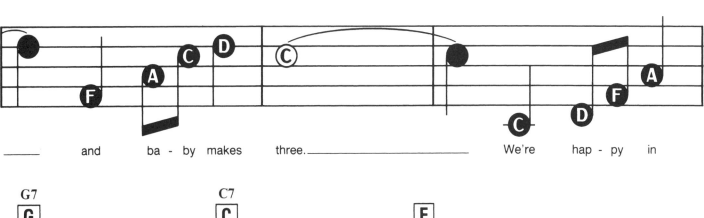

____ and ba - by makes three. _____ We're hap - py in

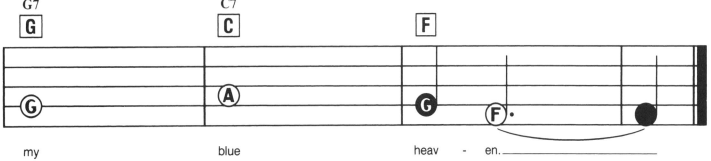

my blue heav - en. _____

My Heart Stood Still
from A CONNECTICUT YANKEE

Registration 4
Rhythm: Swing

Words by Lorenz Hart
Music by Richard Rodgers

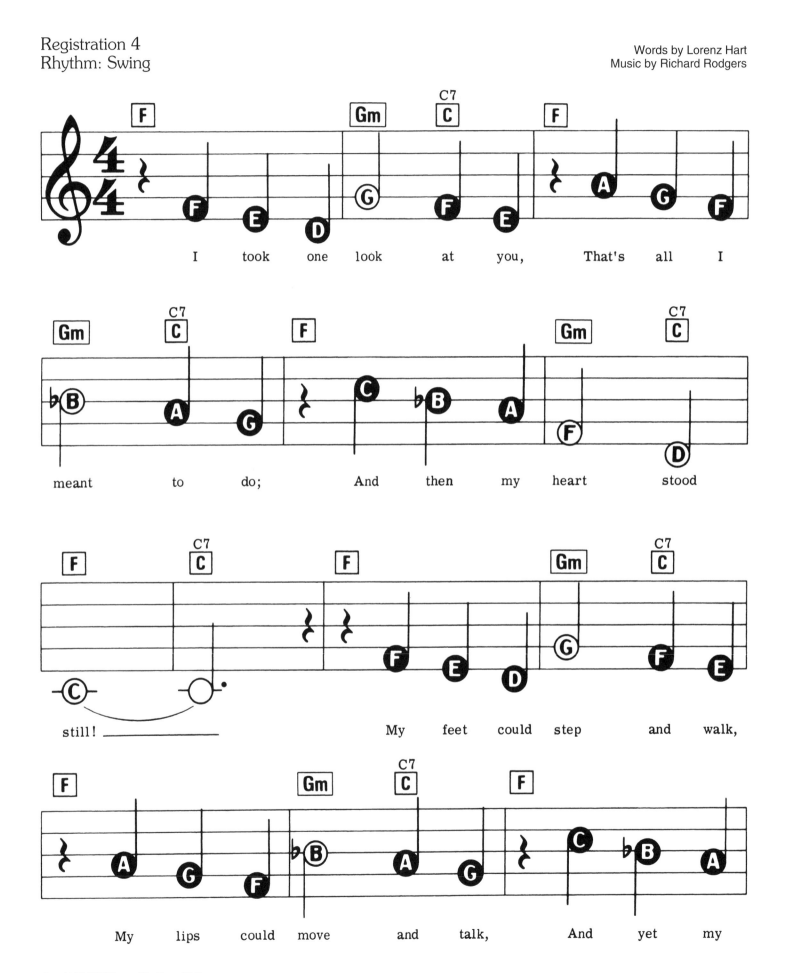

Copyright © 1927 (Renewed) by Chappell & Co.
Rights for the Extended Renewal Term in the U.S. Controlled by Williamson Music, a Division of Rodgers & Hammerstein: an Imagem Company and WB Music Corp.
International Copyright Secured   All Rights Reserved

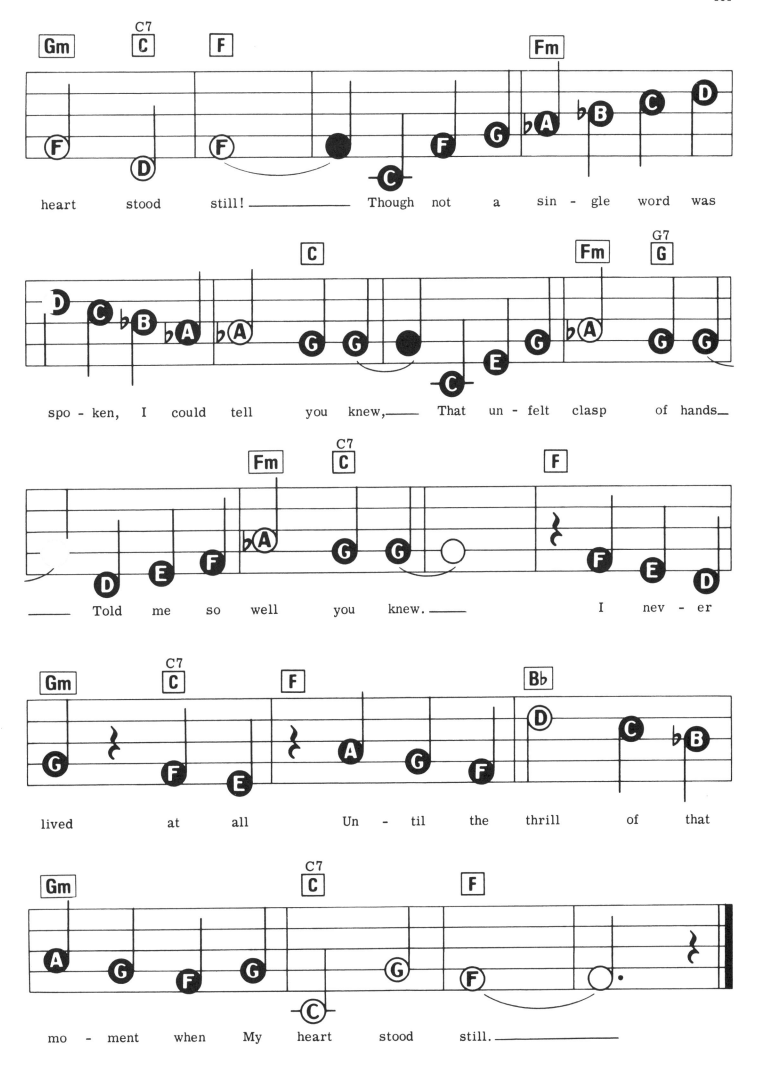

My Man
(Mon homme)
from ZIEGFELD FOLLIES

Registration 2
Rhythm: Fox Trot

Words by Albert Willemetz and Jacques Charles
English Words by Channing Pollock
Music by Maurice Yvain

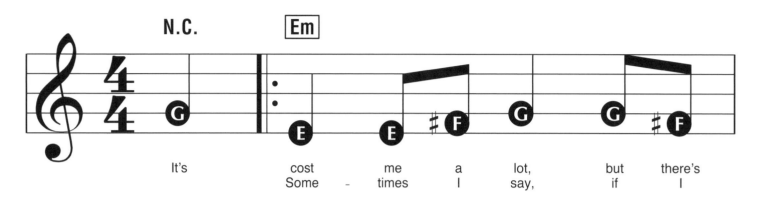

It's / cost / me / a / lot, / but / there's
Some - / times / I / say, / if / I

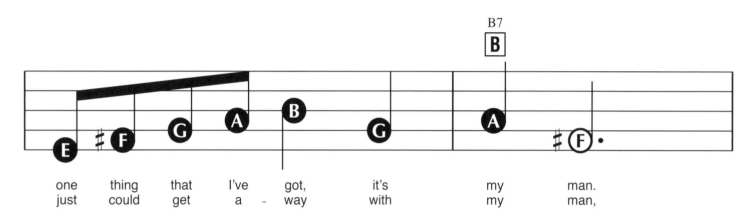

one / thing / that / I've / got, / it's / my / man.
just / could / that / get / a - way / with / my / man,

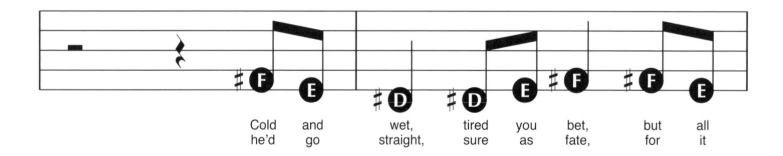

Cold / and / wet, / tired / you / bet, / but / all
he'd / go / straight, / sure / as / fate, / for / it

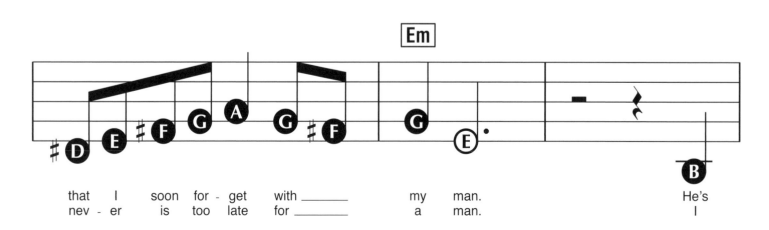

that / I / soon / for - get / with _____ / my / man.
nev - er / is / too / late / for _____ / a / man.

He's
I

Copyright © 2000 by HAL LEONARD CORPORATION
All Rights for Canada Administered by EMI FEIST CATALOG INC. (Publishing) and ALFRED MUSIC (Print)
International Copyright Secured   All Rights Reserved

133

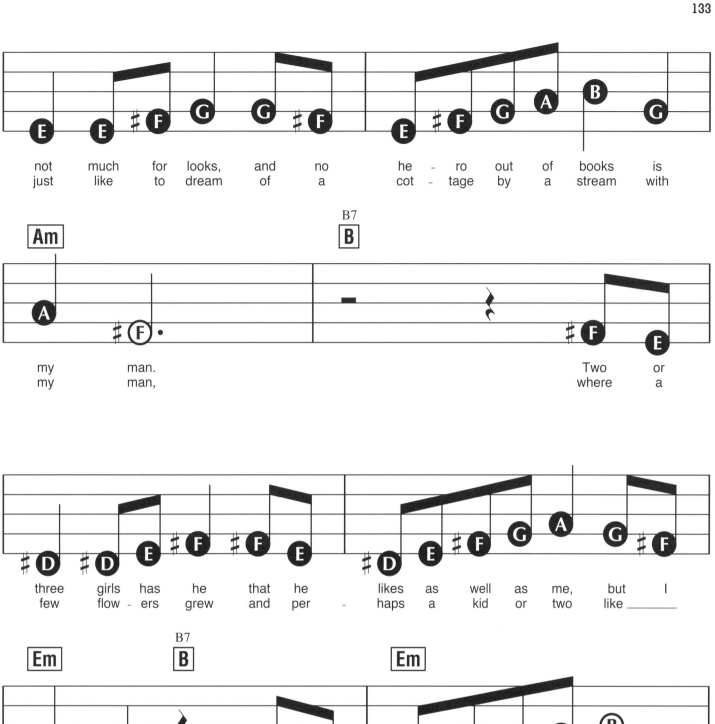

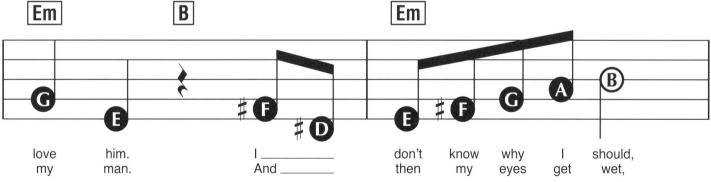

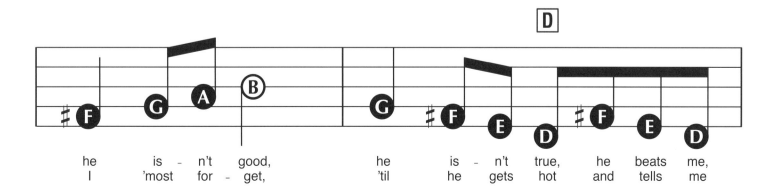

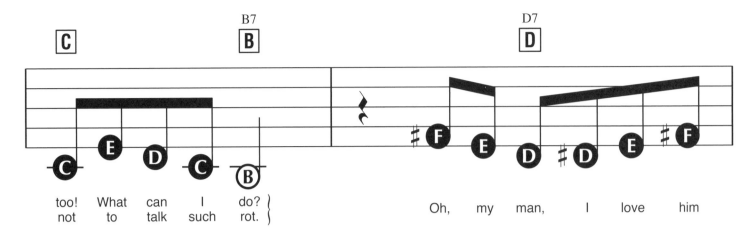

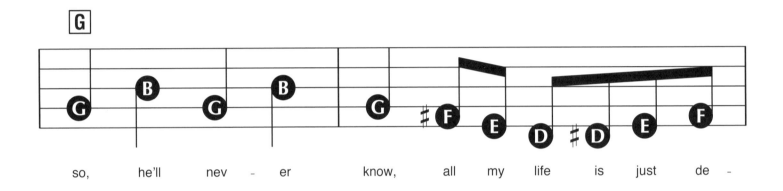

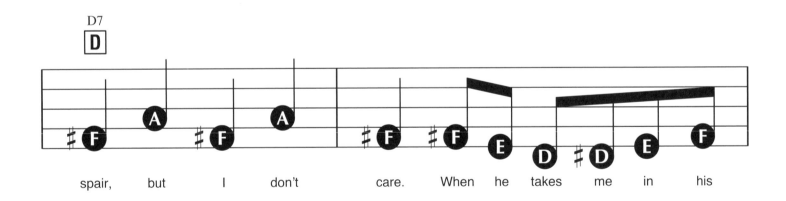

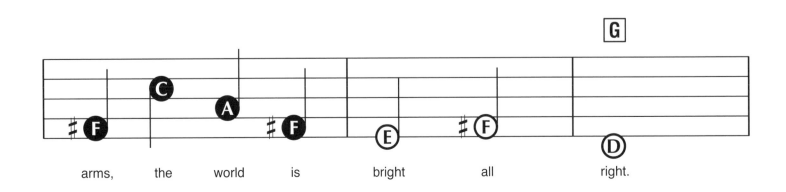

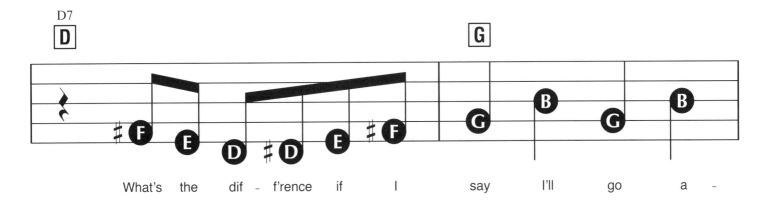

What's the dif - f'rence if I say I'll go a -

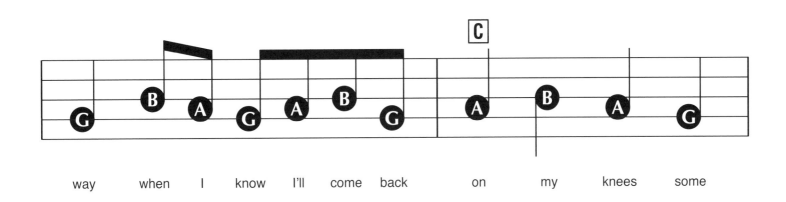

way when I know I'll come back on my knees some

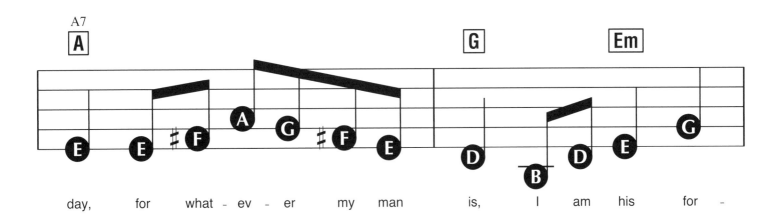

day, for what - ev - er my man is, I am his for -

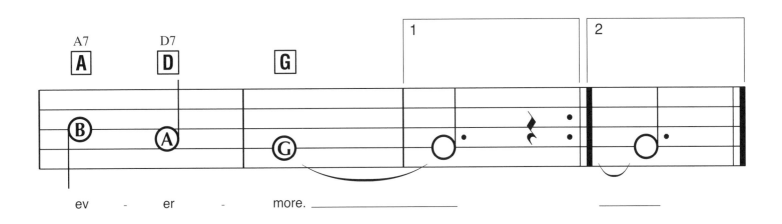

ev - er - more. _____

Oh, Lady Be Good!
from LADY, BE GOOD!

Registration 1
Rhythm: Fox Trot or Swing

Music and Lyrics by George Gershwin
and Ira Gershwin

Oh, sweet and love - ly la - dy, be good!

Oh la - dy, be good! to me!

I am so aw - f'ly mis - un - der - stood,

So la - dy be good to me.

© 1924 (Renewed) WB MUSIC CORP.
All Rights Reserved   Used by Permission

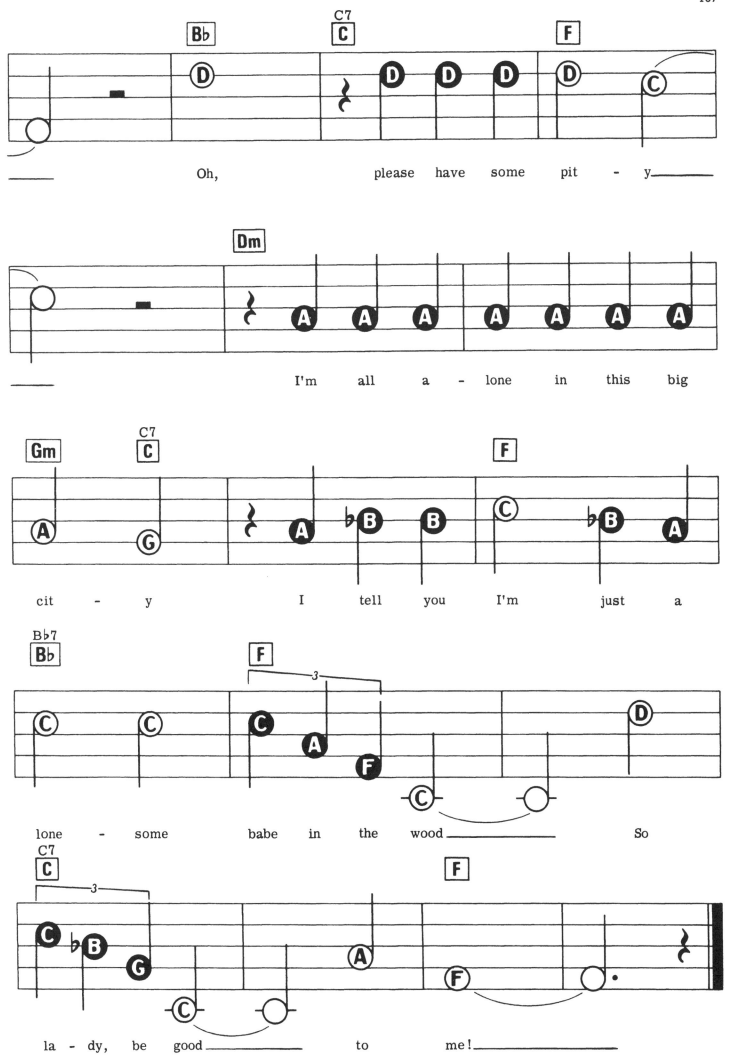

Ol' Man River
from SHOW BOAT

Registration 5
Rhythm: Ballad or Fox Trot

Lyrics by Oscar Hammerstein II
Music by Jerome Kern

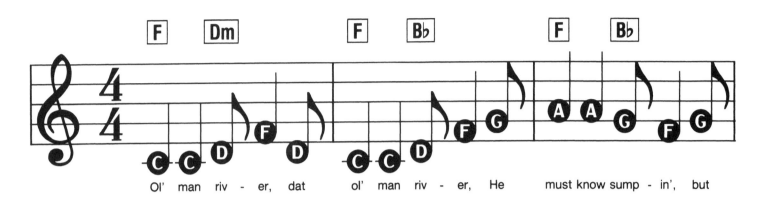

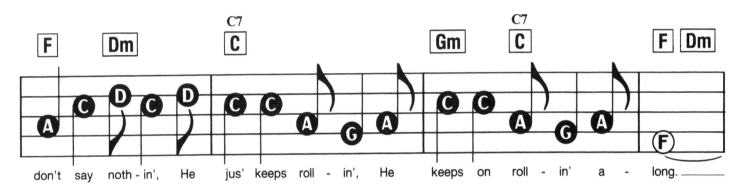

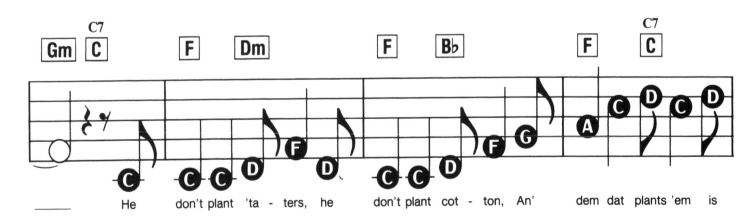

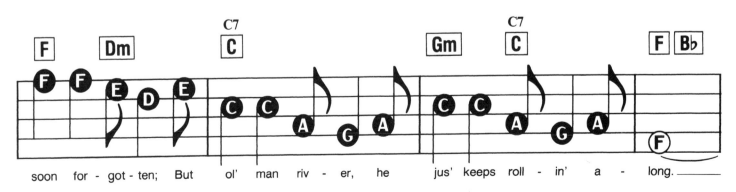

Copyright © 1927 UNIVERSAL - POLYGRAM INTERNATIONAL PUBLISHING, INC.
Copyright Renewed
All Rights Reserved   Used by Permission

139

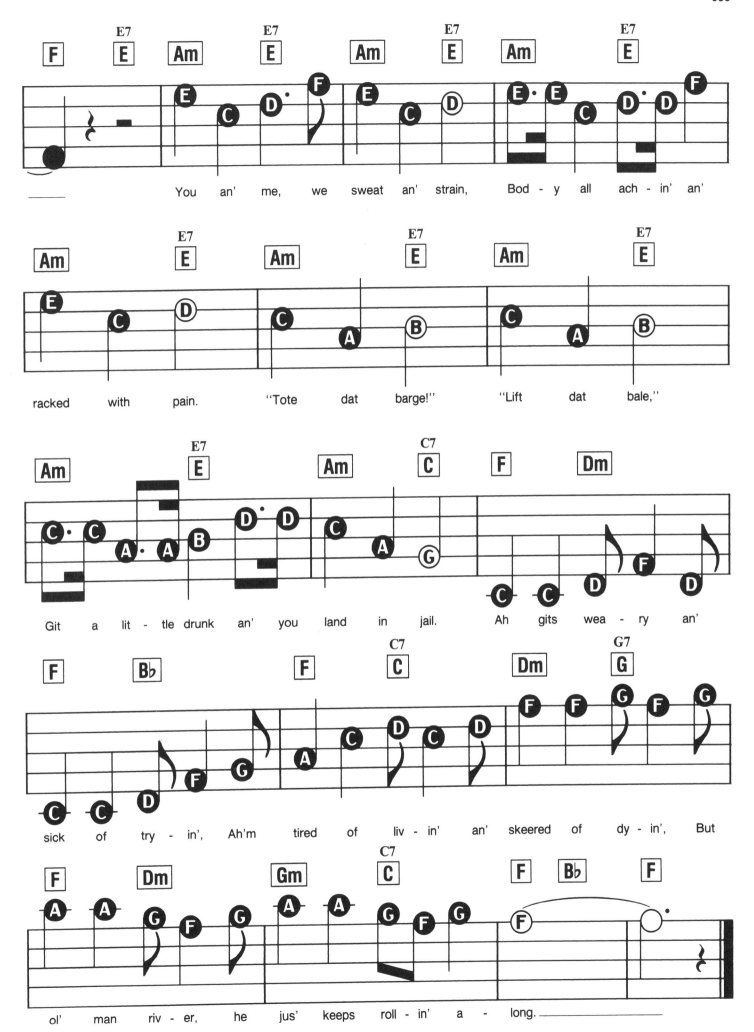

Puttin' on the Ritz
from the Motion Picture PUTTIN' ON THE RITZ

Registration 7
Rhythm: Swing

Words and Music by
Irving Berlin

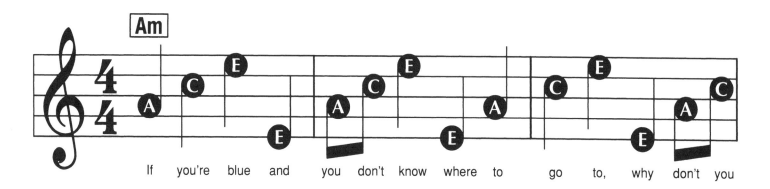

If you're blue and you don't know where to go to, why don't you

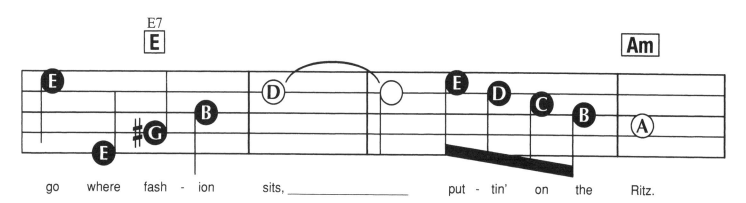

go where fash - ion sits, _____ put - tin' on the Ritz.

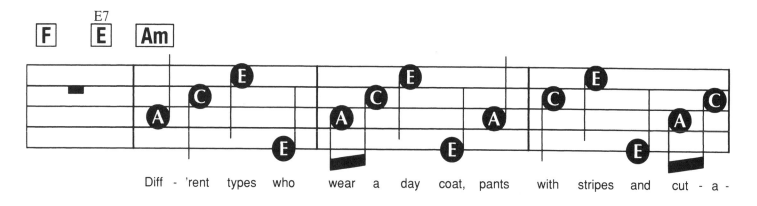

Diff - 'rent types who wear a day coat, pants with stripes and cut - a -

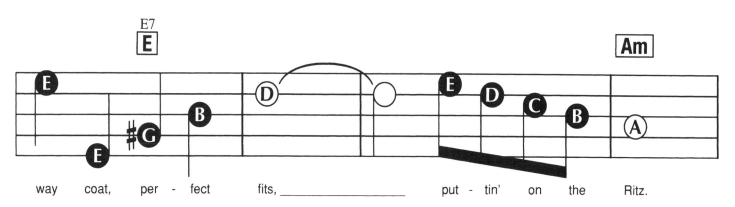

way coat, per - fect fits, _____ put - tin' on the Ritz.

© Copyright 1928, 1929 by Irving Berlin
© Arrangement Copyright 1946 by Irving Berlin
Copyright Renewed
International Copyright Secured All Rights Reserved

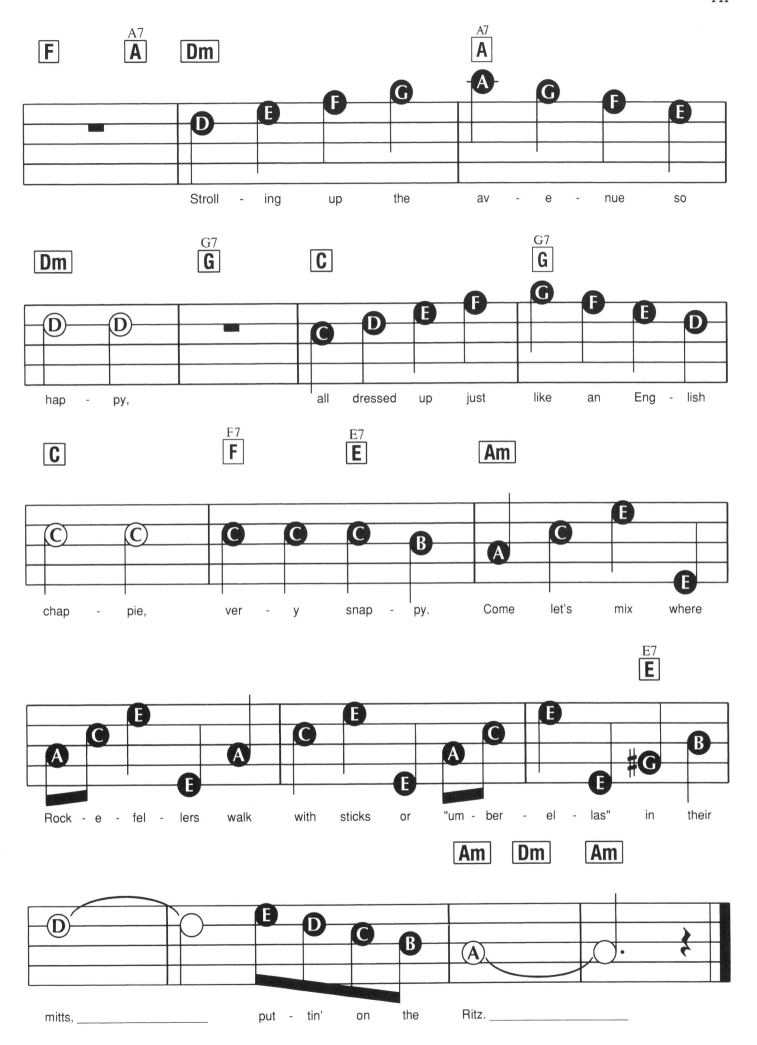

Ramona

Registration 5
Rhythm: Waltz

Words by L. Wolfe Gilbert
Music by Mabel Wayne

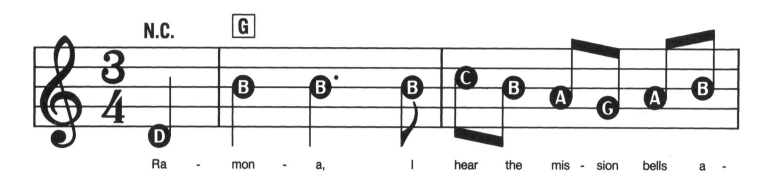

Ra - mon - a, I hear the mis - sion bells a -

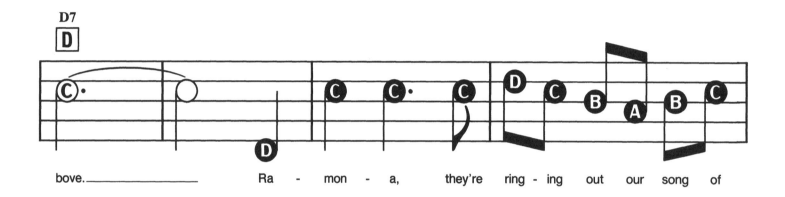

bove._____ Ra - mon - a, they're ring - ing out our song of

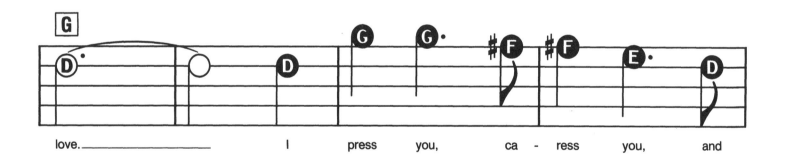

love._____ I press you, ca - ress you, and

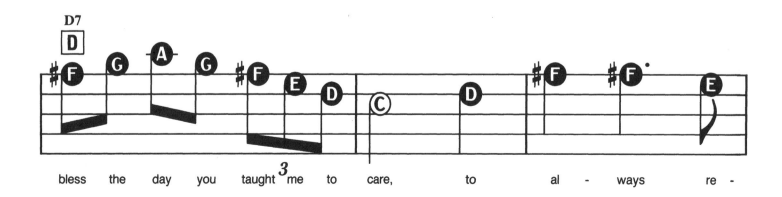

bless the day you taught me to care, to al - ways re -

© 1927 (Renewed) EMI FEIST CATALOG INC.
All Rights Administered by EMI FEIST CATALOG INC. (Publishing) and ALFRED MUSIC (Print)
All Rights Reserved   Used by Permission

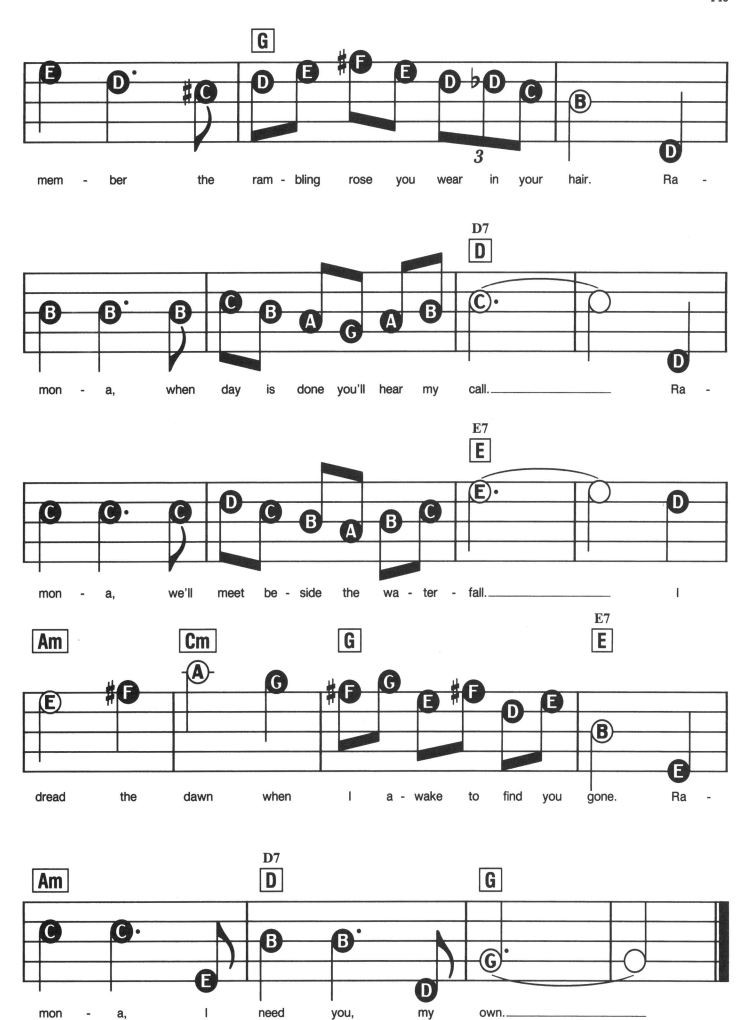

Rhapsody in Blue

Registration 8
Rhythm: None

By George Gershwin

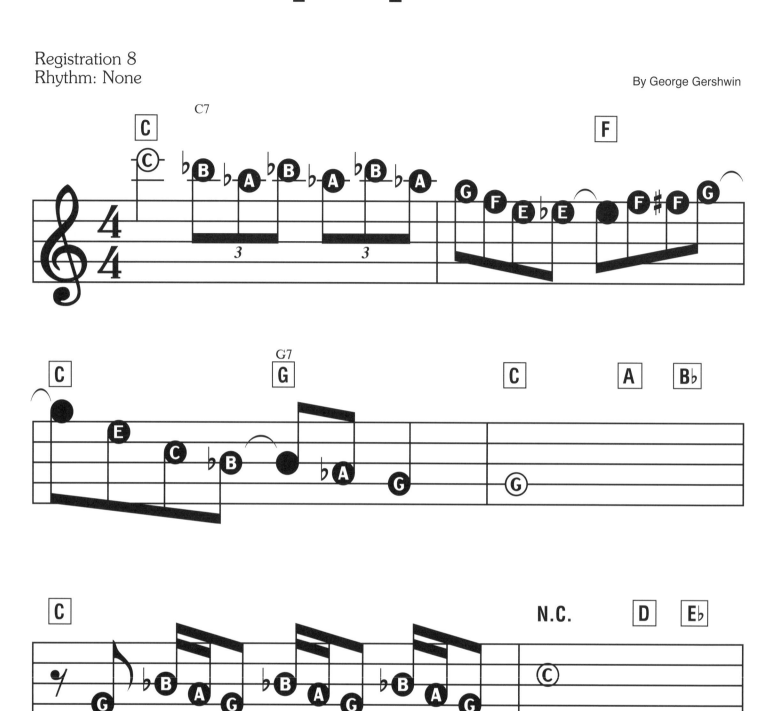

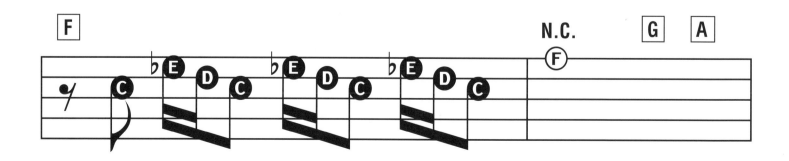

© 1924 (Renewed) WB MUSIC CORP.
All Rights Reserved   Used by Permission

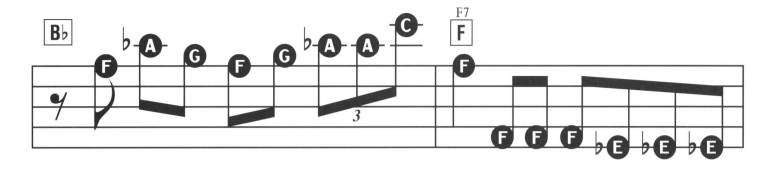

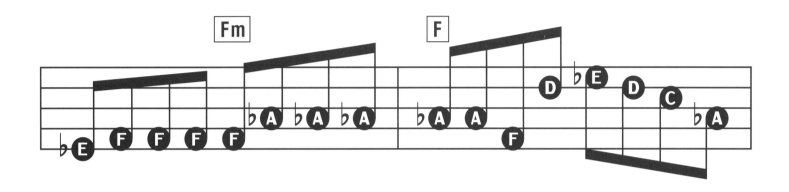

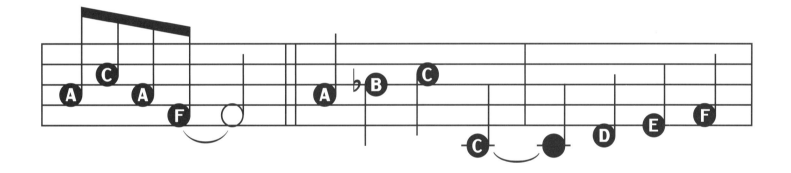

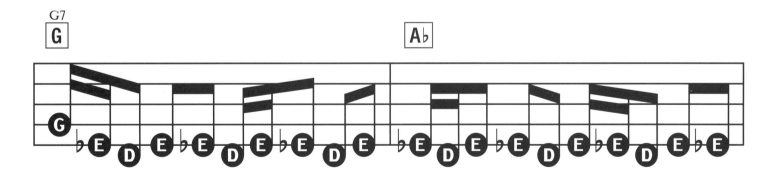

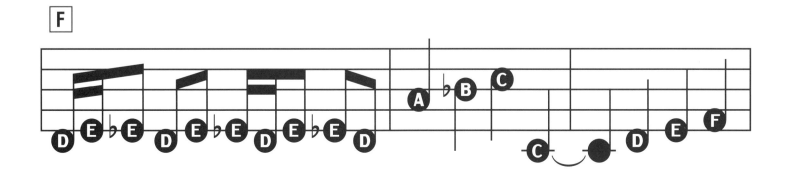

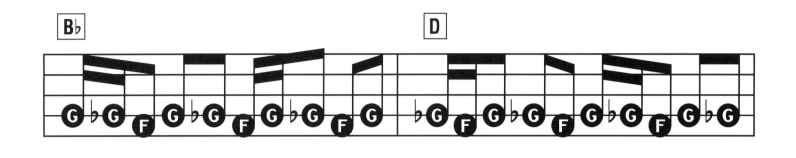

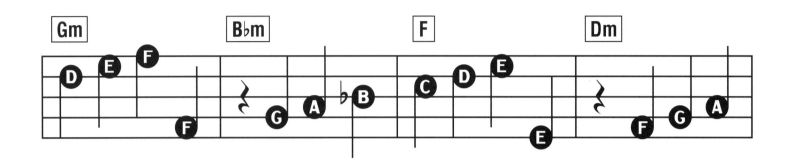

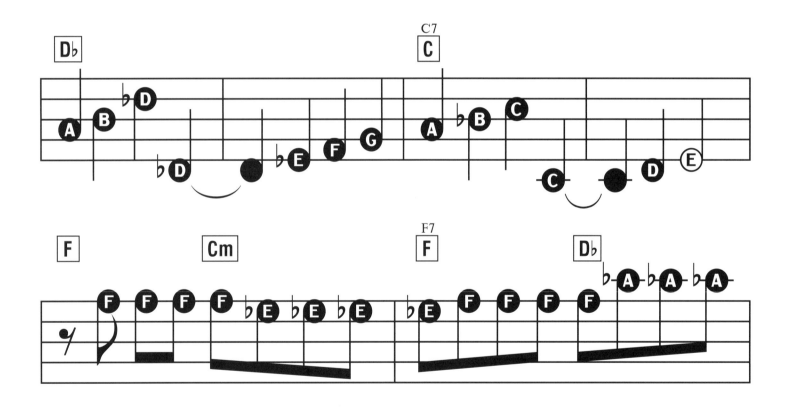

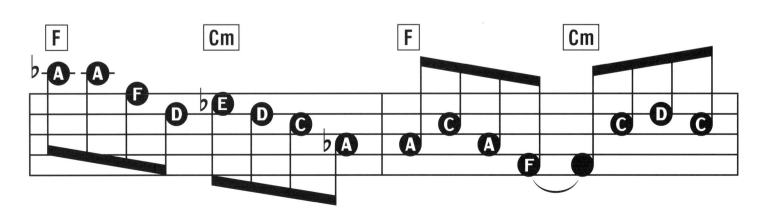

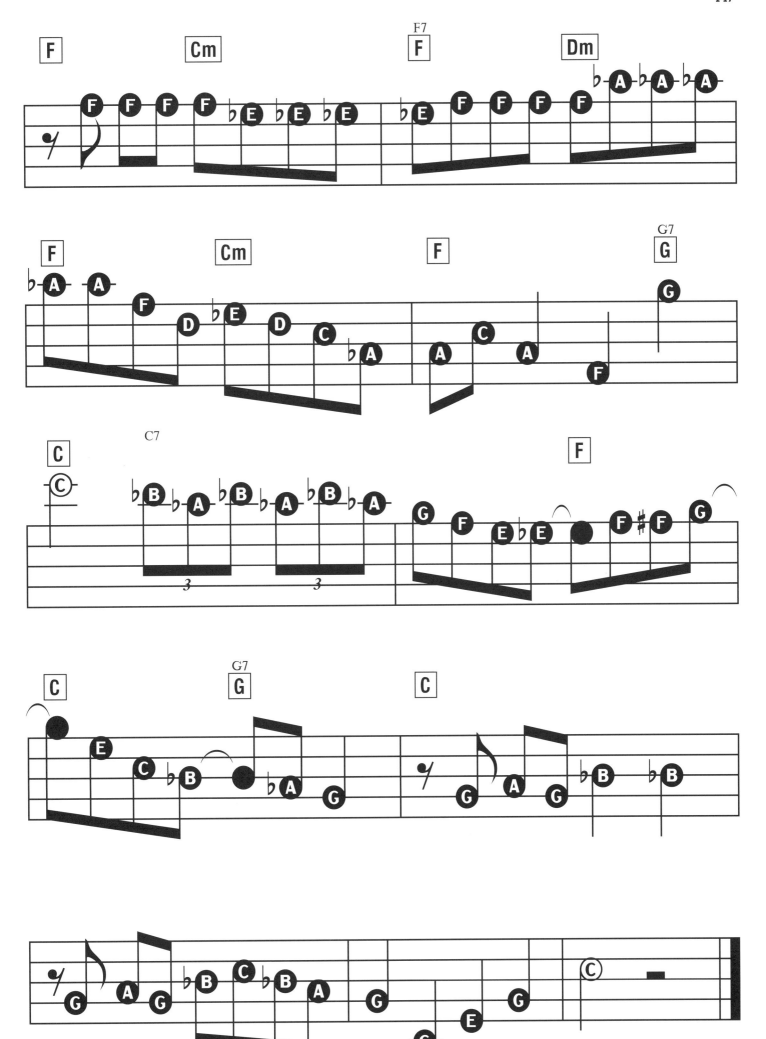

Rockin' Chair

Registration 1
Rhythm: Fox Trot

Words and Music by
Hoagy Carmichael

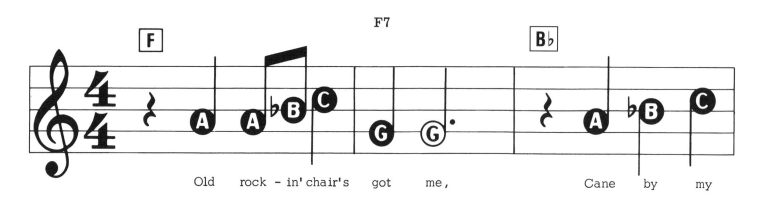

Old rock - in' chair's got me, Cane by my

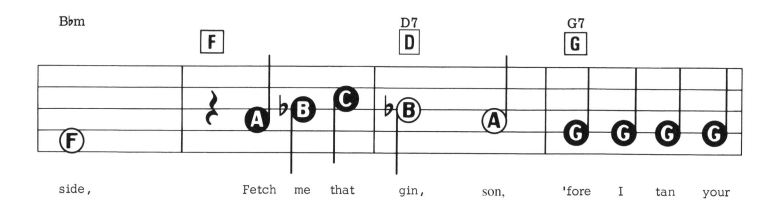

side, Fetch me that gin, son, 'fore I tan your

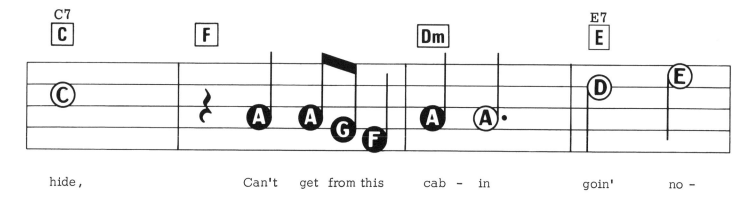

hide, Can't get from this cab - in goin' no -

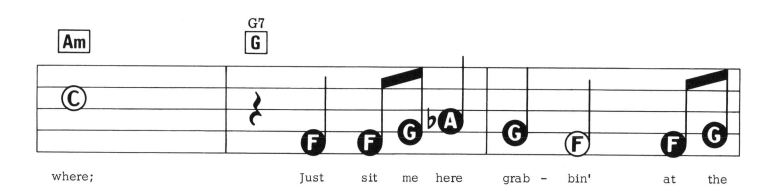

where; Just sit me here grab - bin' at the

Copyright © 1929, 1930 by Songs Of Peer, Ltd.
Copyrights Renewed
International Copyright Secured All Rights Reserved

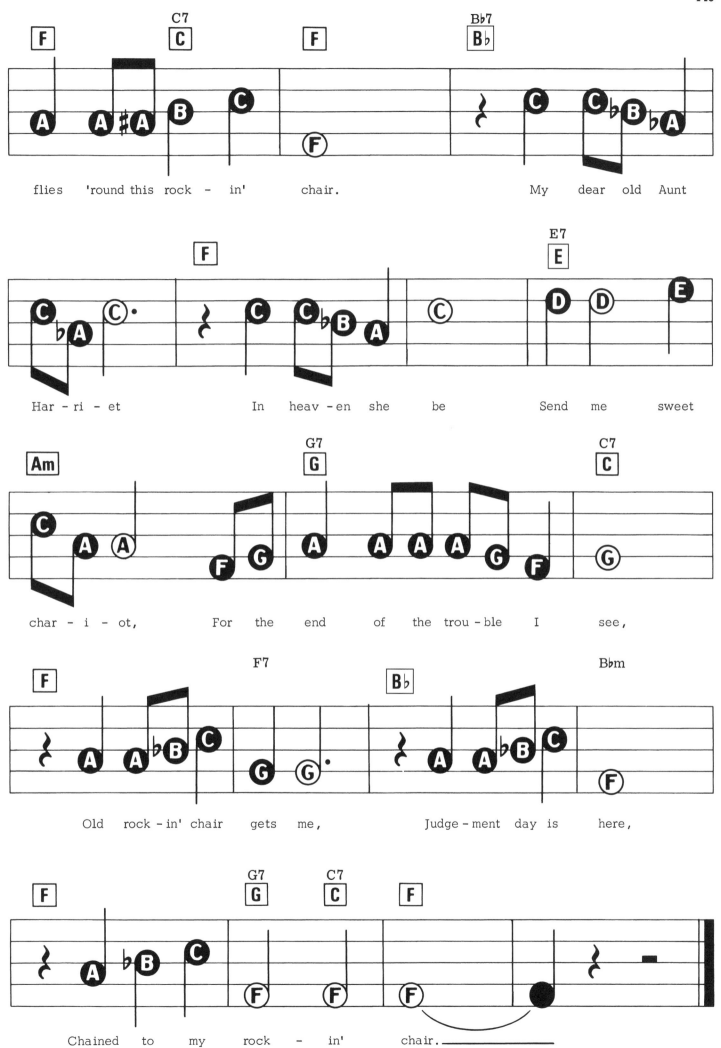

'S Wonderful
from FUNNY FACE
from AN AMERICAN IN PARIS

Registration 5
Rhythm: Swing or Jazz

Music and Lyrics by George Gershwin
and Ira Gershwin

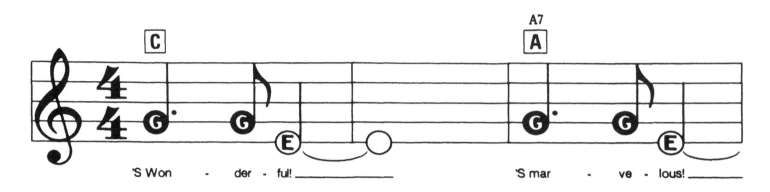

'S Won - der - ful! _____ 'S mar - ve - lous! _____

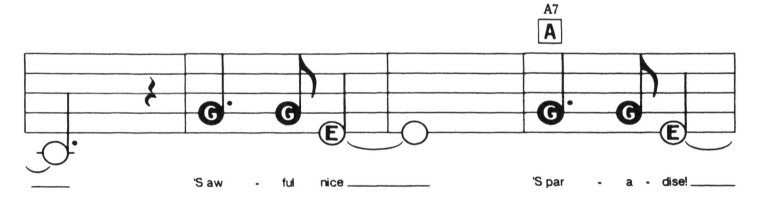

_____ You should care _____ for me! _____

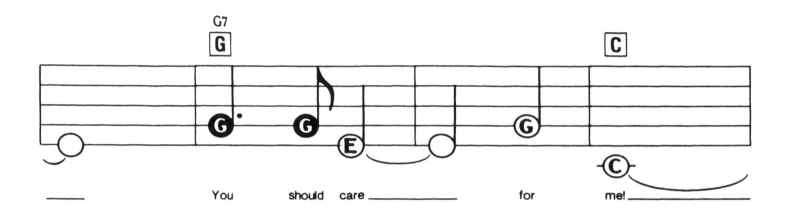

_____ 'S aw - ful nice _____ 'S par - a - dise! _____

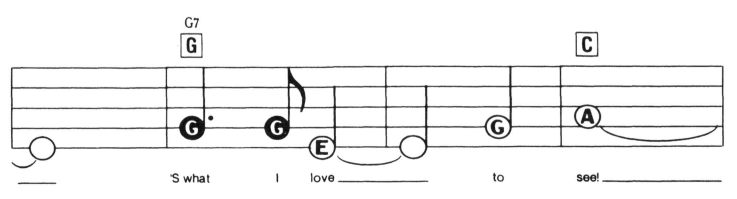

_____ 'S what I love _____ to see! _____

© 1927 (Renewed) WB MUSIC CORP.
All Rights Reserved Used by Permission

St. Louis Blues
from BIRTH OF THE BLUES

Registration 7
Rhythm: Swing

Words and Music by
W.C. Handy

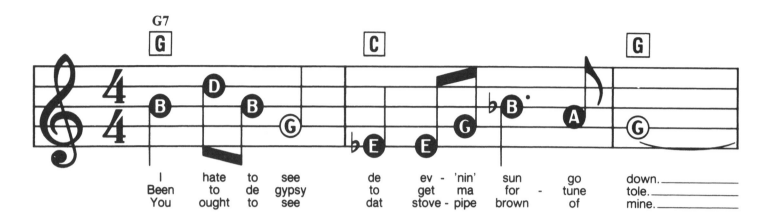

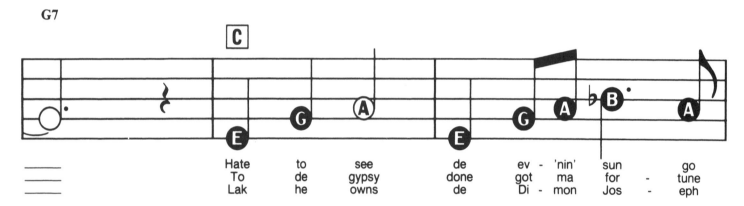

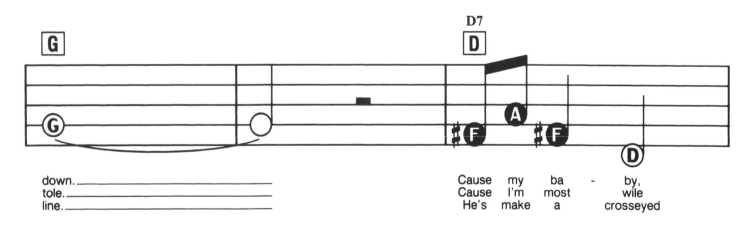

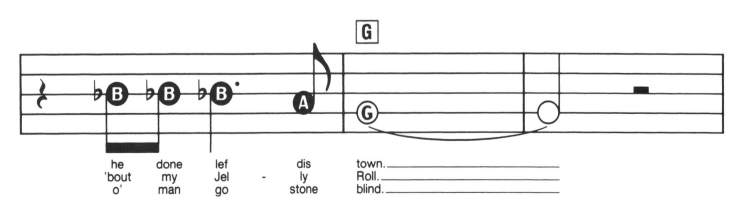

Copyright © 1990 by HAL LEONARD CORPORATION
All Rights Reserved

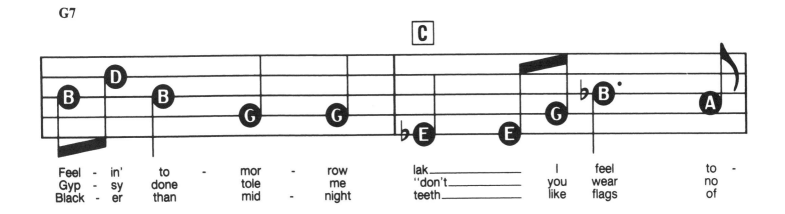

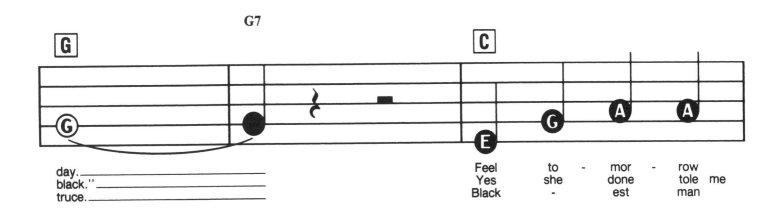

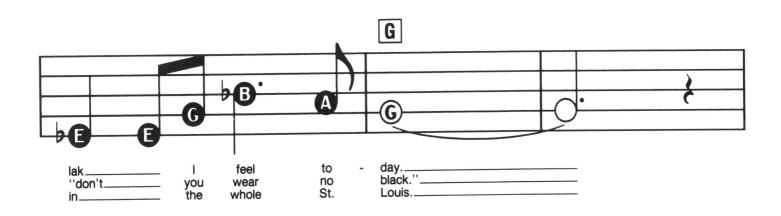

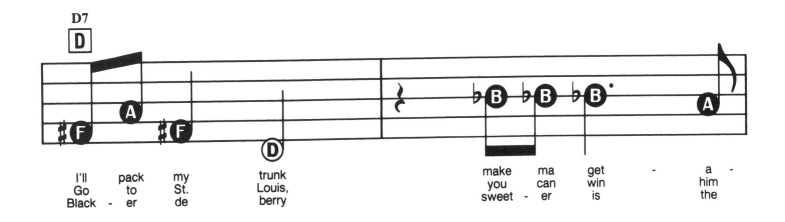

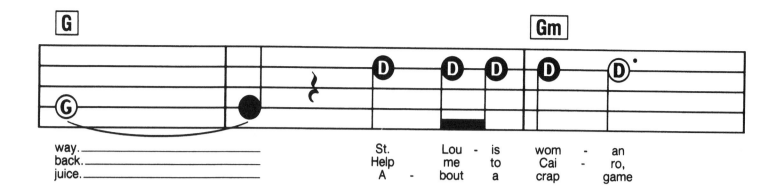

way.
back.
juice.

St. Lou - is wom - an
Help me to Cai - ro,
A - bout a crap game

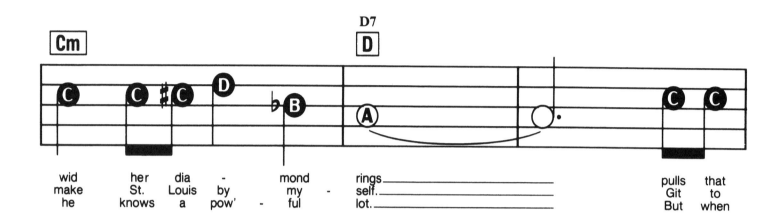

wid her dia - mond rings
make St. Louis by my - self.
he knows a pow' - ful lot.

pulls that
Git to
But when

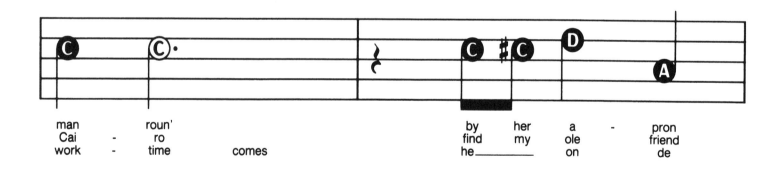

man roun'
Cai - ro
work - time comes

by her a - pron
find my ole friend
he on de

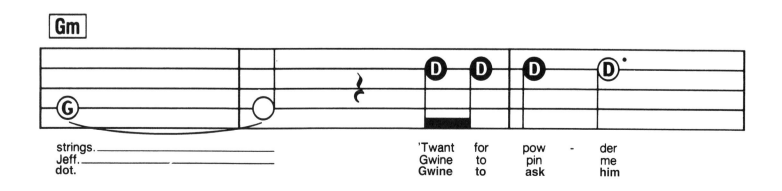

strings.
Jeff.
dot.

'Twant for pow - der
Gwine to pin me
Gwine to ask him

155

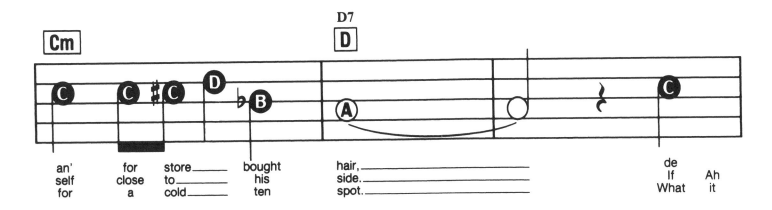

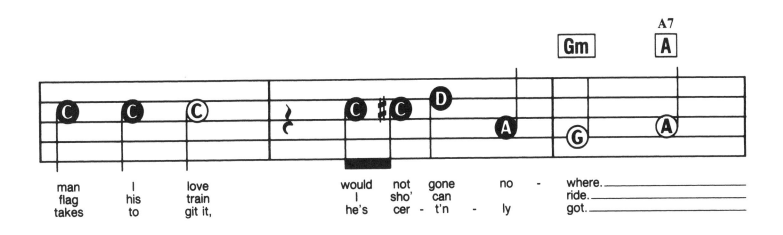

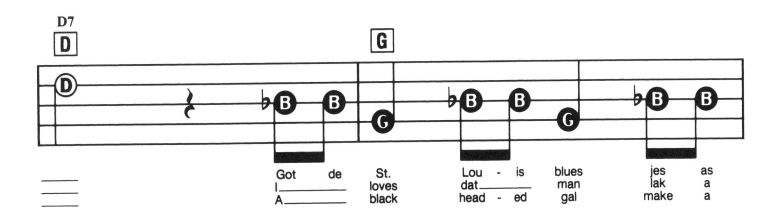

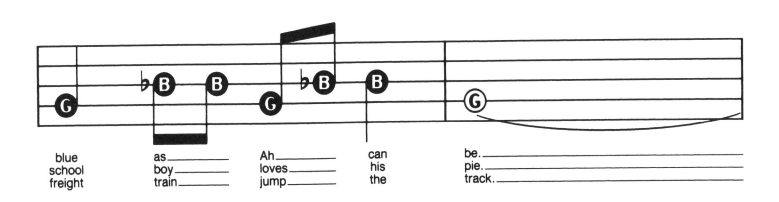

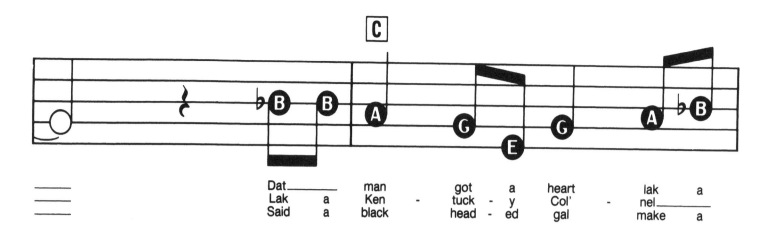

Dat_____ man got a heart lak a
Lak a Ken - tuck - y Col' - nel_____ a
Said a black head - ed gal make a

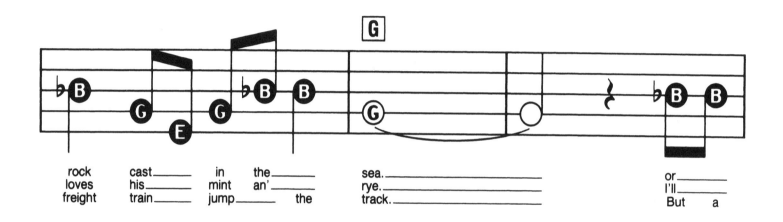

rock cast_____ in the_____ sea._____ or_____
loves his_____ mint an'_____ rye._____ I'll_____
freight train_____ jump_____ the track._____ But a

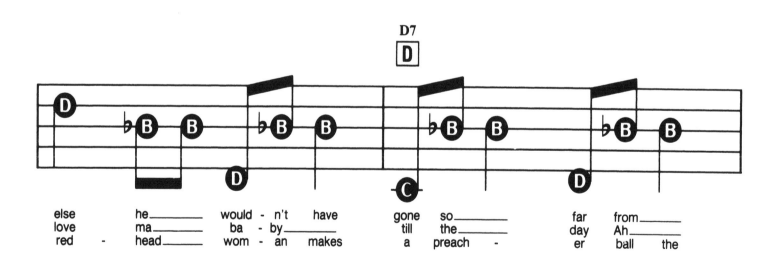

else he_____ would - n't have gone so_____ far from_____
love ma_____ ba - by_____ till the_____ day Ah_____
red - head_____ wom - an makes a preach - er ball the

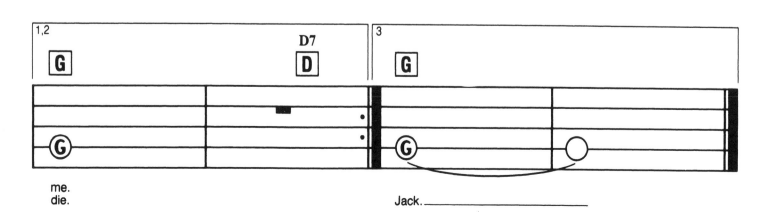

me.
die. Jack._____

Second Hand Rose

Registration 8
Rhythm: Fox Trot

Words by Grant Clarke
Music by James F. Hanley

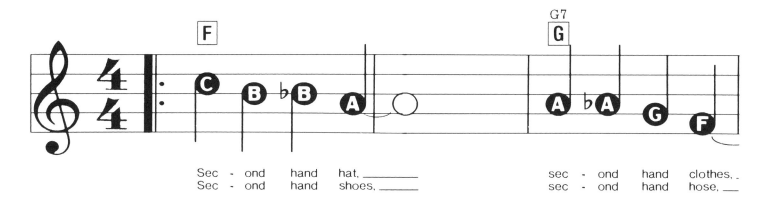

Sec - ond hand hat, _____ sec - ond hand clothes, _____
Sec - ond hand shoes, _____ sec - ond hand hose, _____

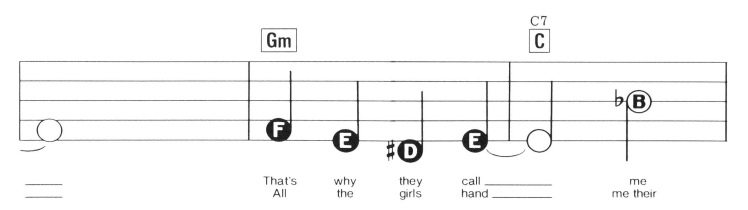

_____ That's why they call _____ me
_____ All the girls hand _____ me their

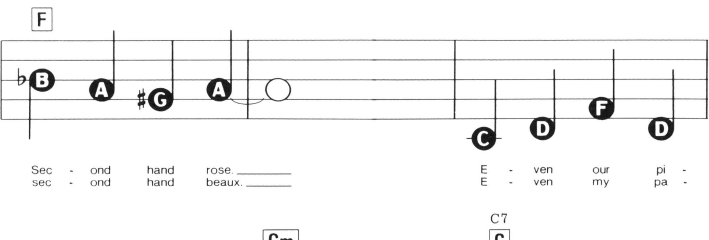

Sec - ond hand rose. _____ E - ven our pi -
sec - ond hand beaux. _____ E - ven my pa -

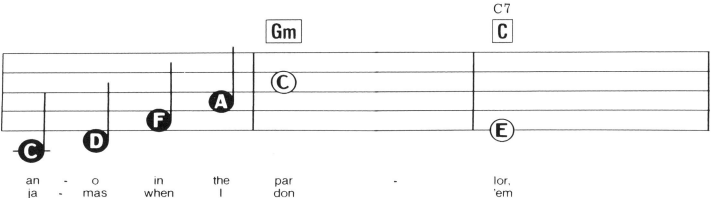

an - o in the par - lor,
ja - mas when I don 'em

Copyright © 2010 by HAL LEONARD CORPORATION
International Copyright Secured All Rights Reserved

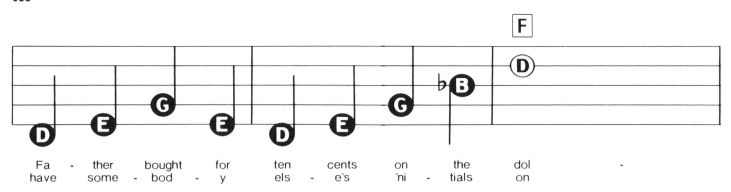

Fa - ther bought for ten cents on the dol -
have some - bod - y els - e's 'ni - tials on

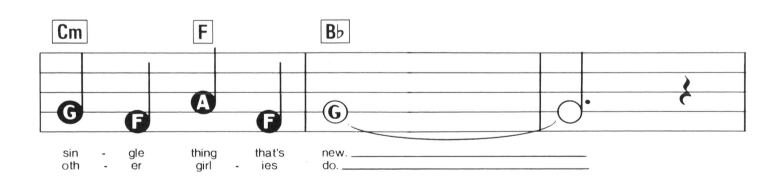

lar.   Sec - ond hand pearls, _____ I'm wear - ing
'em.   Sec - ond hand rings, _____ I'm sick of

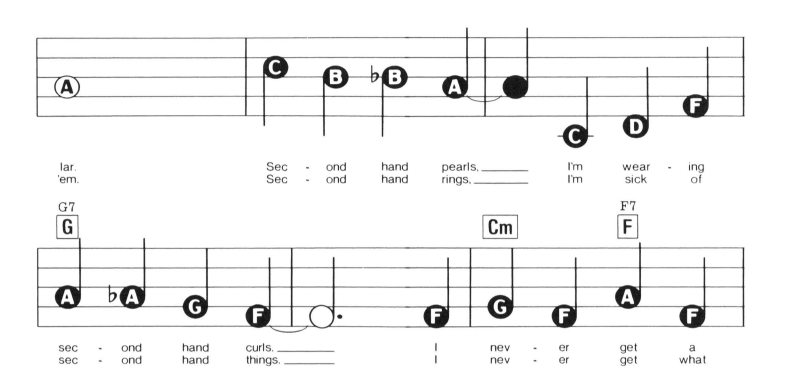

sec - ond hand curls. _____   I nev - er get a
sec - ond hand things. _____   I nev - er get what

sin - gle thing that's new. _____
oth - er girl - ies do. _____

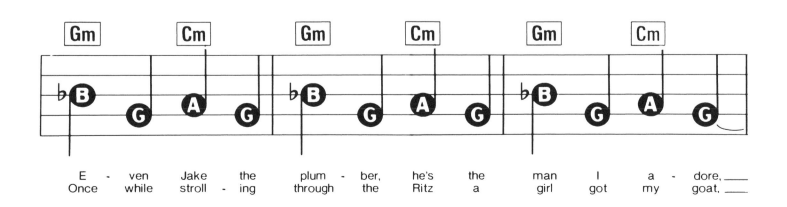

E - ven Jake the plum - ber, he's the man I a - dore, ____
Once while stroll - ing through the Ritz a girl got my goat, ____

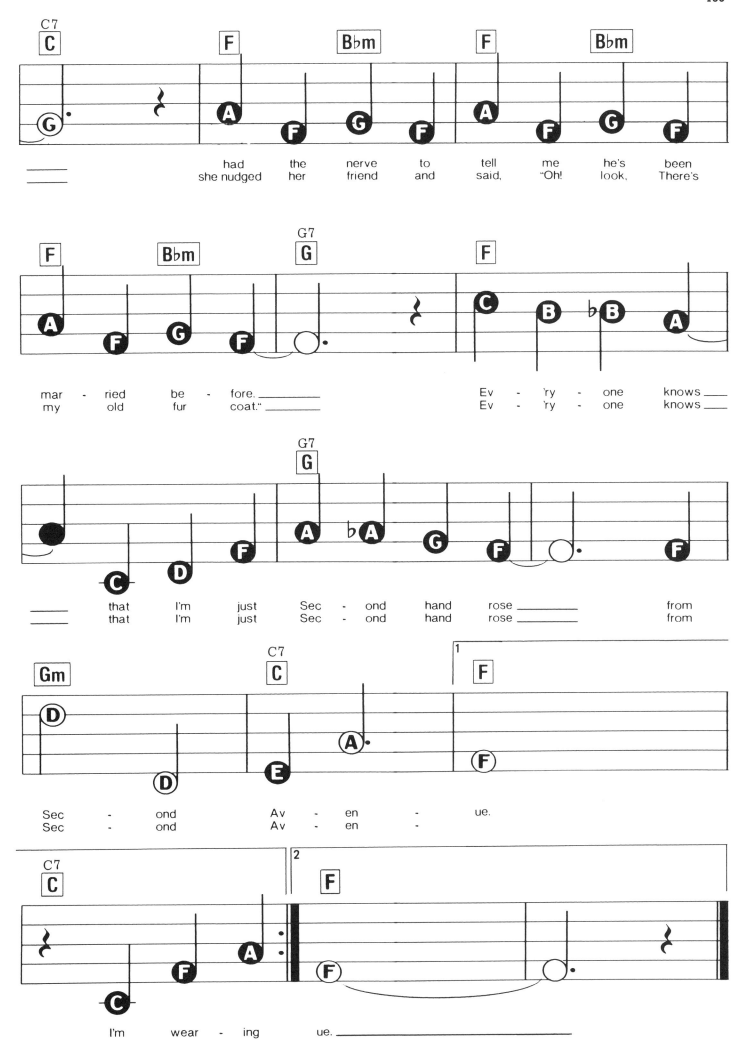

Say It with Music

from the 1921 Stage Production MUSIC BOX REVUE

Registration 4
Rhythm: Fox Trot or Swing

Words and Music by
Irving Berlin

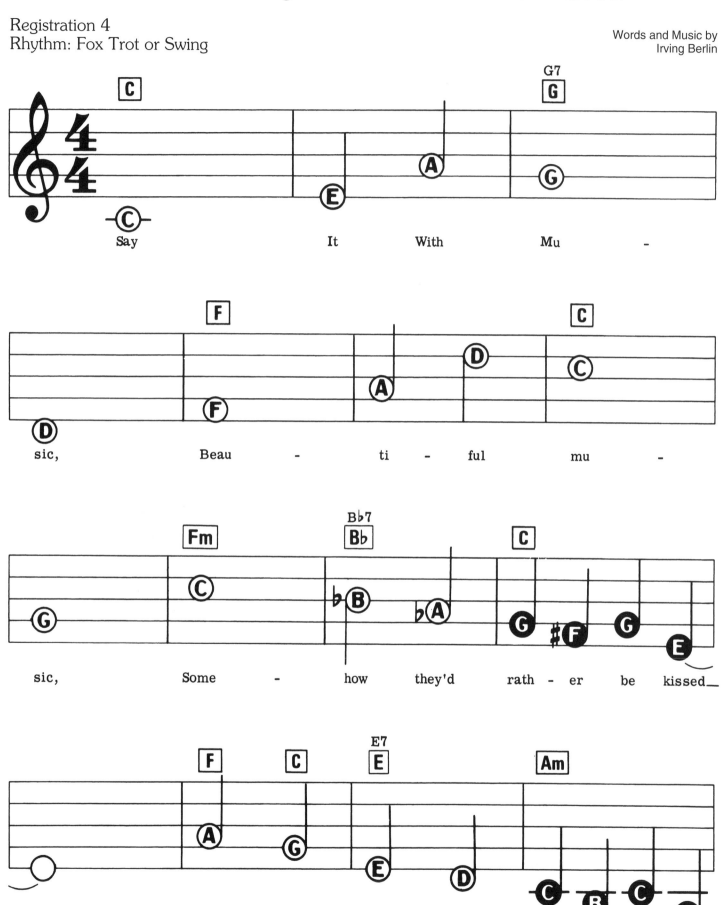

© Copyright 1921 by Irving Berlin
Copyright Renewed
International Copyright Secured   All Rights Reserved

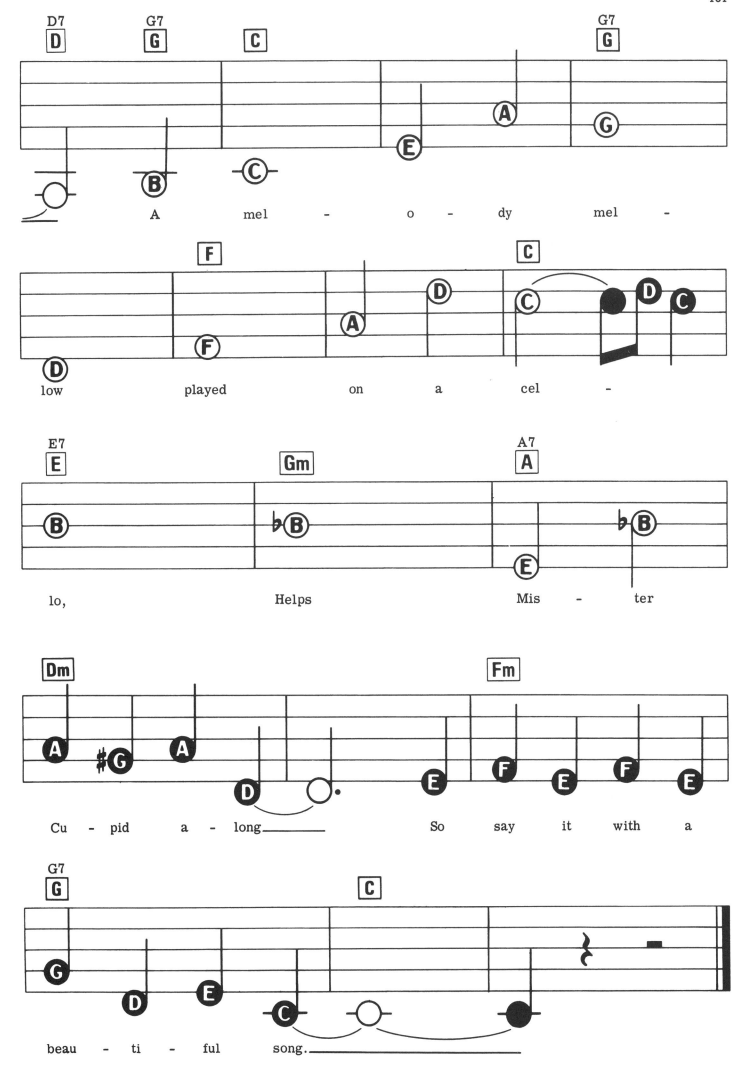

Sentimental Me
from the Broadway Musical THE GARRICK GAIETIES

Registration 4
Rhythm: Ballad or Fox Trot

Words by Lorenz Hart
Music by Richard Rodgers

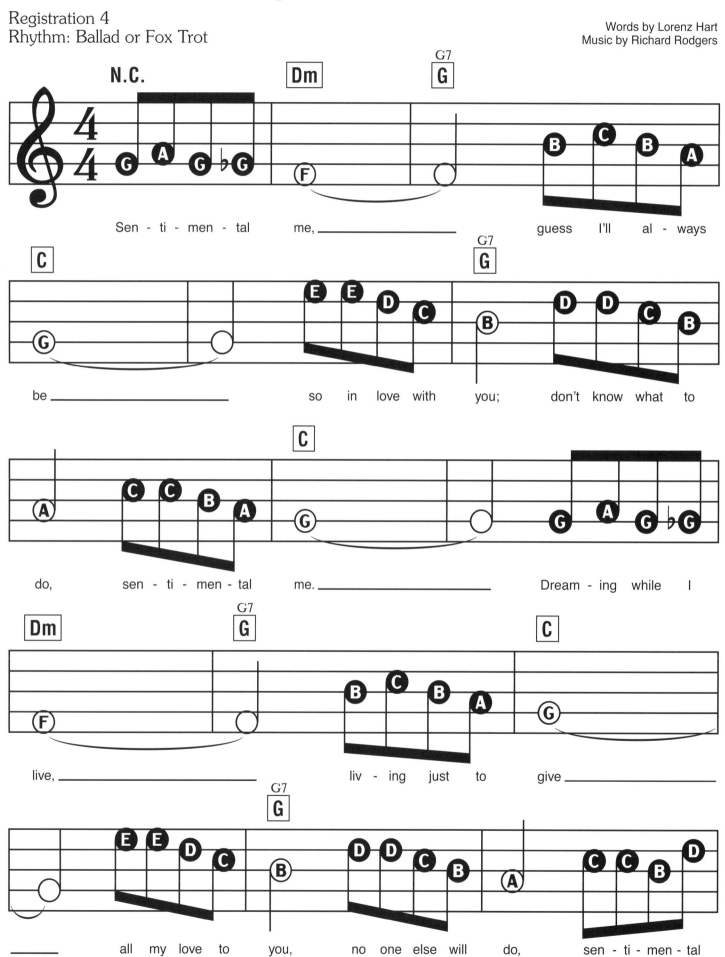

Copyright © 1925 by Edward B. Marks Music Company
Copyright Renewed
International Copyright Secured   All Rights Reserved
Used By Permission

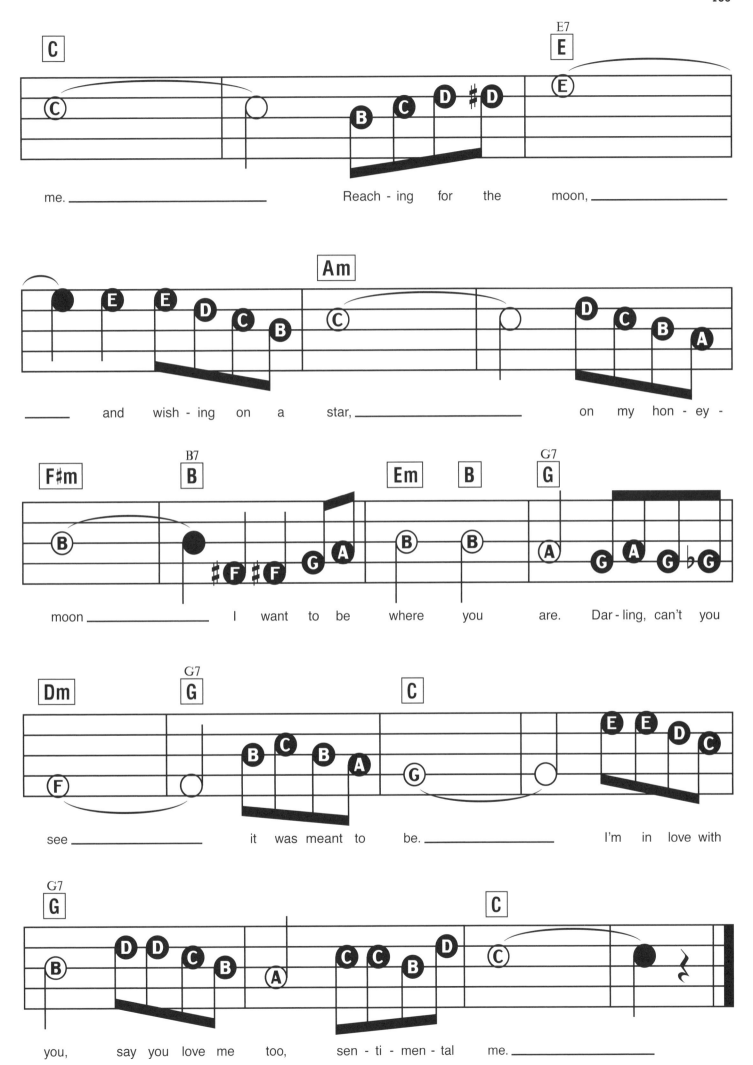

Side by Side

Registration 7
Rhythm: Fox Trot or Swing

Words and Music by
Harry Woods

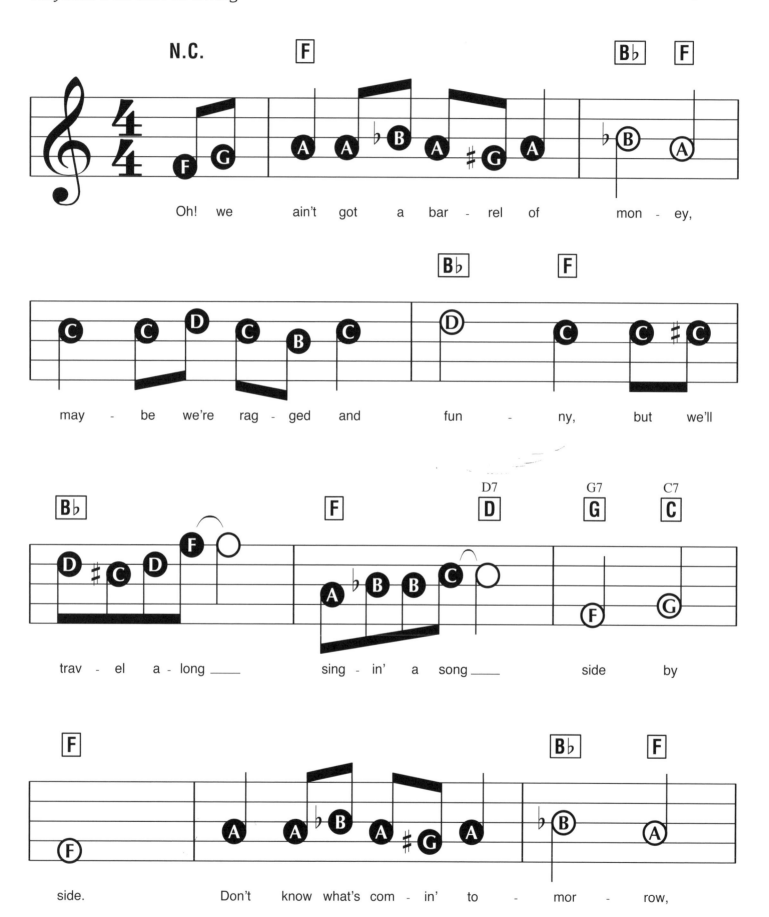

Copyright © 1927 Shapiro, Bernstein & Co., Inc., New York
Copyright Renewed
International Copyright Secured   All Rights Reserved
Used by Permission

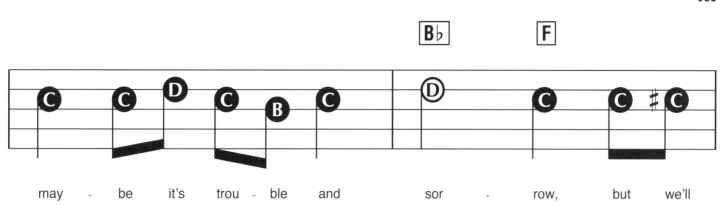

may - be it's trou - ble and sor - row, but we'll

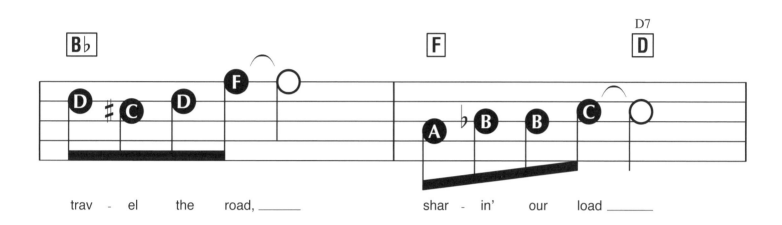

trav - el the road, _____ shar - in' our load _____

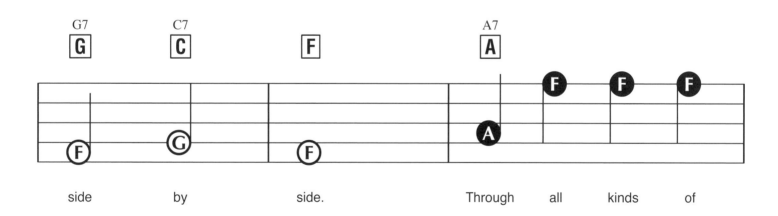

side by side. Through all kinds of

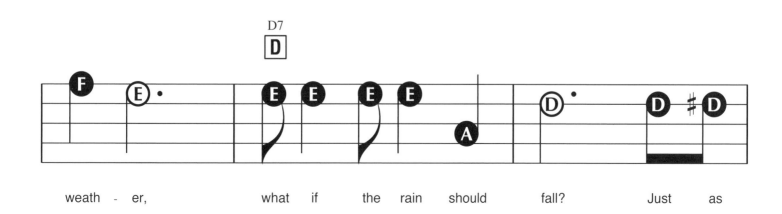

weath - er, what if the rain should fall? Just as

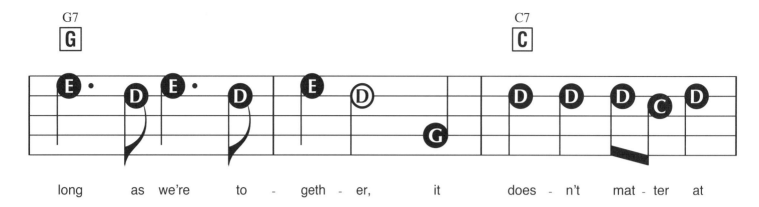

long   as   we're   to - geth - er,   it   does - n't   mat - ter   at

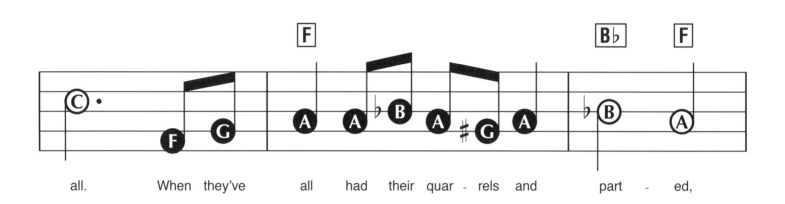

all.   When they've   all   had   their   quar - rels   and   part - ed,

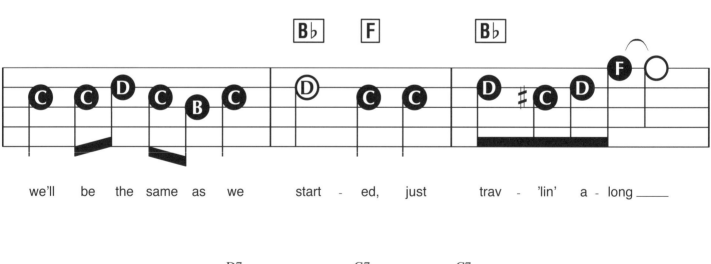

we'll   be   the same as   we   start - ed,   just   trav - 'lin'   a - long ____

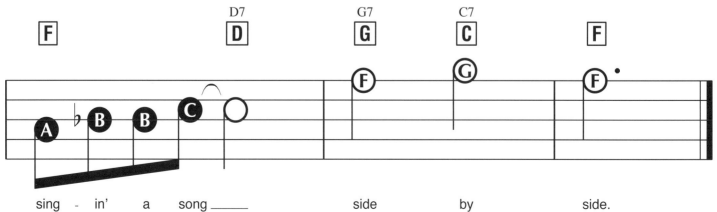

sing - in'   a   song ____   side   by   side.

Some of These Days

Registration 1
Rhythm: Swing or Shuffle

Words and Music by
Shelton Brooks

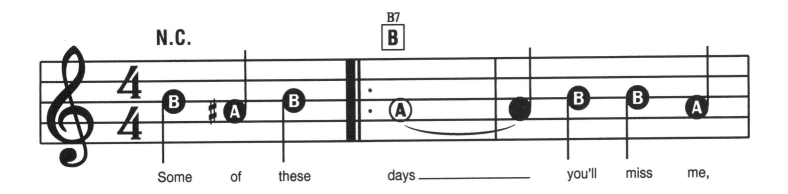

Some of these days _____ you'll miss me,

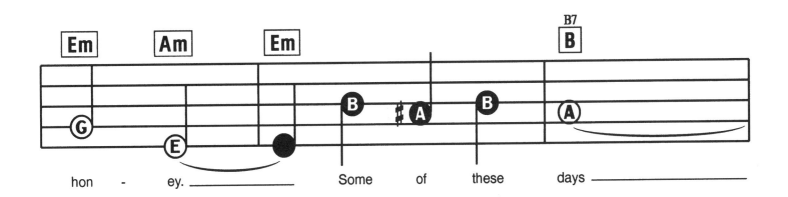

hon - ey. _____ Some of these days _____

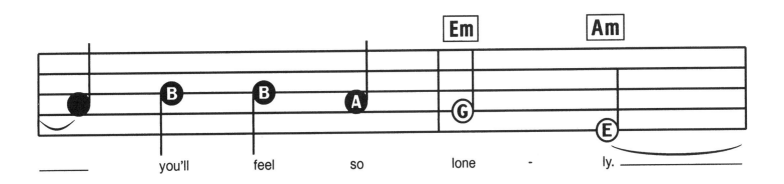

_____ you'll feel so lone - ly.

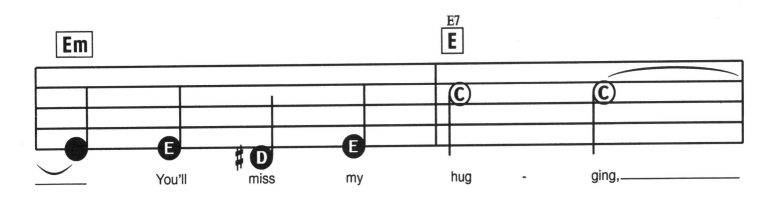

You'll miss my hug - ging, _____

Copyright © 1991 by HAL LEONARD CORPORATION
International Copyright Secured   All Rights Reserved

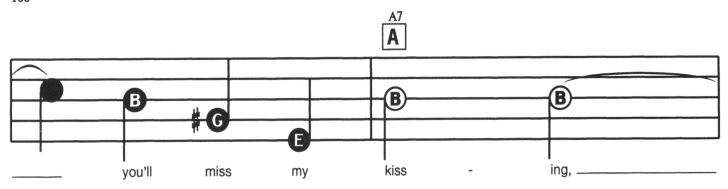

you'll miss my kiss - ing, _____

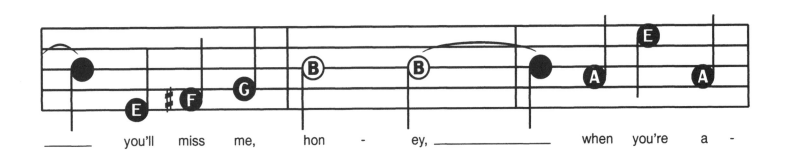

you'll miss me, hon - ey, _____ when you're a -

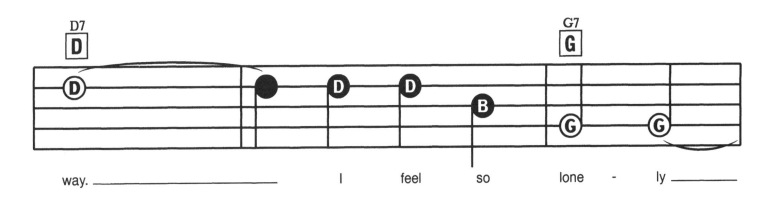

way. _____ I feel so lone - ly _____

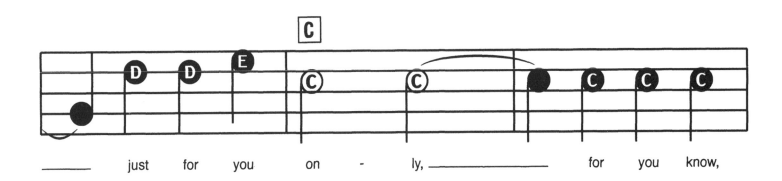

_____ just for you on - ly, _____ for you know,

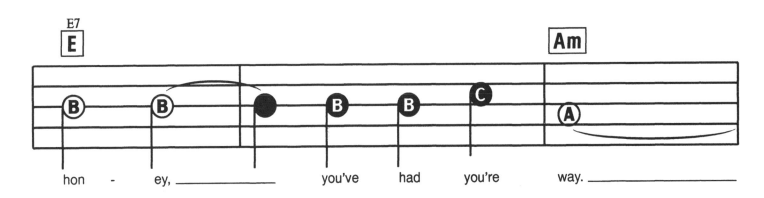

hon - ey, _____ you've had you're way. _____

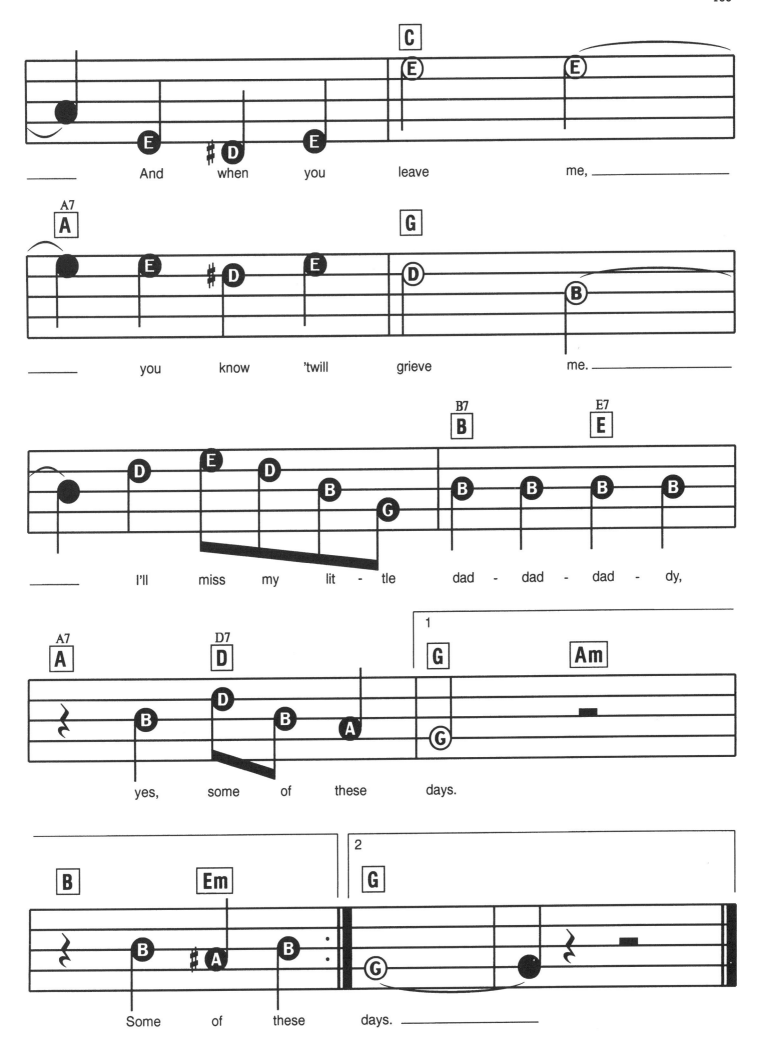

Sleepy Time Gal

Registration 9
Rhythm: Swing

Words by Joseph Alden and Raymond Egan
Music by Angelo Lorenzo and Richard Whiting

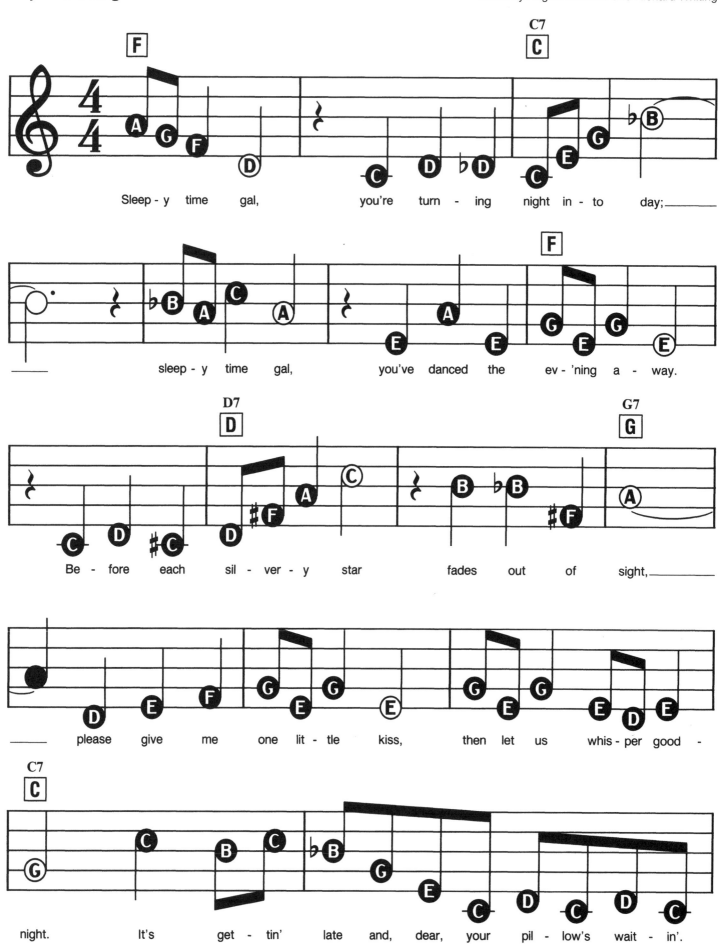

© 1924, 1925 (Copyrights Renewed) EMI FEIST CATALOG INC. and EMI APRIL MUSIC INC.
All Rights for EMI FEIST CATALOG INC. Administered by EMI FEIST CATALOG INC. (Publishing) and ALFRED MUSIC (Print)
All Rights Reserved   Used by Permission

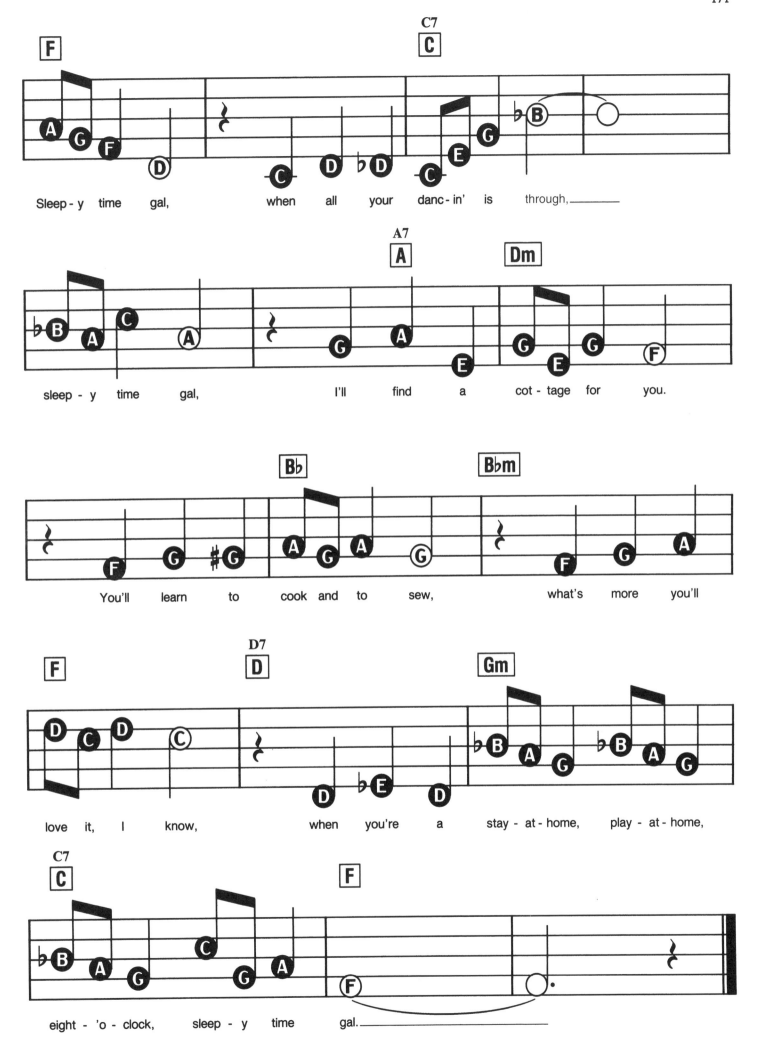

Softly as in a Morning Sunrise
from THE NEW MOON

Registration 1
Rhythm: Slow Rock or Ballad

Lyrics by Oscar Hammerstein II
Music by Sigmund Romberg

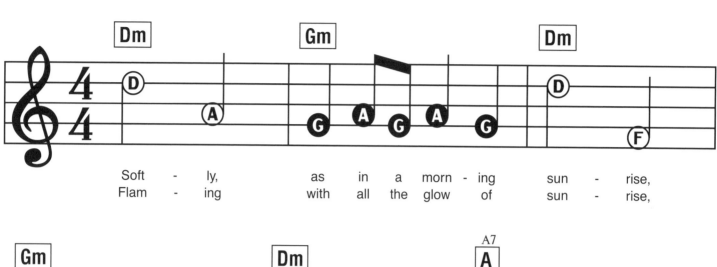

Soft - ly, as in a morn - ing sun - rise,
Flam - ing with all the glow of sun - rise,

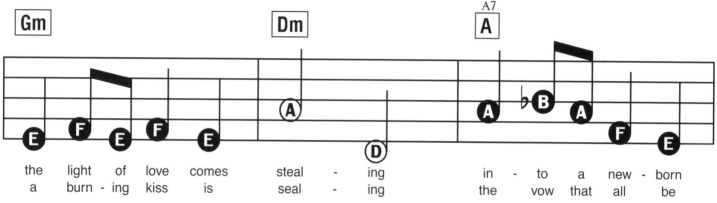

the light of love comes steal - ing in - to a new - born
a burn - ing love kiss is seal - ing the vow that all be

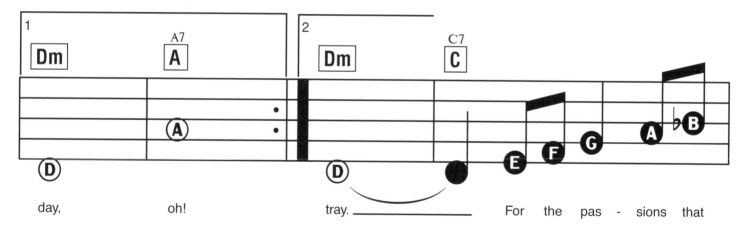

day, oh! tray. _____ For the pas - sions that

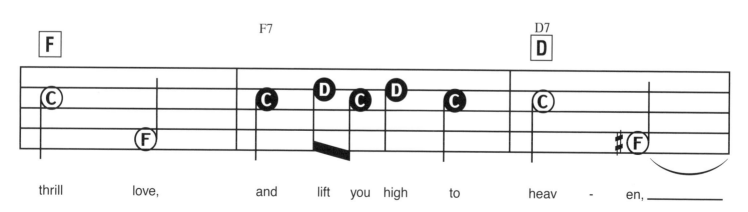

thrill love, and lift you high to heav - en, _____

Copyright © 1928 by Bambalina Music Publishing Co. and Warner Bros. Inc. in the United States
Copyright Renewed
All Rights on behalf of Bambalina Music Publishing Co. Administered by Williamson Music, a Division of Rodgers & Hammerstein: an Imagem Company
International Copyright Secured   All Rights Reserved

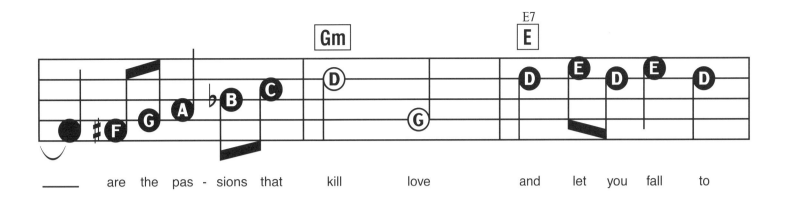

_____ are the pas - sions that kill love and let you fall to

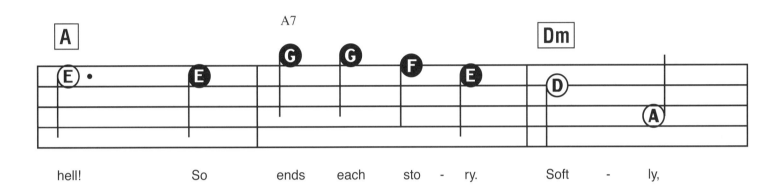

hell! So ends each sto - ry. Soft - ly,

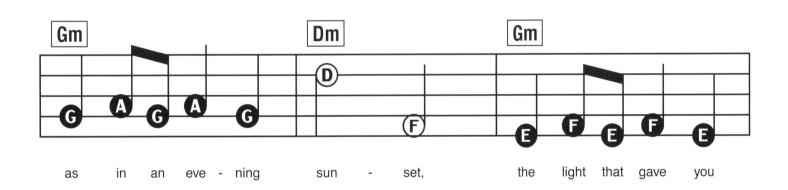

as in an eve - ning sun - set, the light that gave you

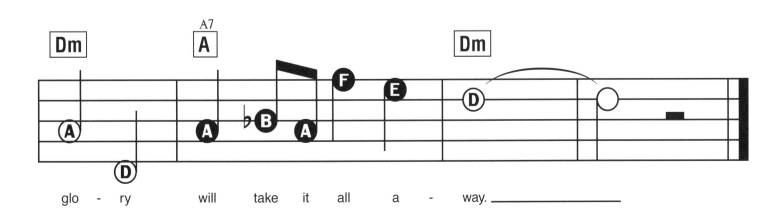

glo - ry will take it all a - way. _____

Somebody Loves Me
from GEORGE WHITE'S SCANDALS OF 1924

Registration 4
Rhythm: Fox Trot or Swing

Music by George Gershwin
Lyrics by B.G. DeSylva and Ballard MacDonald
French Version by Emelia Renaud

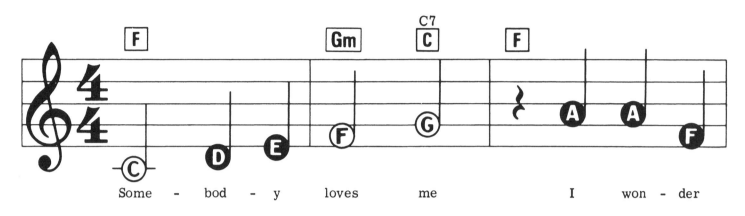

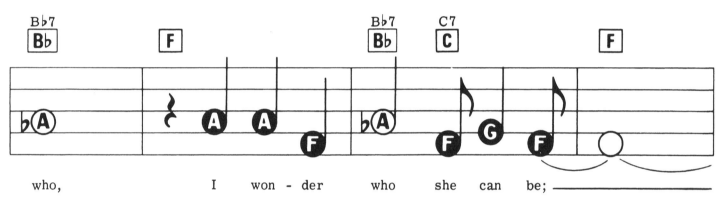

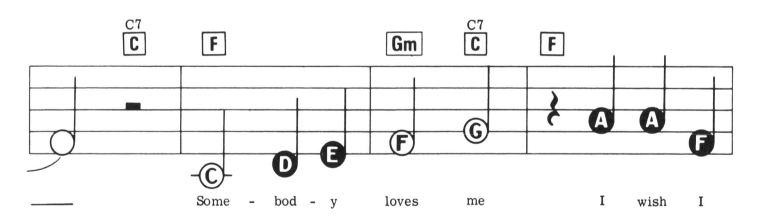

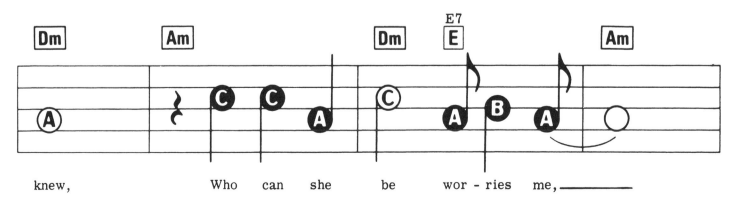

Copyright © 1924 Stephen Ballentine Music and WB Music Corp.
Copyright Renewed
All Rights for Stephen Ballentine Music Administered by The Songwriters Guild Of America
International Copyright Secured   All Rights Reserved

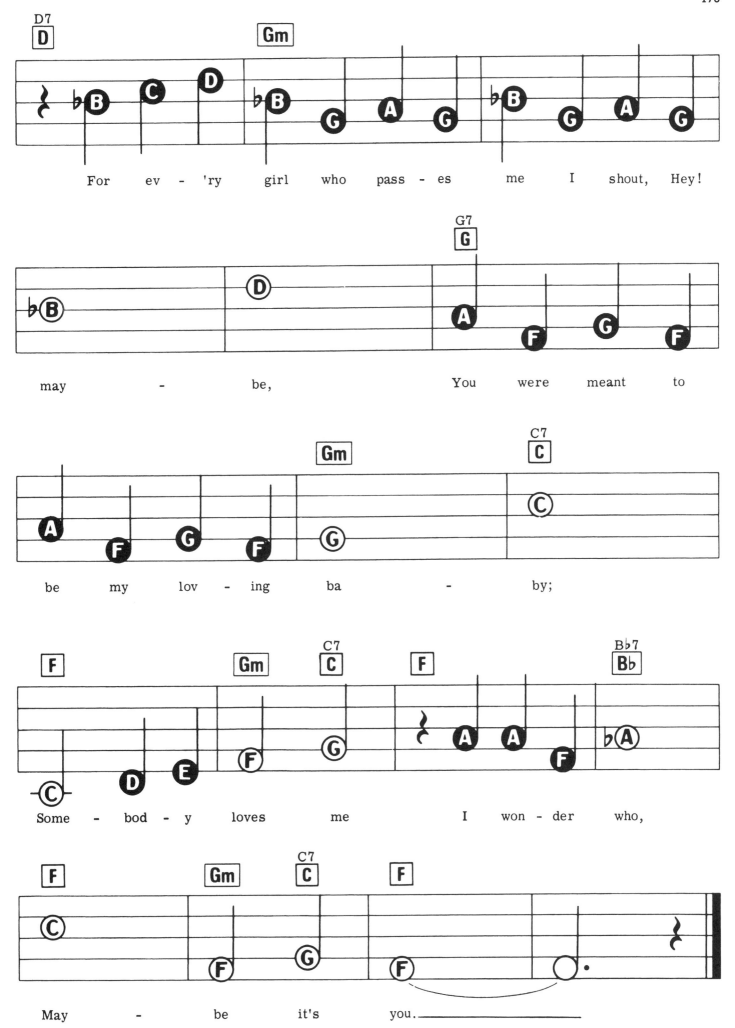

Someone to Watch Over Me

from OH, KAY!

Registration 7
Rhythm: Ballad or Swing

Music and Lyrics by George Gershwin
and Ira Gershwin

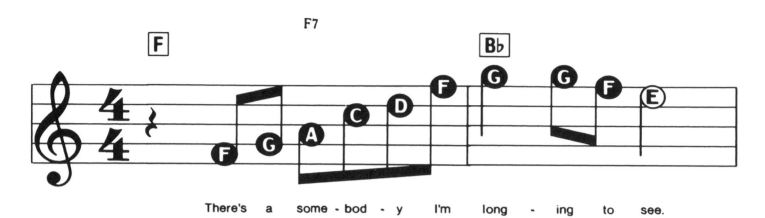

There's a some-bod-y I'm long - ing to see.

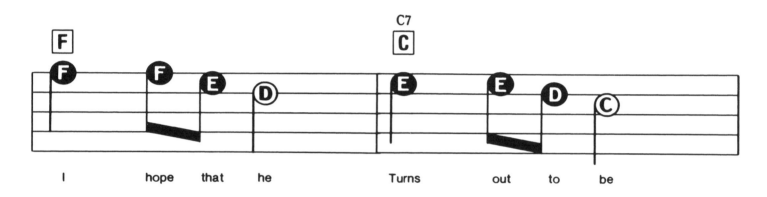

I hope that he Turns out to be

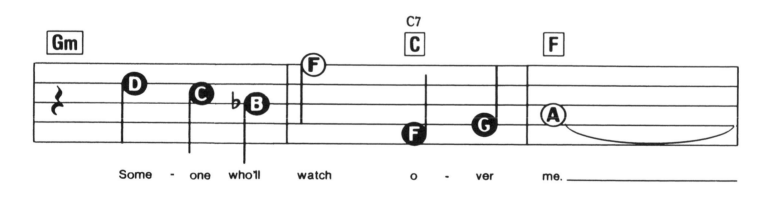

Some - one who'll watch o - ver me. _____

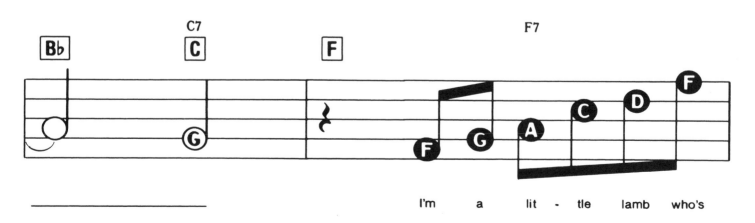

I'm a lit - tle lamb who's

© 1926 (Renewed) WB MUSIC CORP.
All Rights Reserved   Used by Permission

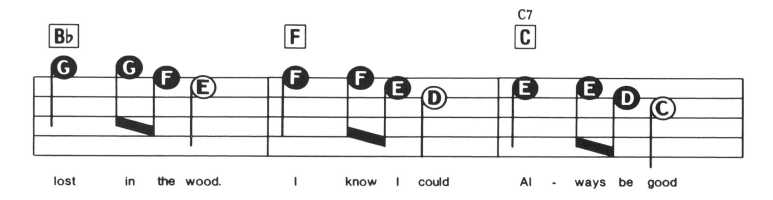

lost   in   the   wood.   I   know   I   could   Al - ways be good

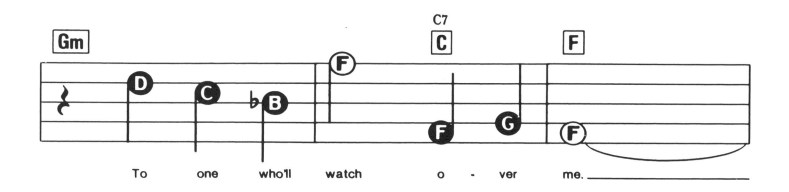

To   one   who'll   watch   o   -   ver   me.

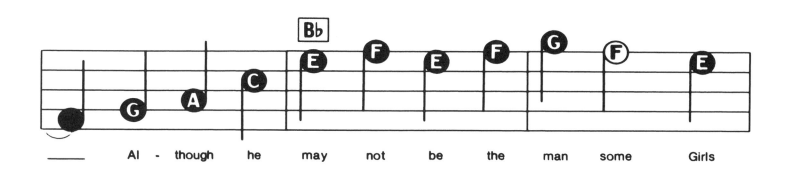

Al - though   he   may   not   be   the   man   some   Girls

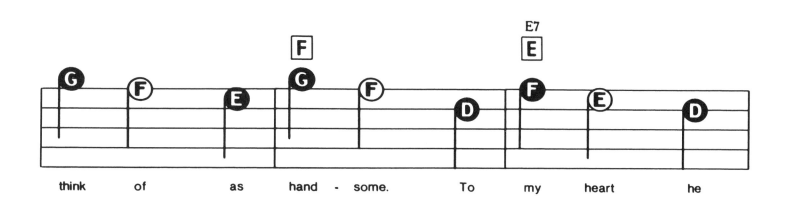

think   of   as   hand - some.   To   my   heart   he

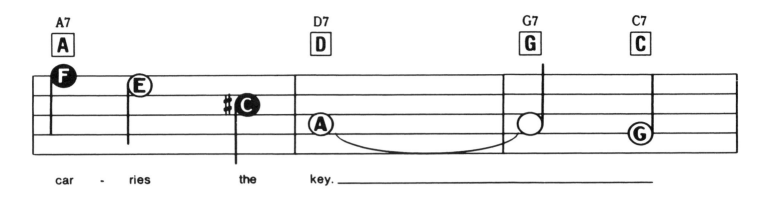

car - ries the key. _____

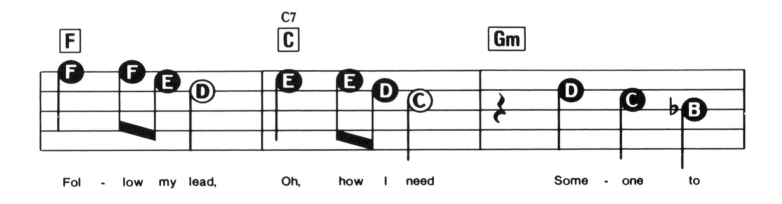

Won't you tell him please to put on some speed,

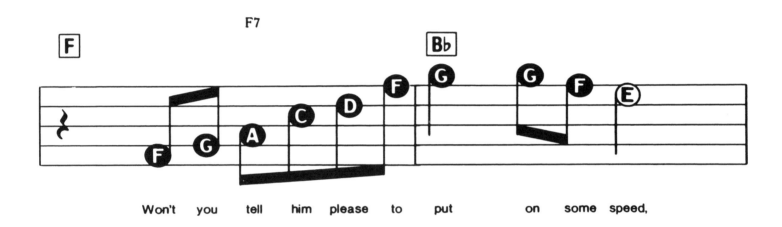

Fol - low my lead, Oh, how I need Some - one to

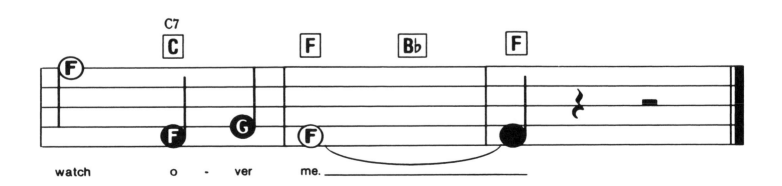

watch o - ver me. _____

When You're Smiling
(The Whole World Smiles with You)

Registration 9
Rhythm: Swing

Words and Music by Mark Fisher,
Joe Goodwin and Larry Shay

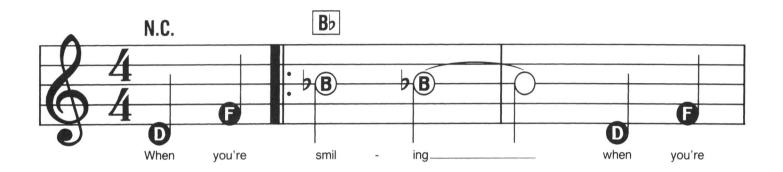

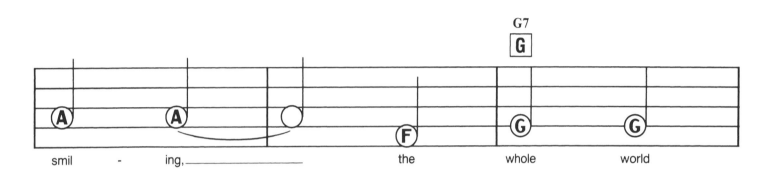

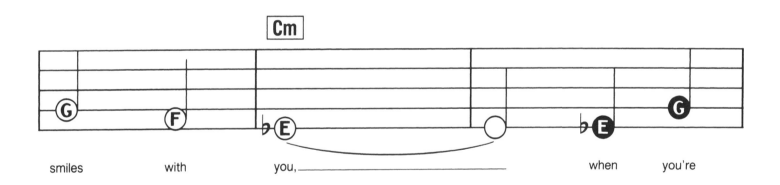

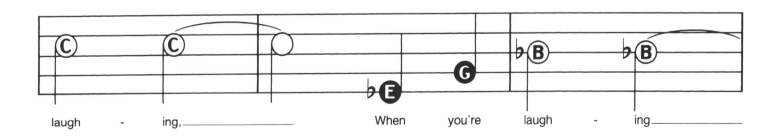

Copyright © 1928 EMI Mills Music Inc. and Music By Shay
Copyright Renewed
All Rights for EMI Mills Music Inc. Administered by EMI Mills Music Inc. (Publishing) and Alfred Music (Print)
All Rights for Music By Shay Administered by The Songwriters Guild Of America
International Copyright Secured   All Rights Reserved

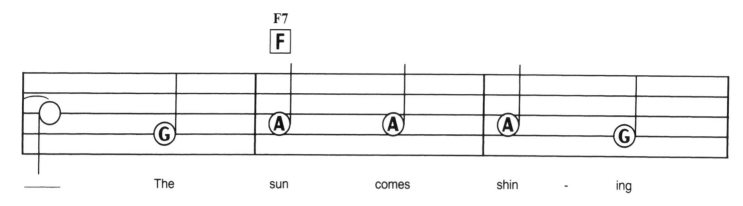

The sun comes shin - ing

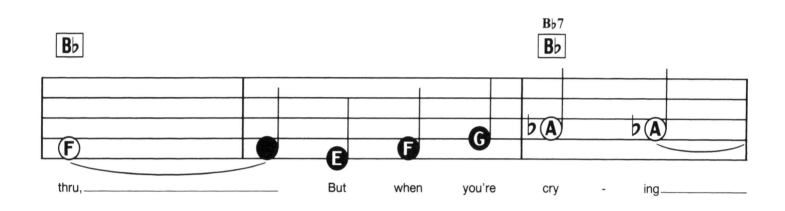

thru,_____ But when you're cry - ing_____

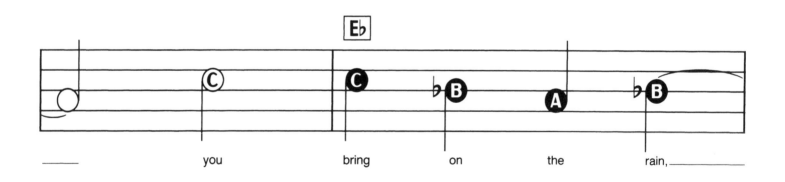

_____ you bring on the rain,

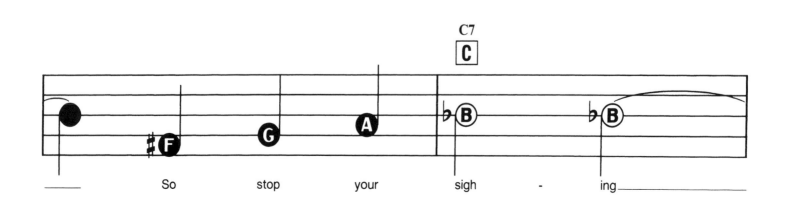

So stop your sigh - ing_____

181

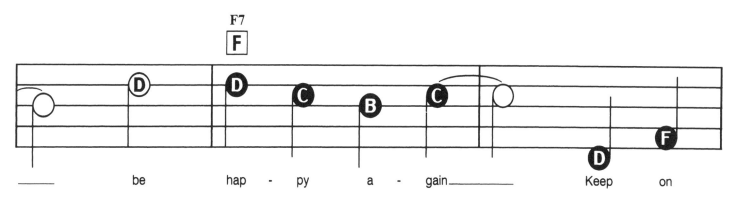

be hap - py a - gain_____ Keep on

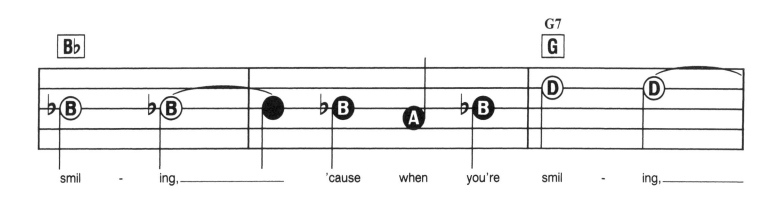

smil - ing,_____ 'cause when you're smil - ing,_____

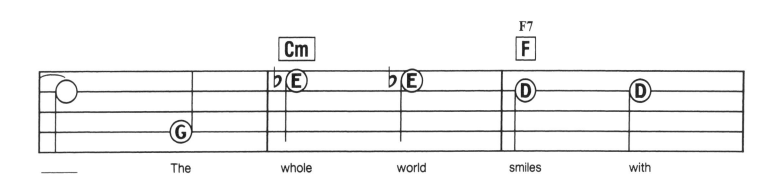

_____ The whole world smiles with

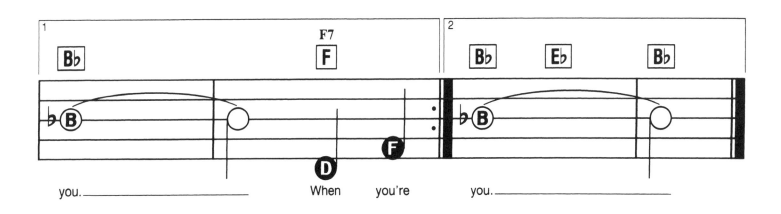

you._____ When you're you._____

The Song Is Ended
(But the Melody Lingers On)

Registration 10
Rhythm: Waltz

Words and Music by
Irving Berlin

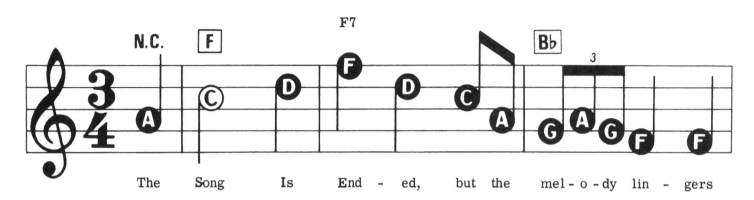

The Song Is End - ed, but the mel - o - dy lin - gers

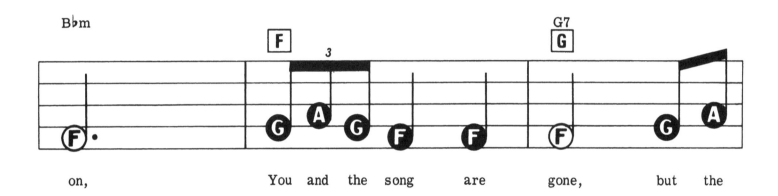

on, You and the song are gone, but the

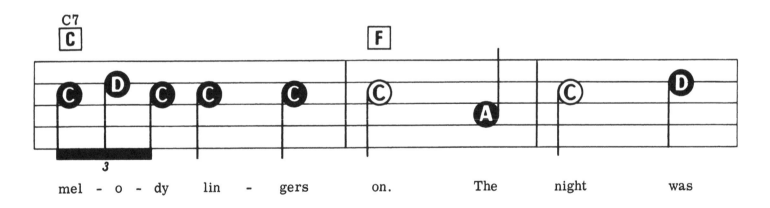

mel - o - dy lin - gers on. The night was

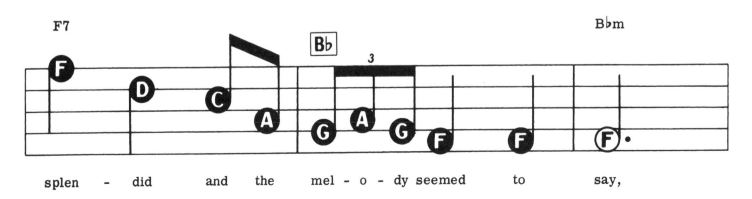

splen - did and the mel - o - dy seemed to say,

© Copyright 1927 by Irving Berlin
© Arrangement Copyright 1951 by Irving Berlin
Copyright Renewed
International Copyright Secured   All Rights Reserved

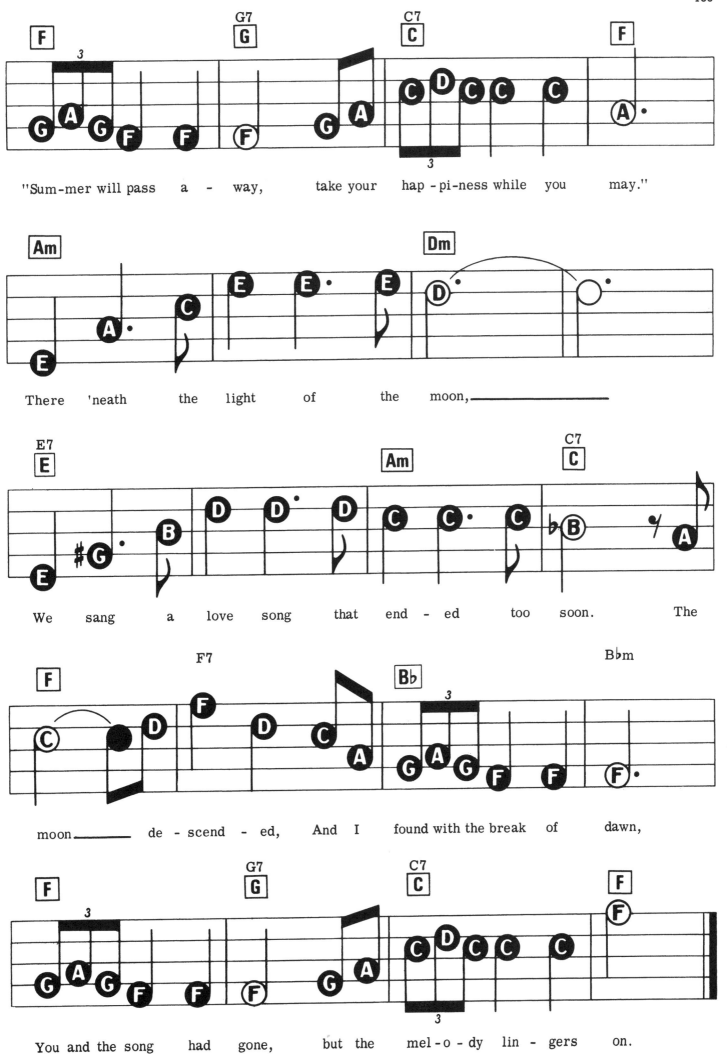

Squeeze Me

Registration 8
Rhythm: Blues or Fox Trot

Words and Music by Clarence Williams
and Thomas "Fats" Waller

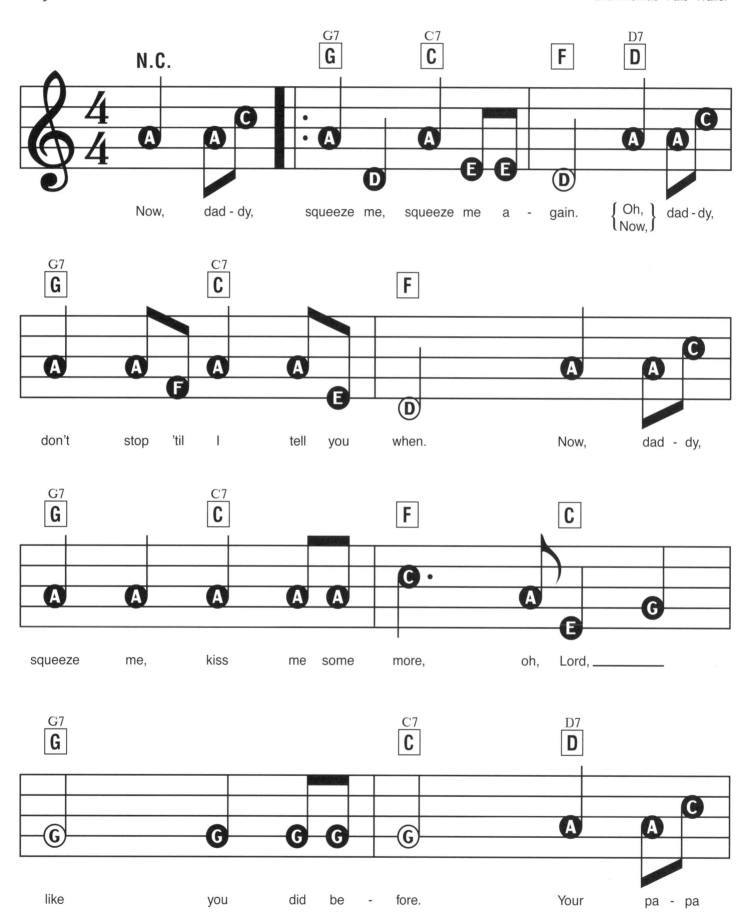

Copyright © 1925 UNIVERSAL MUSIC CORP. and GREAT STANDARDS MUSIC PUBLISHING COMPANY
Copyright Renewed
All Rights for GREAT STANDARDS MUSIC PUBLISHING COMPANY Controlled and Administered by THE SONGWRITERS GUILD OF AMERICA
All Rights Reserved   Used by Permission

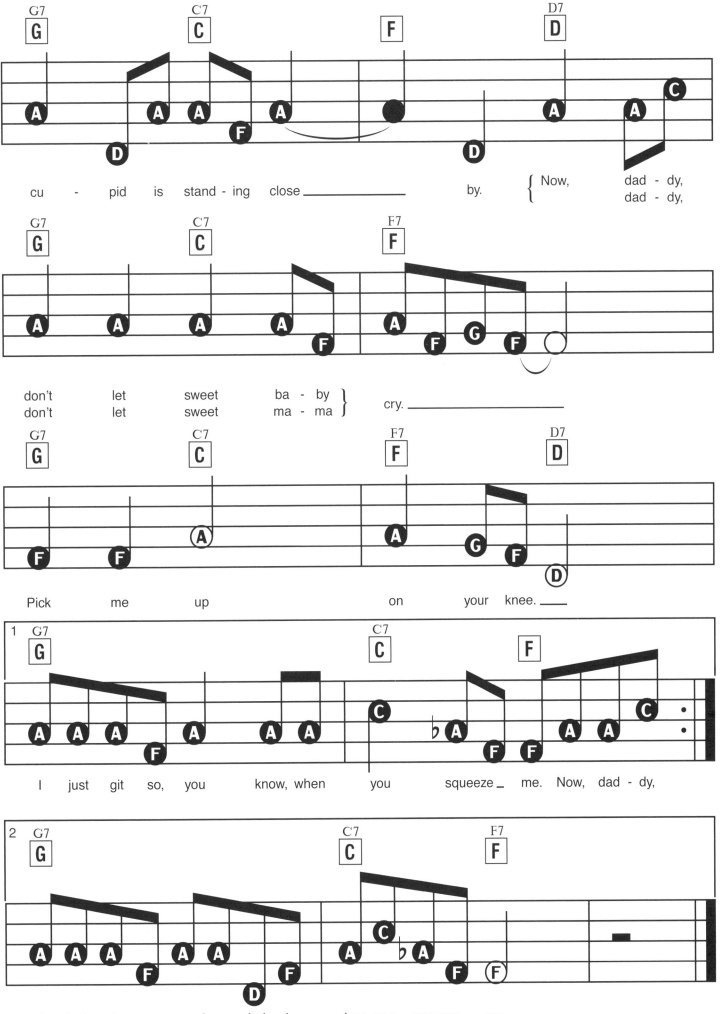

Stardust

Registration 5
Rhythm: Swing or Jazz

Words by Mitchell Parish
Music by Hoagy Carmichael

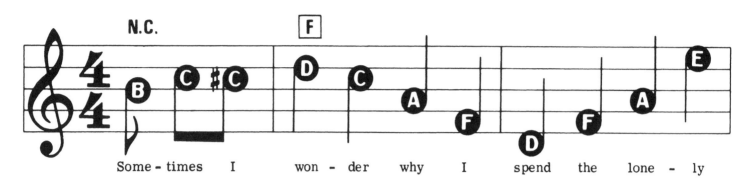

Some - times I won - der why I spend the lone - ly

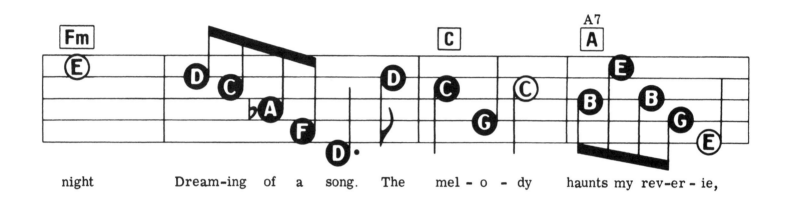

night Dream-ing of a song. The mel - o - dy haunts my rev-er-ie,

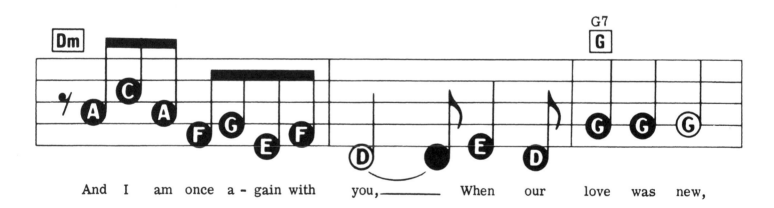

And I am once a - gain with you,_____ When our love was new,

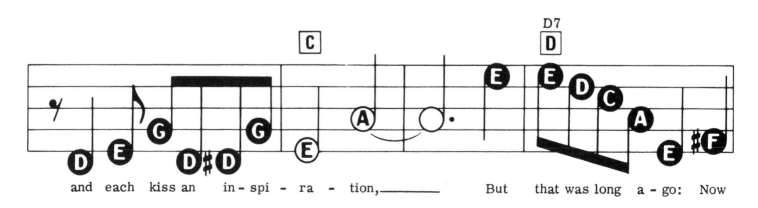

and each kiss an in - spi - ra - tion,_____ But that was long a - go: Now

Copyright © 1928, 1929 by Songs Of Peer, Ltd. and EMI Mills Music, Inc.
Copyrights Renewed
All Rights outside the USA Controlled by EMI Mills Music, Inc. (Publishing) and Alfred Music (Print)
International Copyright Secured   All Rights Reserved

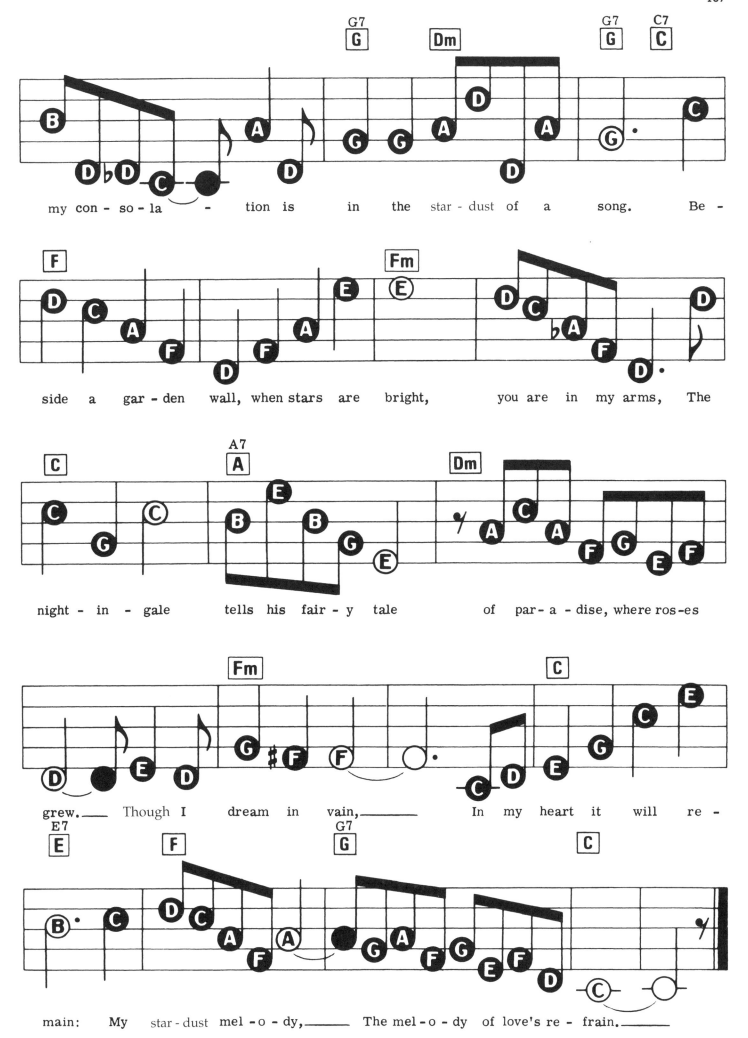

Swanee

Registration 9
Rhythm: Fox Trot or Swing

Words by Irving Caesar
Music by George Gershwin

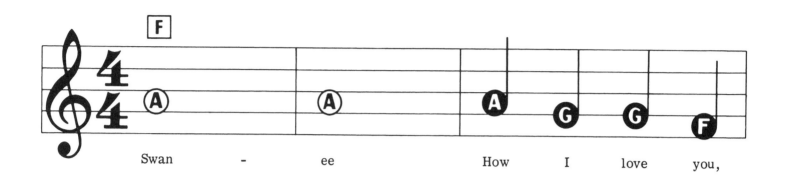

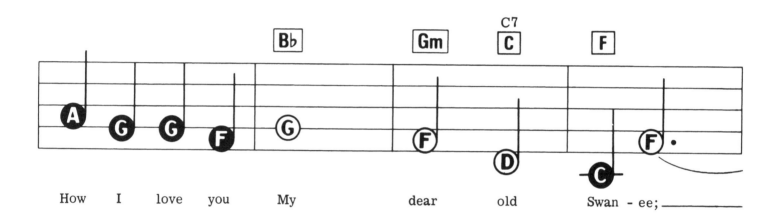

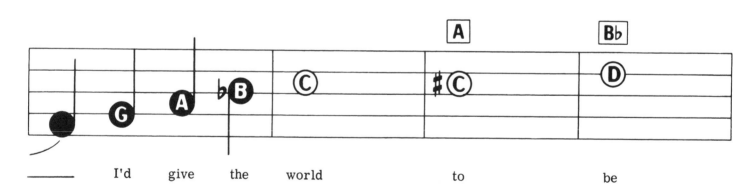

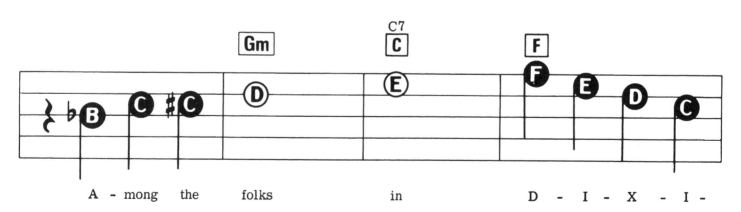

Copyright © 2007 by HAL LEONARD CORPORATION
International Copyright Secured   All Rights Reserved

189

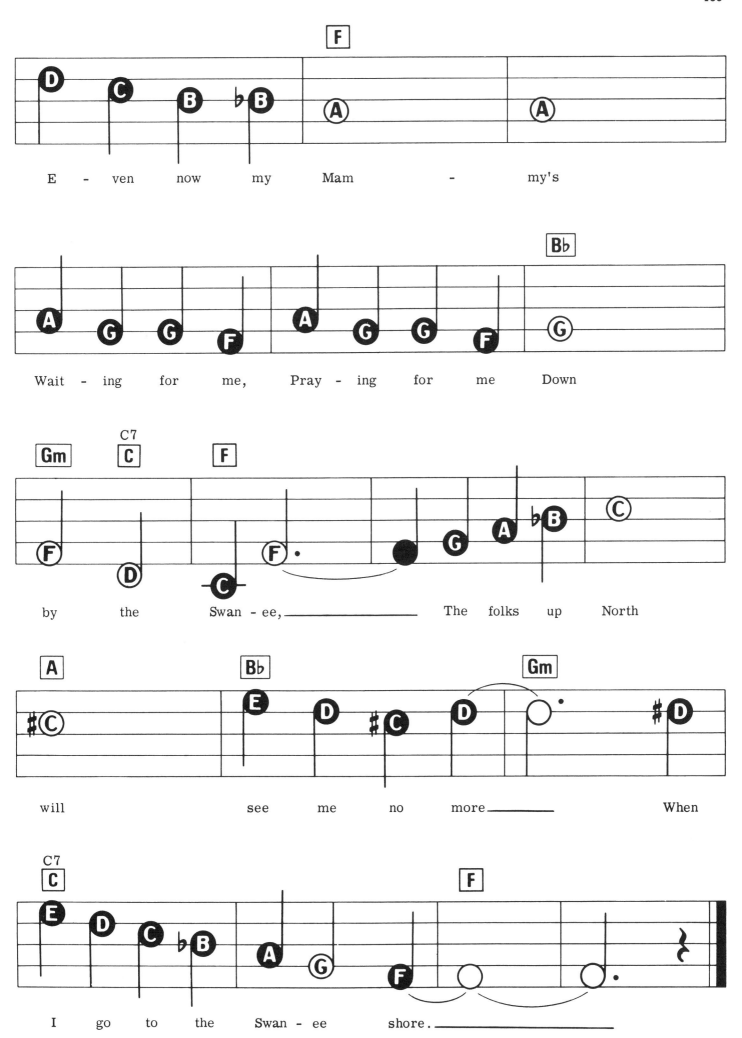

Sweet Georgia Brown

Registration 7
Rhythm: Fox Trot or Swing

Words and Music by Ben Bernie,
Maceo Pinkard and Kenneth Casey

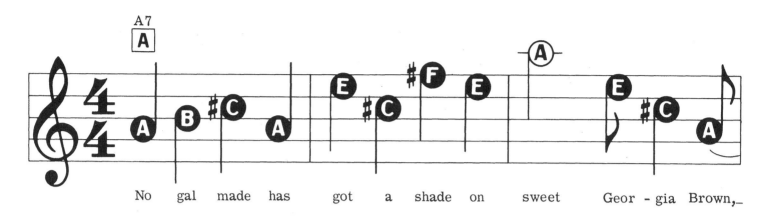

No gal made has got a shade on sweet Geor - gia Brown,_

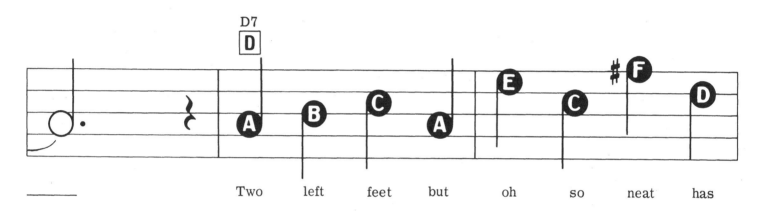

Two left feet but oh so neat has

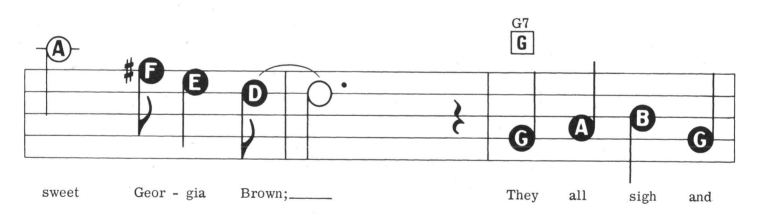

sweet Geor - gia Brown;_____ They all sigh and

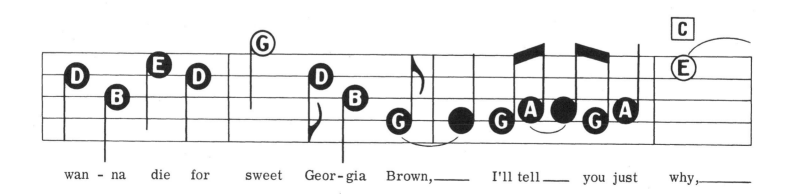

wan - na die for sweet Geor-gia Brown,_____ I'll tell ___ you just why,_____

© 1925 (Renewed) WB MUSIC CORP.
All Rights Reserved   Used by Permission

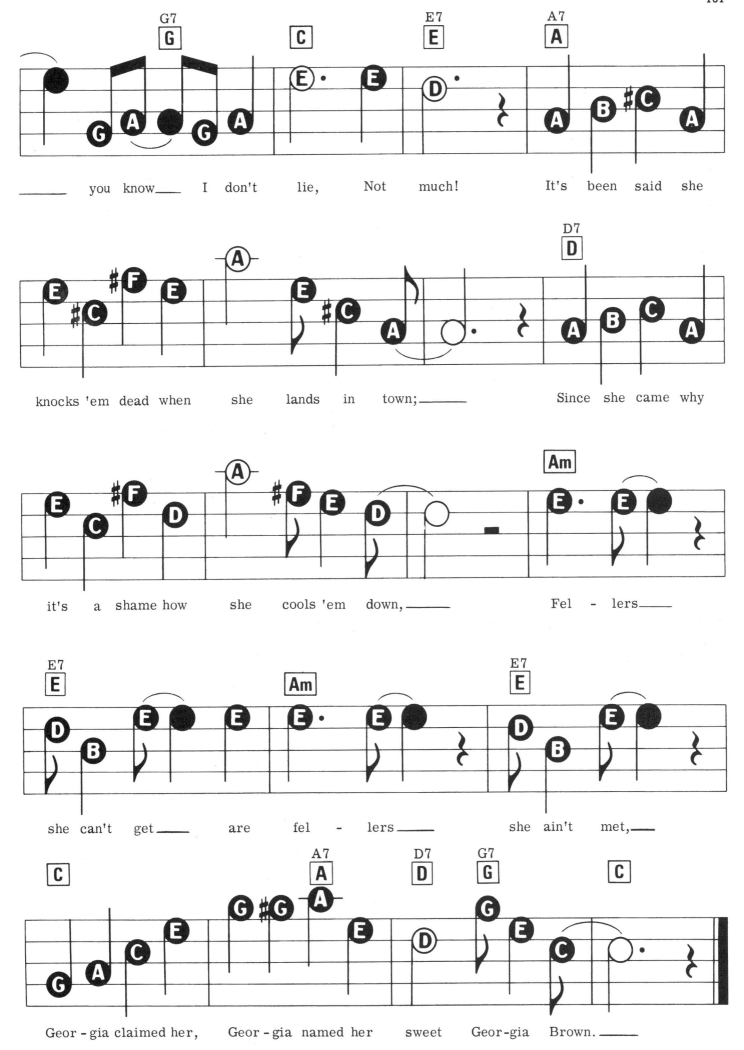

Sweet Lorraine

Registration 1
Rhythm: Swing

Words by Mitchell Parish
Music by Cliff Burwell

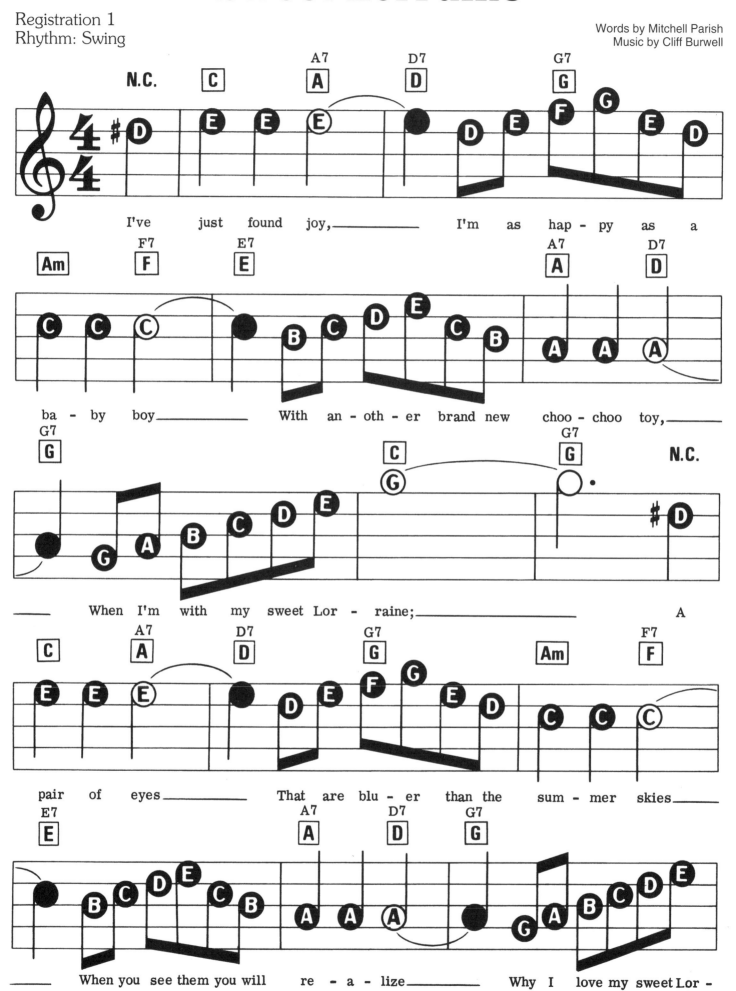

© 1928 (Renewed) EMI MILLS MUSIC INC.
All Rights Administered by EMI MILLS MUSIC INC. (Publishing) and ALFRED MUSIC (Print)
All Rights Reserved   Used by Permission

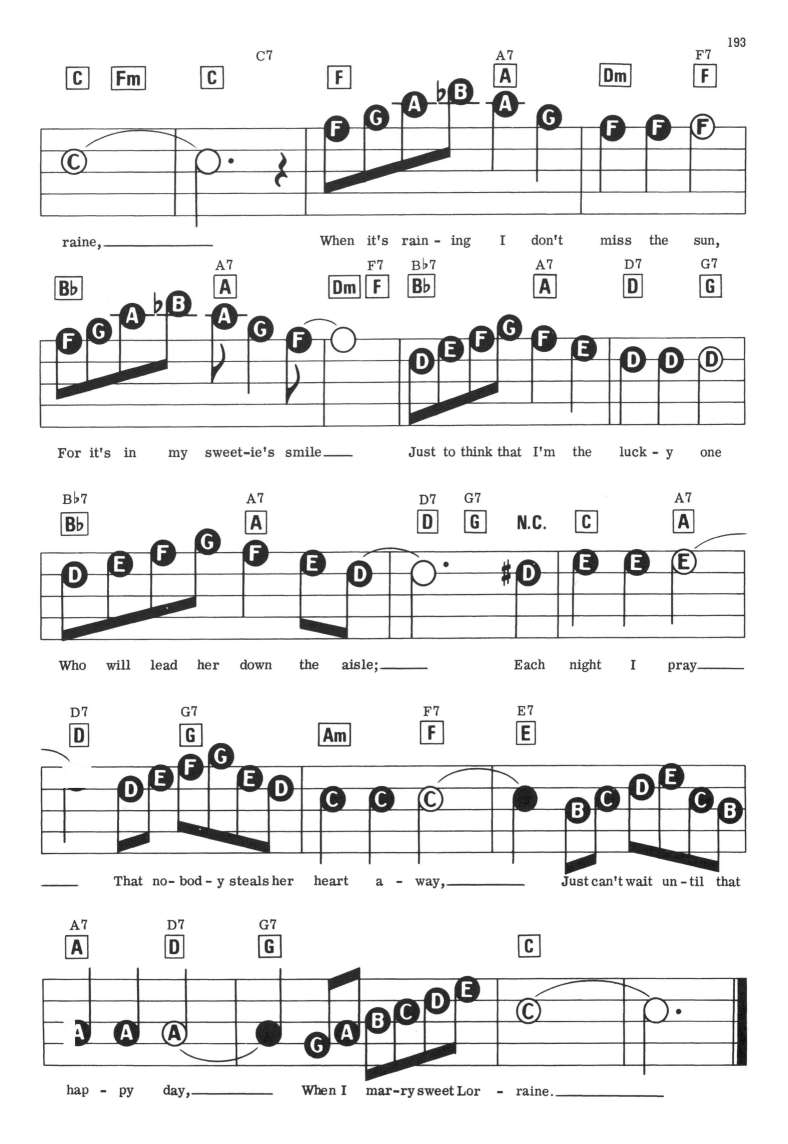

Tea for Two
from NO, NO NANETTE

Words by Irving Caesar
Music by Vincent Youmans

Registration 8
Rhythm: Shuffle or Swing

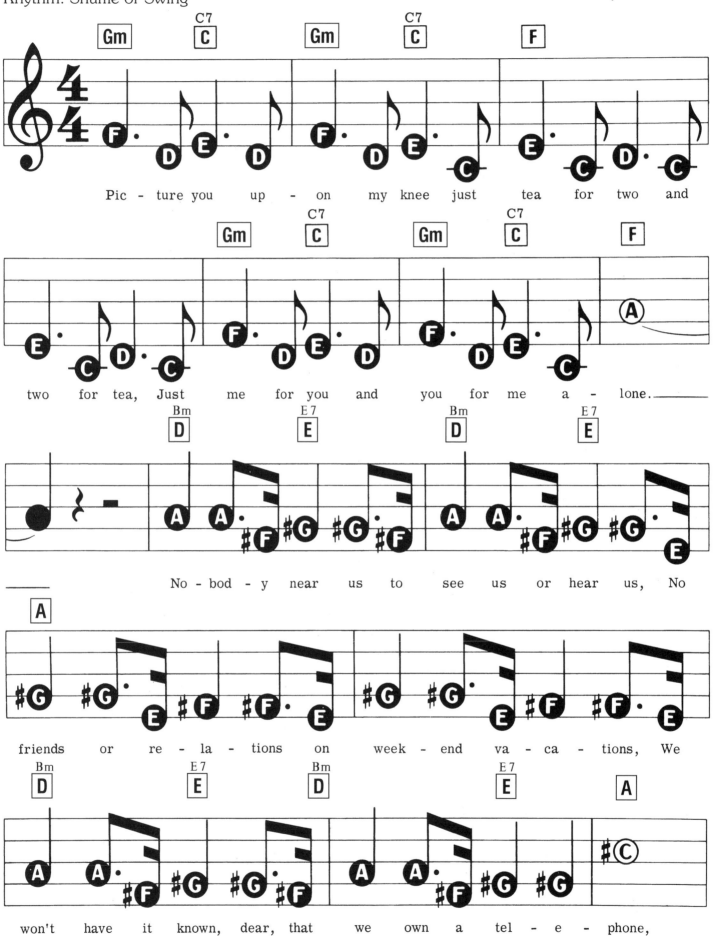

© 1924 (Renewed) WB MUSIC CORP. and IRVING CAESAR MUSIC CORP.
All Rights Administered by WB MUSIC CORP.
All Rights Reserved   Used by Permission

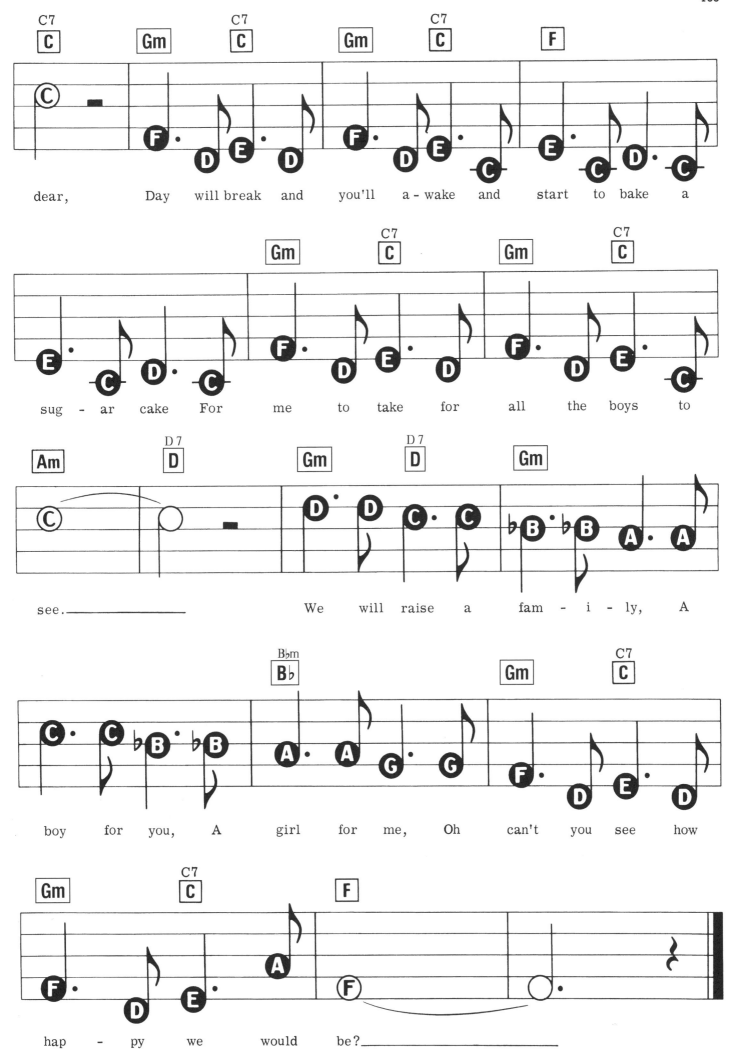

Thou Swell
from A CONNECTICUT YANKEE
from WORDS AND MUSIC

Registration 2
Rhythm: Fox Trot or Swing

Words by Lorenz Hart
Music by Richard Rodgers

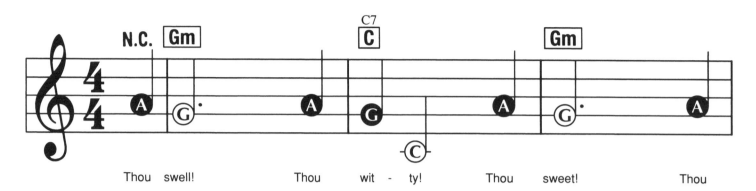

Thou swell! Thou wit - ty! Thou sweet! Thou

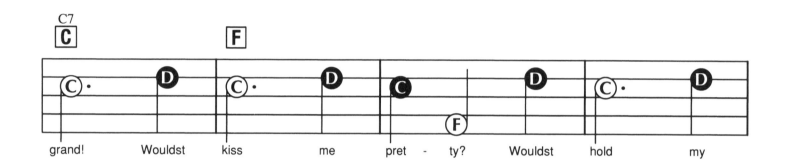

grand! Wouldst kiss me pret - ty? Wouldst hold my

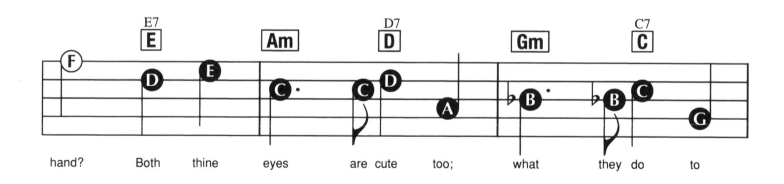

hand? Both thine eyes are cute too; what they do to

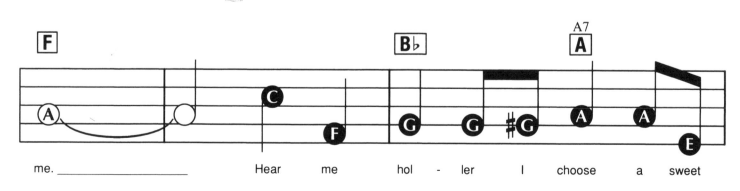

me. _____ Hear me hol - ler I choose a sweet

Copyright © 1927 by Harms, Inc.
Copyright Renewed
Copyright Assigned to Williamson Music and WB Music Corp. for the extended renewal period of copyright in the USA
International Copyright Secured All Rights Reserved

197

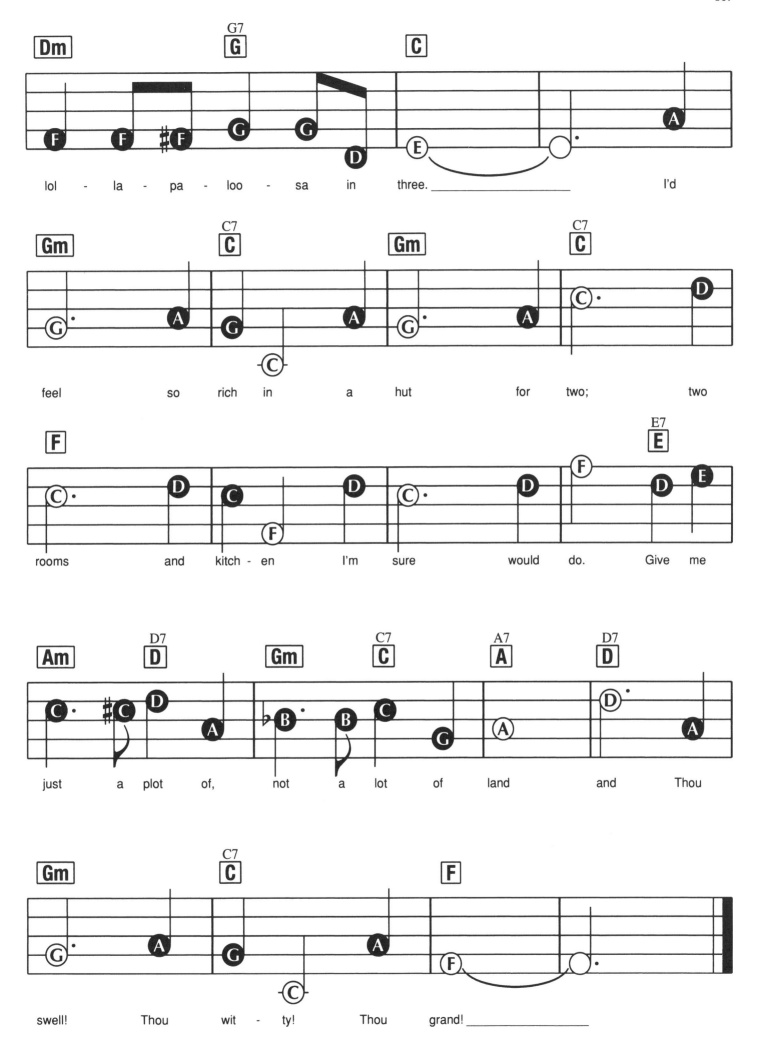

Three O'Clock in the Morning

Registration 10
Rhythm: Waltz

Words by Dorothy Terriss
Music by Julian Robledo

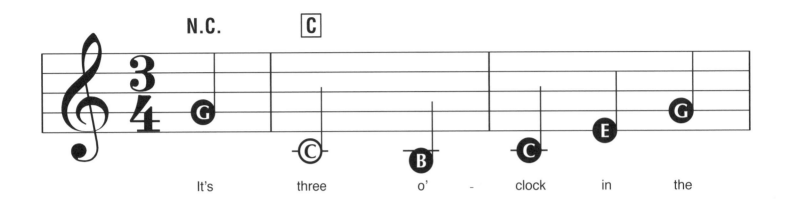

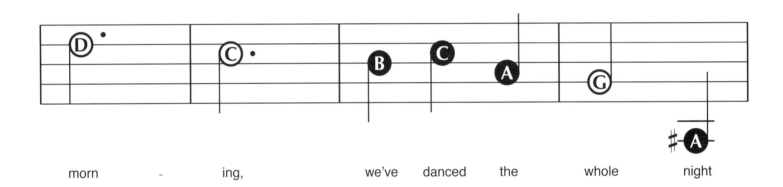

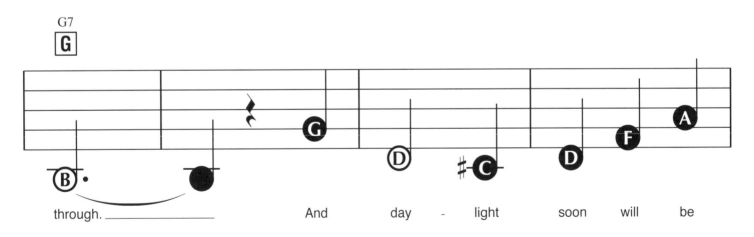

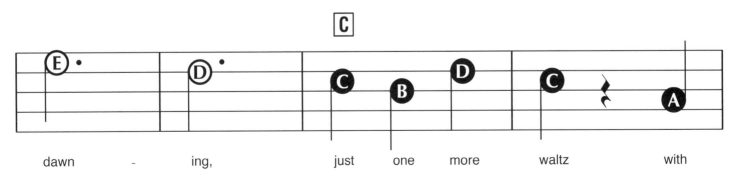

Copyright © 2000 by HAL LEONARD CORPORATION
International Copyright Secured   All Rights Reserved

199

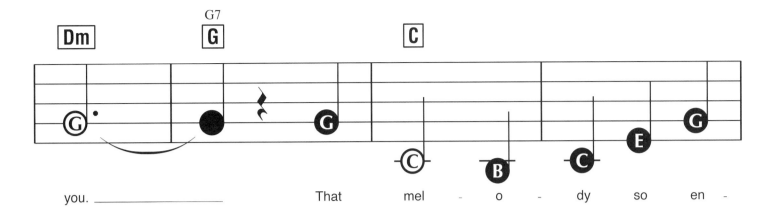

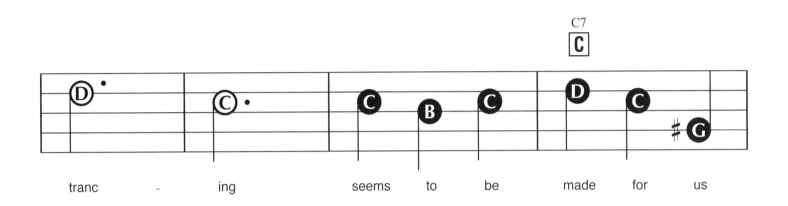

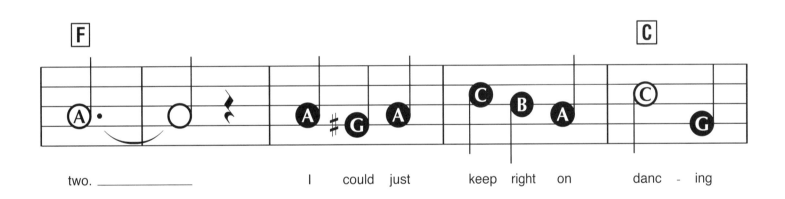

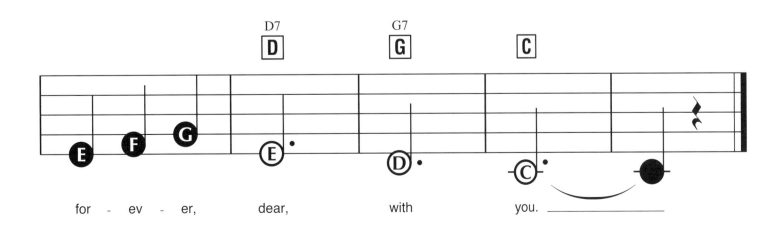

Tip-Toe Thru' the Tulips with Me

Registration 2
Rhythm: Swing or Jazz

Words by Al Dubin
Music by Joe Burke

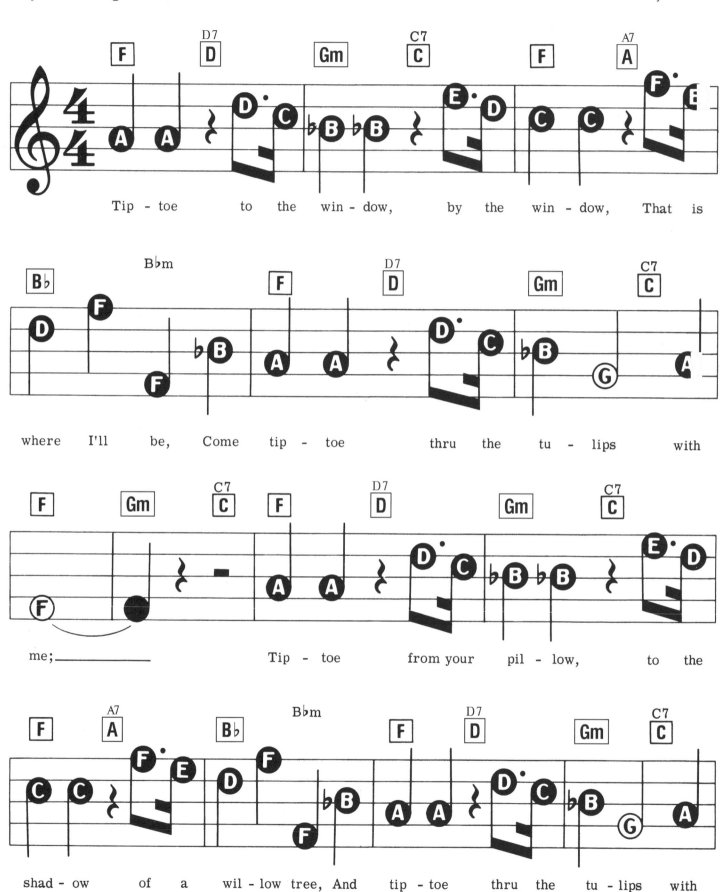

© 1929 (Renewed) WB MUSIC CORP.
All Rights Reserved   Used by Permission

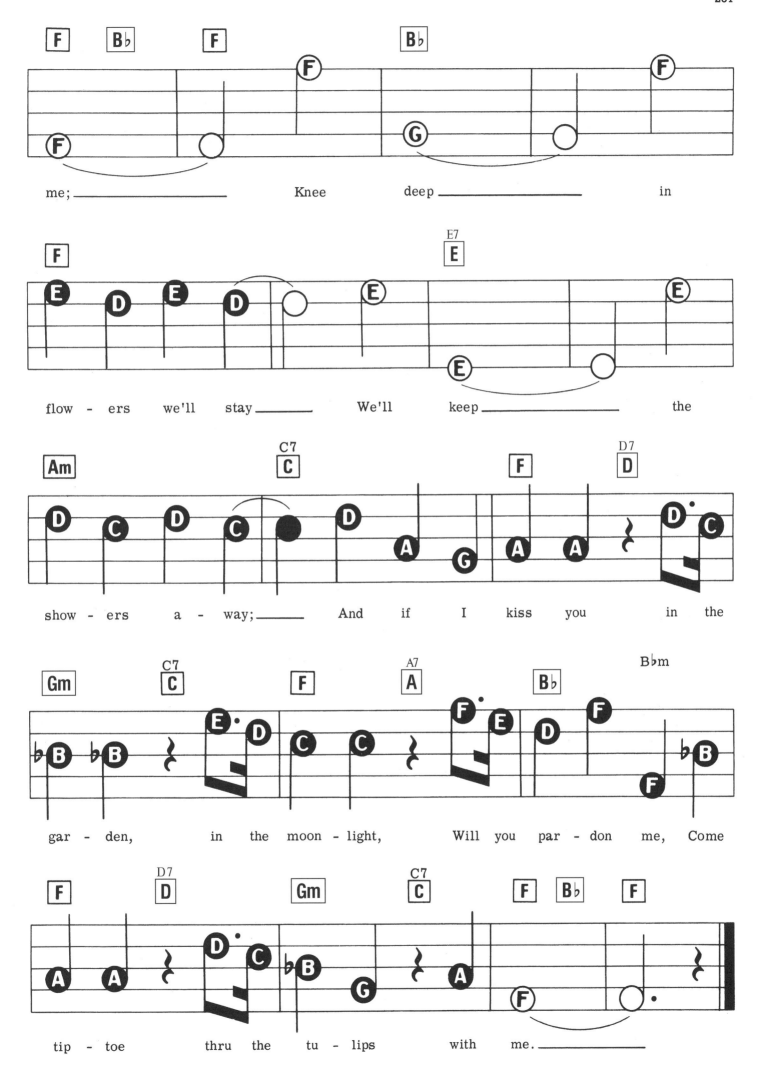

Toot, Toot, Tootsie!
(Good-bye!)
from THE JAZZ SINGER

Registration 4
Rhythm: Swing

Words and Music by Gus Kahn, Ernie Erdman,
Dan Russo and Ted Fiorito

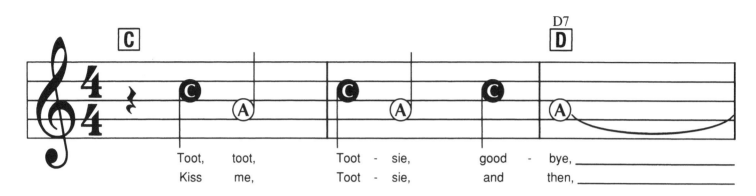

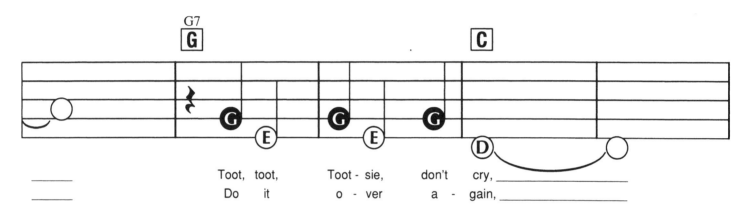

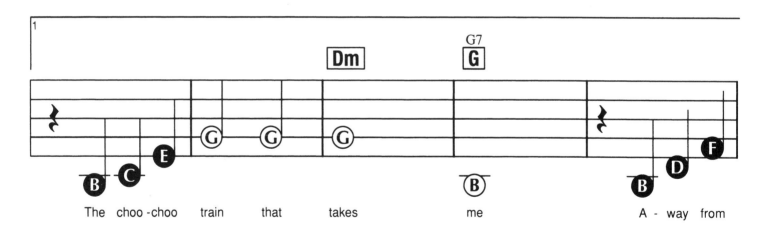

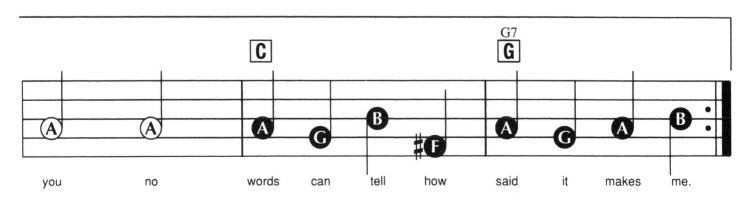

Copyright © 1998 by HAL LEONARD CORPORATION
International Copyright Secured   All Rights Reserved

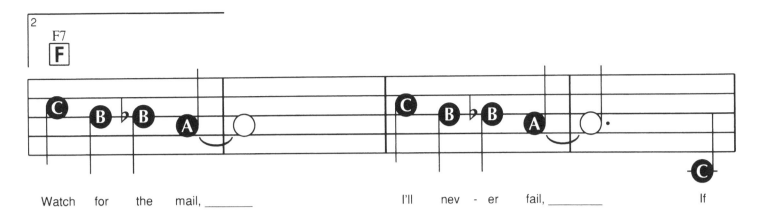

Watch for the mail, _____ I'll nev - er fail, _____ If

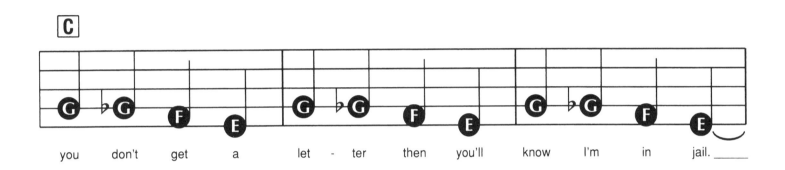

you don't get a let - ter then you'll know I'm in jail. _____

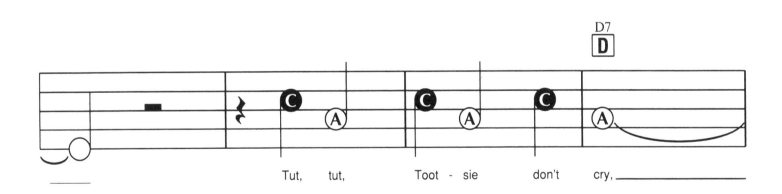

_____ Tut, tut, Toot - sie don't cry, _____

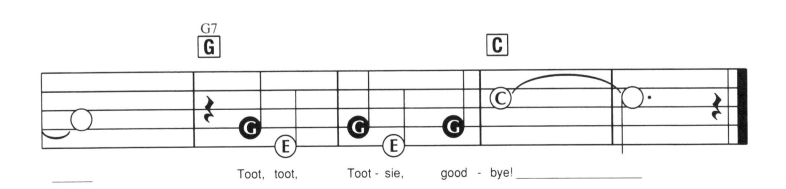

Toot, toot, Toot - sie, good - bye! _____

'Way Down Yonder in New Orleans

Registration 7
Rhythm: Swing

Words and Music by Henry Creamer and
J. Turner Layton

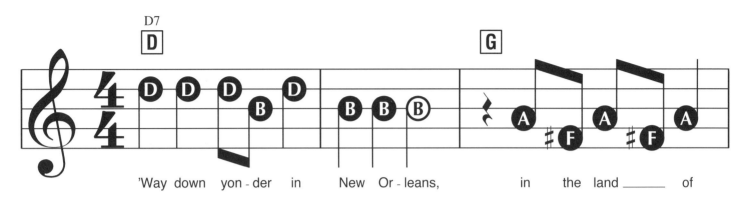

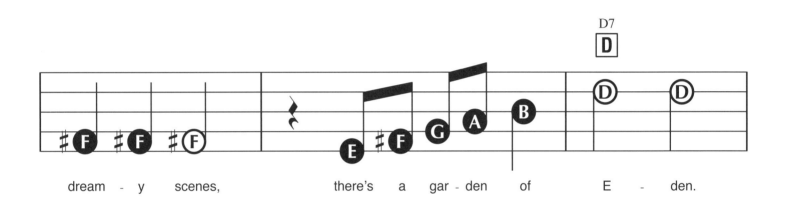

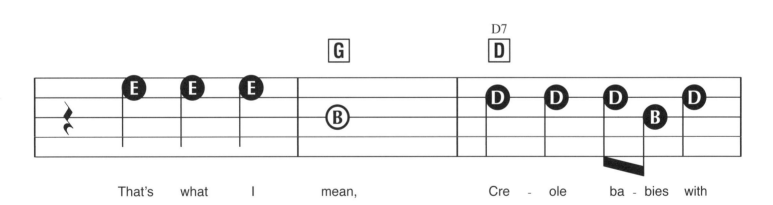

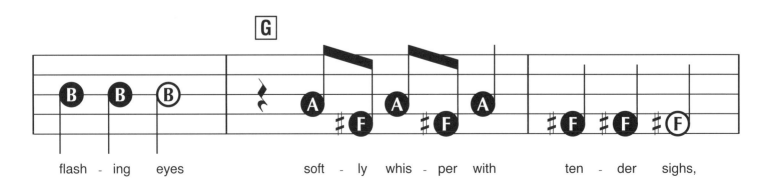

Copyright © 2002 by HAL LEONARD CORPORATION
International Copyright Secured   All Rights Reserved

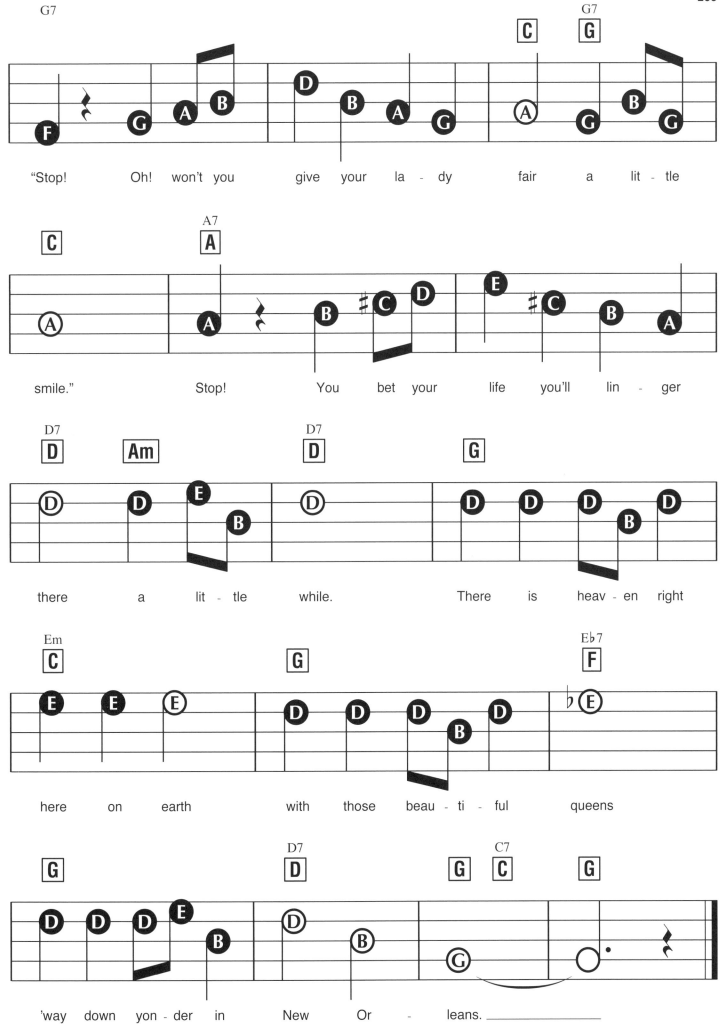

What'll I Do?
from MUSIC BOX REVUE OF 1924

Registration 2
Rhythm: Waltz

Words and Music by Irving Berlin
© Copyright 1924 by Irving Berlin

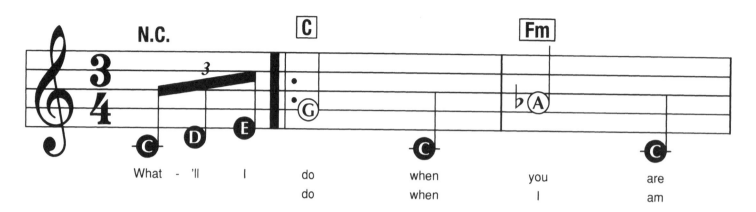

What - 'll I do when you are
do when I am

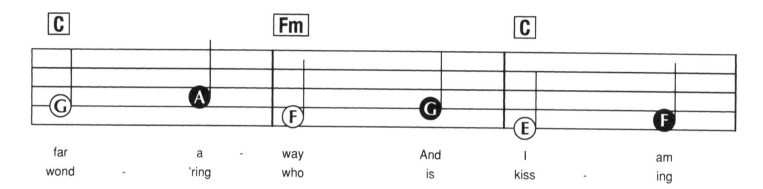

far a - way And I am
wond - 'ring who is kiss - ing

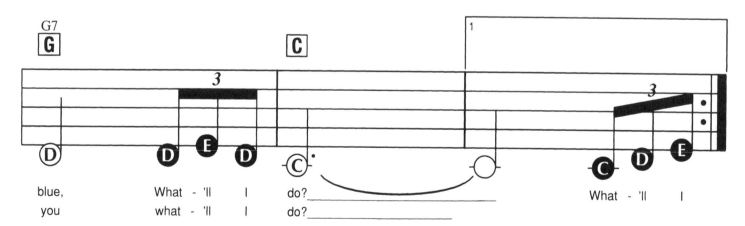

blue, What - 'll I do?_____ What - 'll I
you what - 'll I do?_____

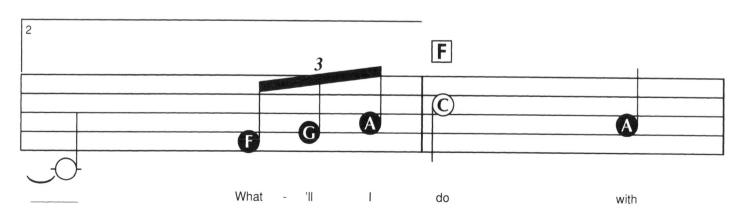

What - 'll I do with

© Copyright 1924 by Irving Berlin
© Arrangement Copyright 1947 by Irving Berlin
Copyright Renewed
International Copyright Secured All Rights Reserved

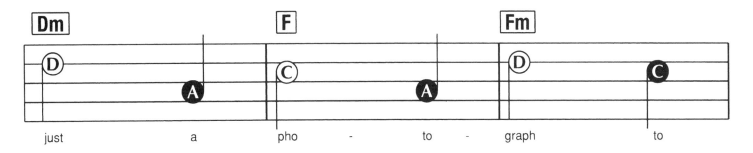

just a pho - to - graph to

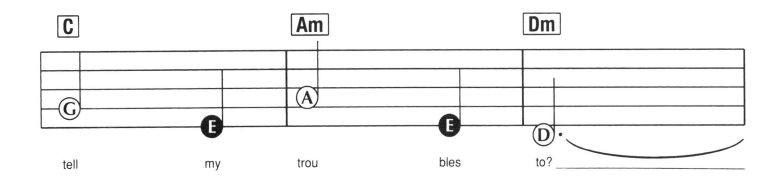

tell my trou bles to? _____

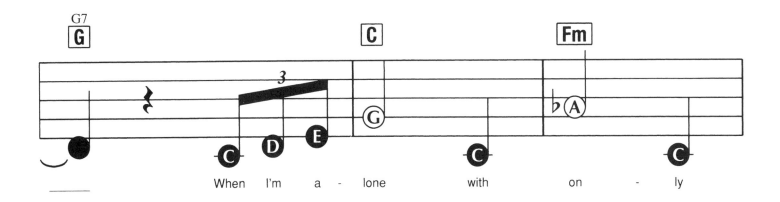

_____ When I'm a - lone with on - ly

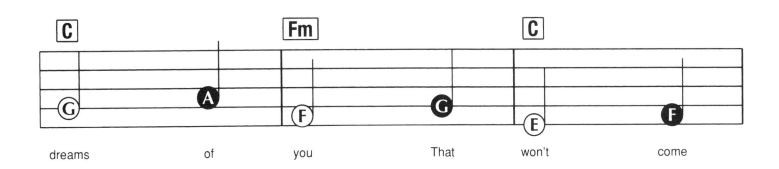

dreams of you That won't come

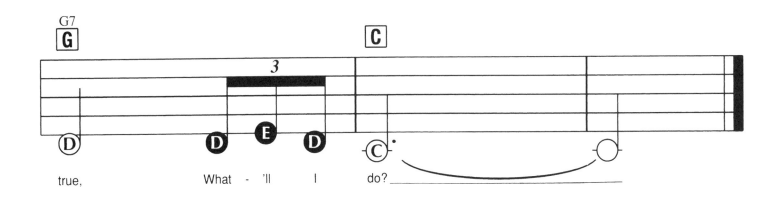

true, What - 'll I do? _____

When My Baby Smiles at Me

Registration 1
Rhythm: Fox Trot or Swing

Words and Music by Harry von Tilzer,
Andrew B. Sterling, Bill Munro and Ted Lewis

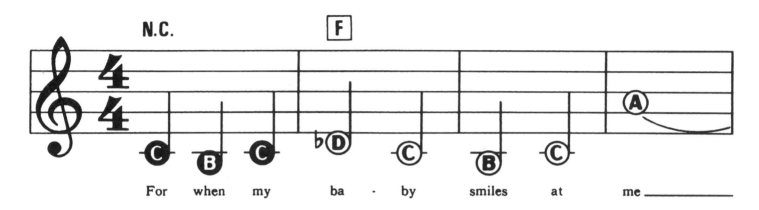

For when my ba - by smiles at me ____

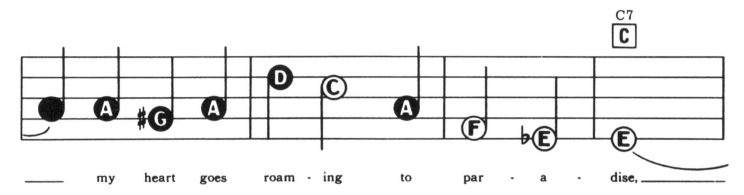

____ my heart goes roam - ing to par - a - dise, ____

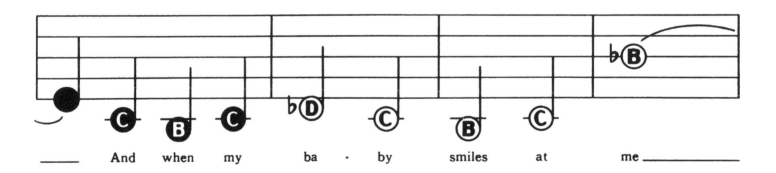

____ And when my ba - by smiles at me ____

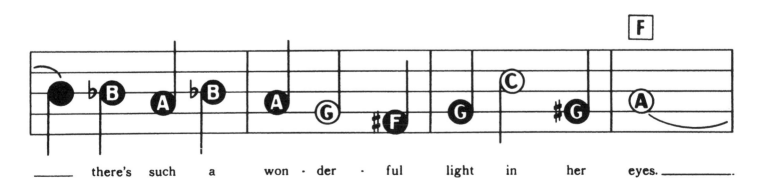

____ there's such a won - der - ful light in her eyes. ____.

Copyright © 2004 by HAL LEONARD CORPORATION
International Copyright Secured All Rights Reserved

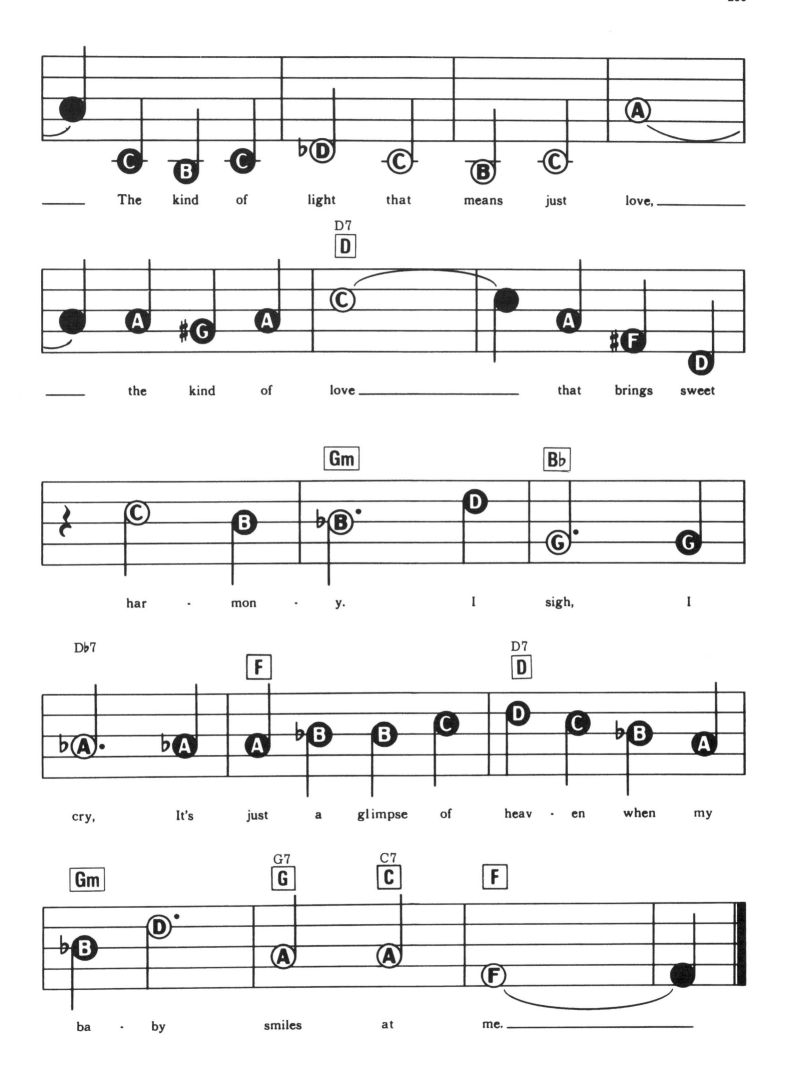

The kind of light that means just love,
the kind of love that brings sweet
D7 D
har - mon - y. I sigh, I
Gm Bb
cry, It's just a glimpse of heav - en when my
Db7 F D7 D
ba - by smiles at me.
Gm G7 G C7 C F

Whispering

Registration 1
Rhythm: Fox Trot

Words and Music by Richard Coburn,
John Schonberger and Vincent Rose

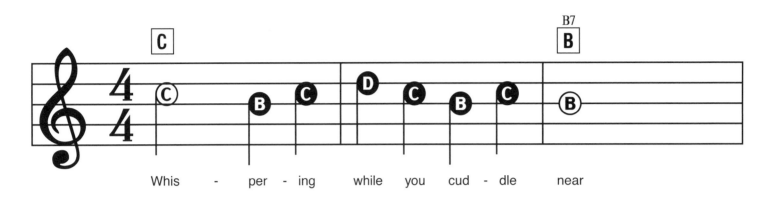

Whis - per - ing while you cud - dle near

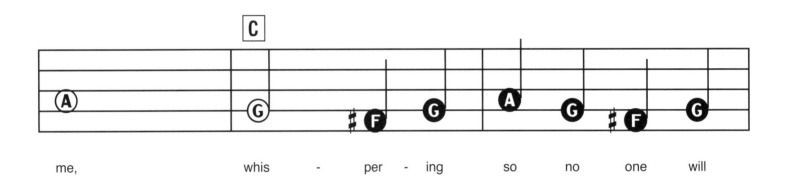

me, whis - per - ing so no one will

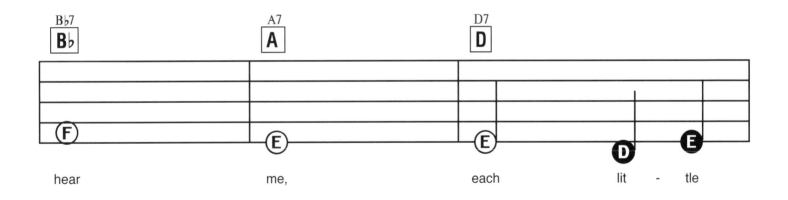

hear me, each lit - tle

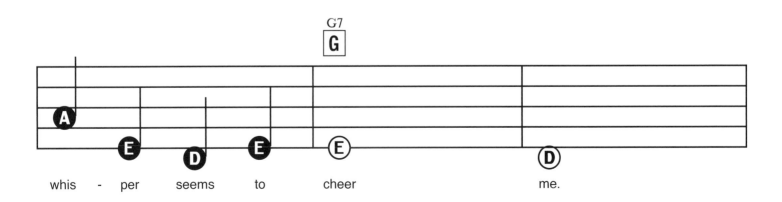

whis - per seems to cheer me.

Copyright © 2007 by HAL LEONARD CORPORATION
International Copyright Secured   All Rights Reserved

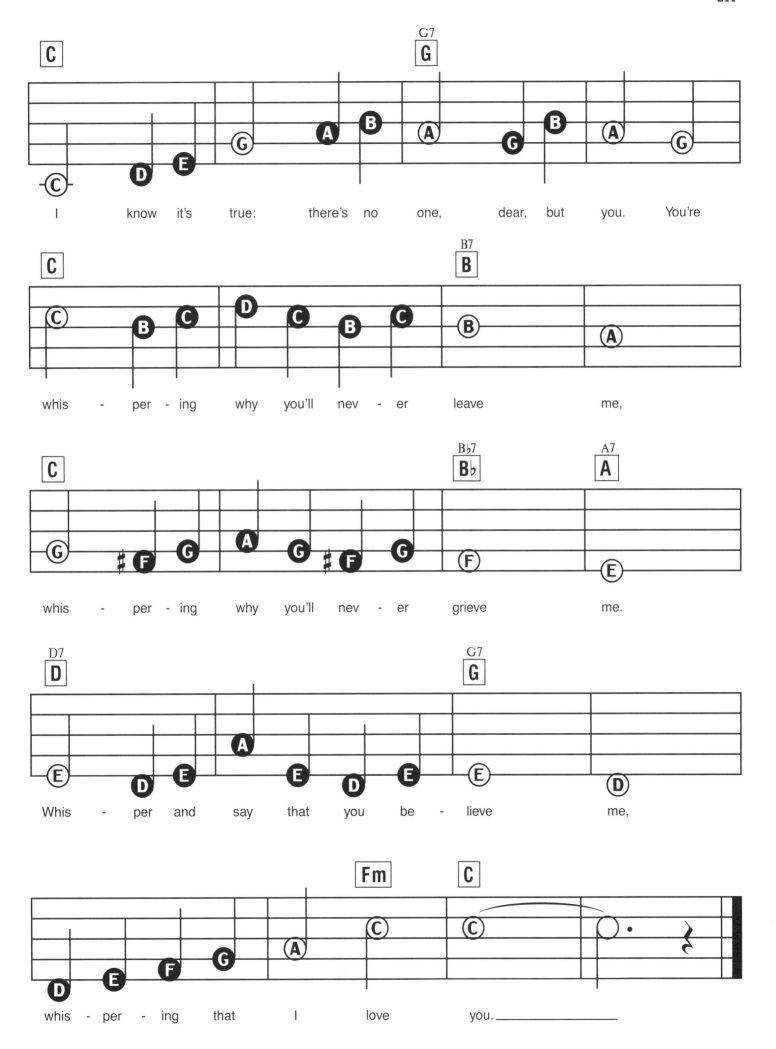

Who?
from SUNNY

Registration 1
Rhythm: Fox Trot or Swing

Lyrics by Otto Harbach and Oscar Hammerstein II
Music by Jerome Kern

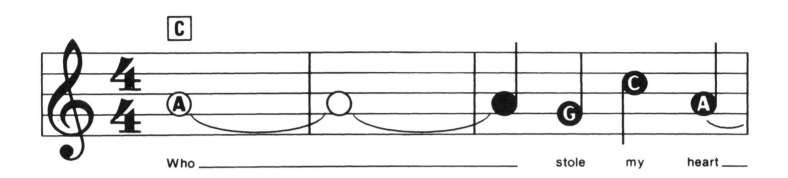

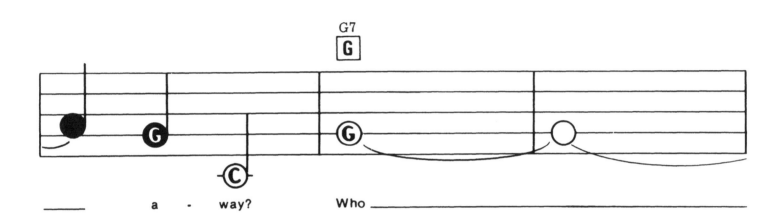

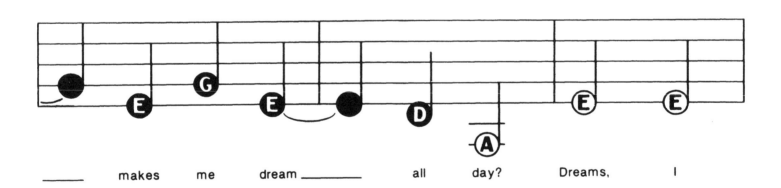

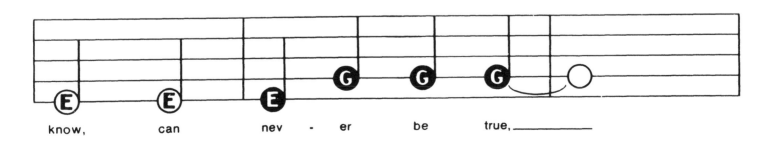

Copyright © 1925 UNIVERSAL - POLYGRAM INTERNATIONAL PUBLISHING, INC.
Copyright Renewed
All Rights Reserved   Used by Permission

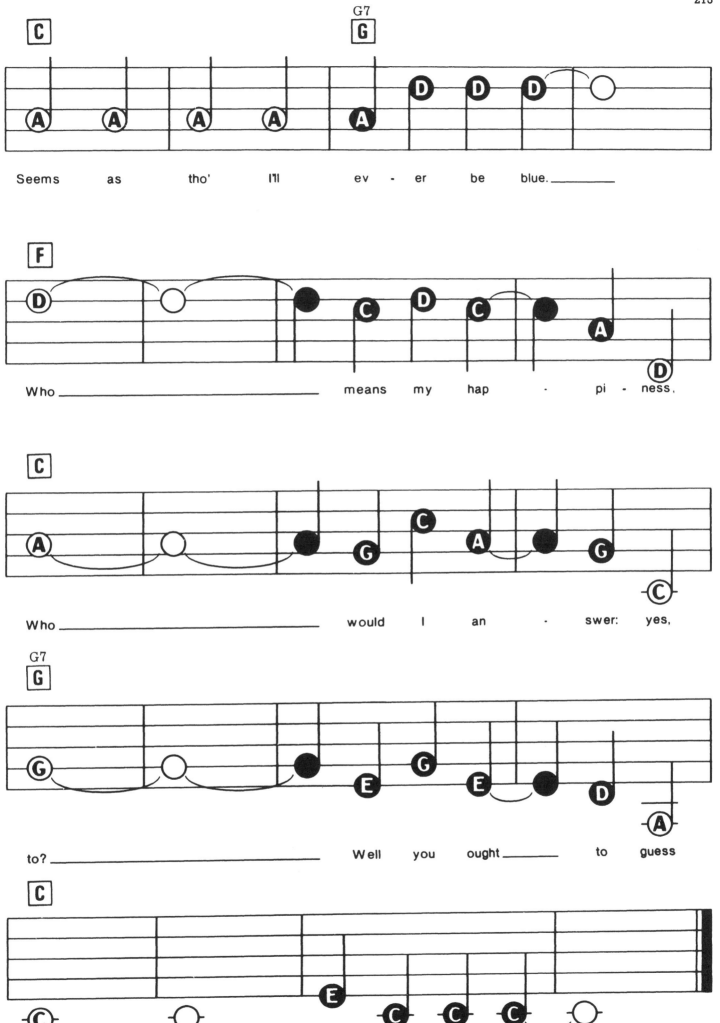

Who's Sorry Now
from THREE LITTLE WORDS

Registration 1
Rhythm: Fox Trot or Swing

Words by Bert Kalmar and Harry Ruby
Music by Ted Snyder

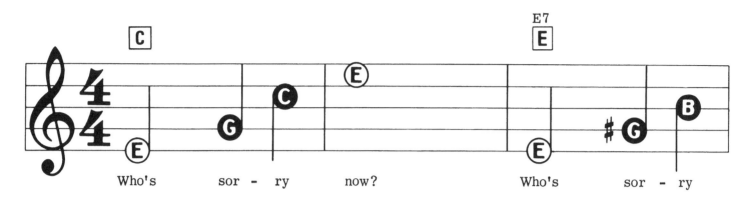

Who's   sor - ry   now?   Who's   sor - ry

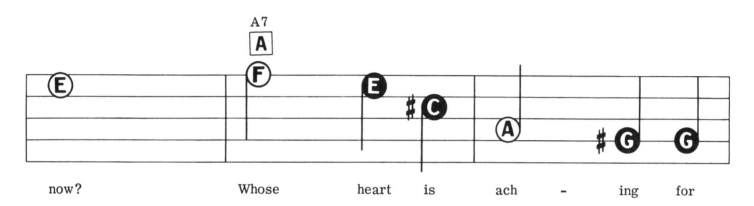

now?   Whose   heart   is   ach - ing   for

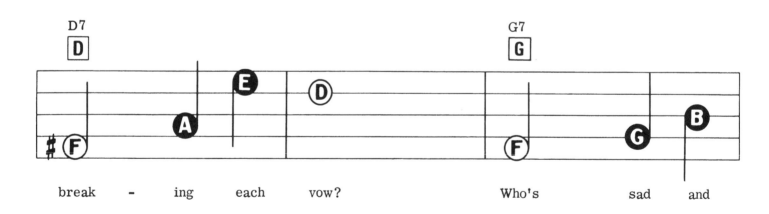

break - ing   each   vow?   Who's   sad   and

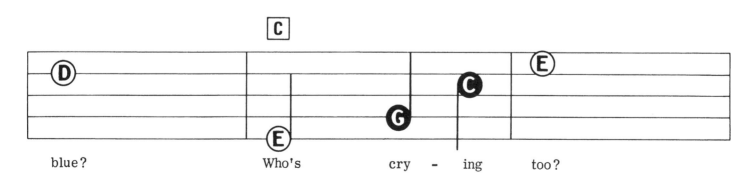

blue?   Who's   cry - ing   too?

© 1923 (Renewed 1951) BMG FIREFLY, HARRY RUBY MUSIC, TED SNYDER MUSIC PUBLISHING CO. and EMI MILLS MUSIC INC.
All Rights for BMG FIREFLY Administered by BMG RIGHTS MANAGEMENT (US) LLC
All Rights for HARRY RUBY MUSIC and TED SNYDER MUSIC PUBLISHING CO. Administered by THE SONGWRITERS GUILD OF AMERICA
All Rights for EMI MILLS MUSIC INC. Administered by EMI MILLS MUSIC INC. (Publishing) and ALFRED MUSIC (Print)
All Rights for HARRY RUBY MUSIC in Canada Administered by MEMORY LANE MUSIC GROUP
All Rights for TED SNYDER MUSIC PUBLISHING CO. in Canada Administered by REDWOOD MUSIC LTD.
All Rights Reserved   Used by Permission

215

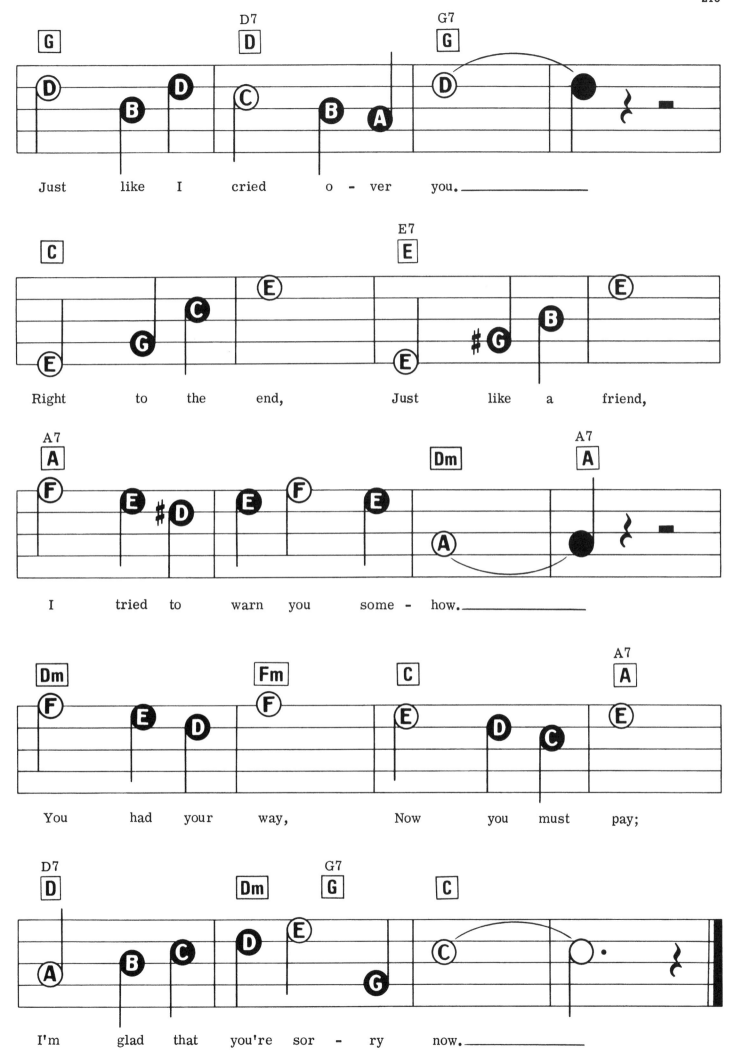

With ~ Song in My Heart

from SPRING IS HERE

Registration 5
Rhythm: Fox Trot

Words by Lorenz Hart
Music by Richard Rodgers

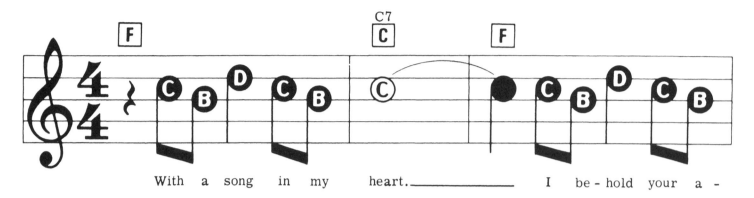

With a song in my heart._____ I be - hold your a -

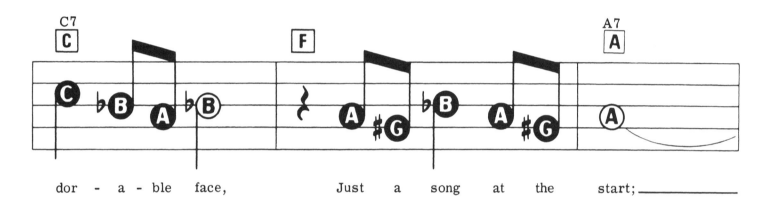

dor - a - ble face,   Just a song at the start;_____

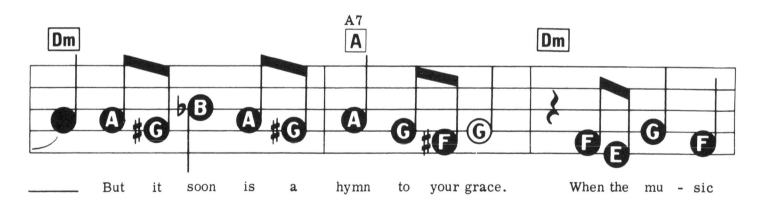

_____ But it soon is a hymn to your grace.   When the mu - sic

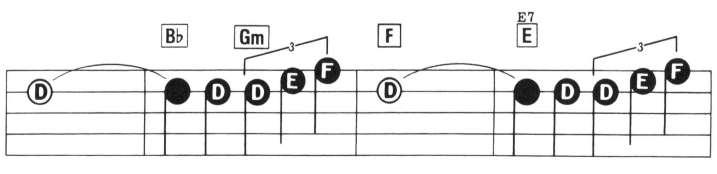

swells_____ I'm touch-ing your hand;_____ It tells that you're

Copyright © 1929 (Renewed) by Chappell & Co.
Rights for the Extended Renewal Term in the U.S. Controlled by Williamson Music, a Division of Rodgers & Hammerstein:
an Imagem Company and WB Music Corp. o/b/o The Estate Of Lorenz Hart
International Copyright Secured   All Rights Reserved

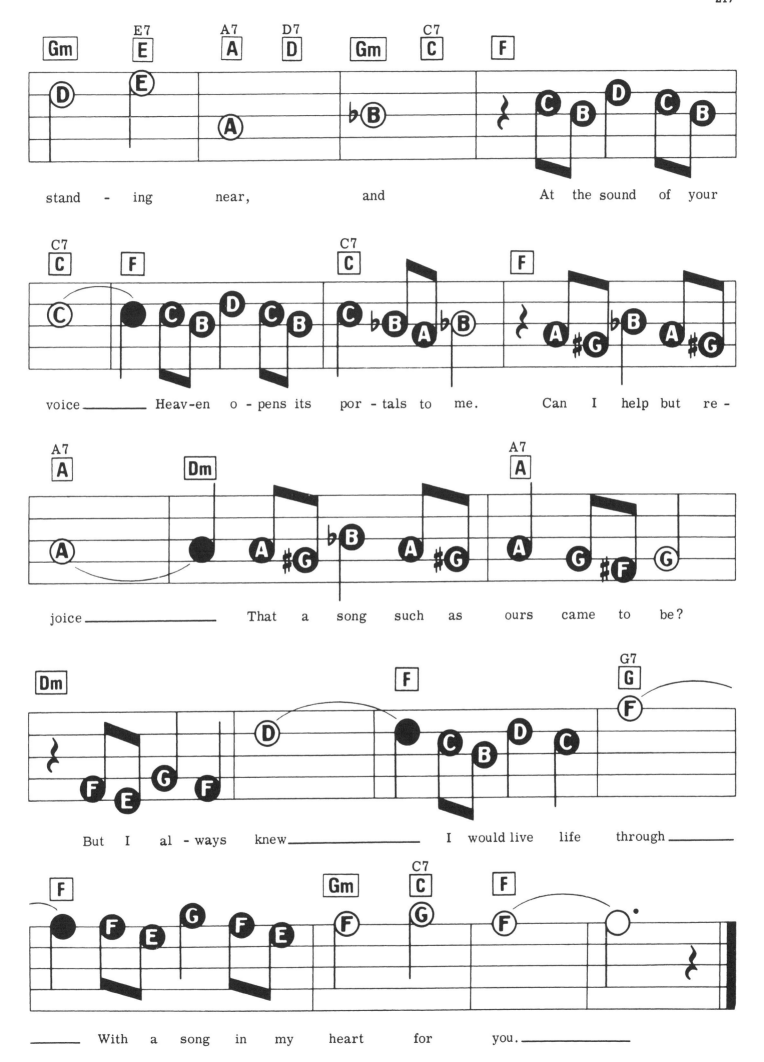

Yes Sir, That's My Baby

Registration 8
Rhythm: Fox Trot, Dixie, or Polka

Lyrics by Gus Kahn
Music by Walter Donaldson

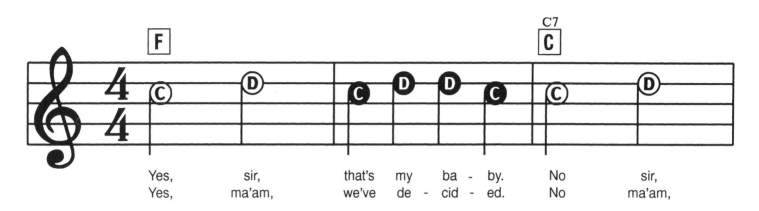

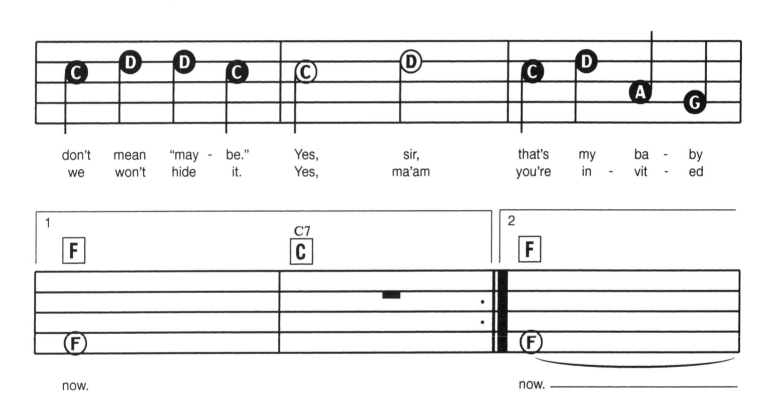

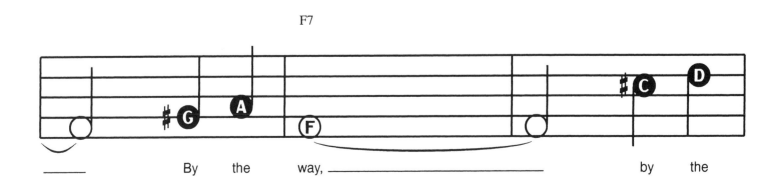

Copyright © 1925 (Renewed) by Donaldson Publishing Co. and Gilbert Keyes Music Co.
Gus Kahn's Canadian Rights Controlled by Bourne Co.
International Copyright Secured   All Rights Reserved

219

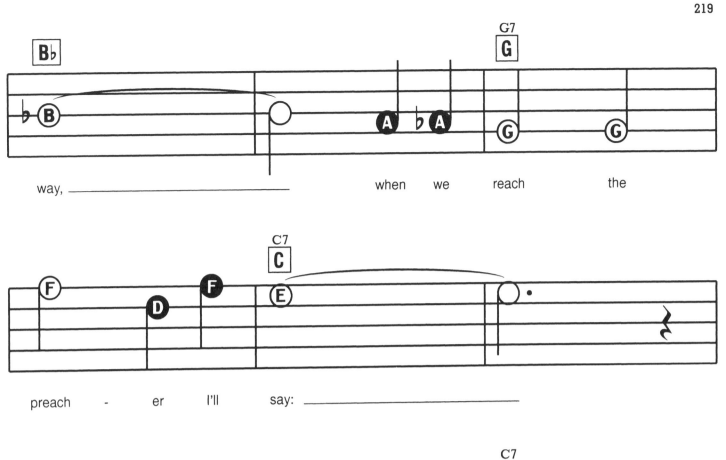

way, _____ when we reach the

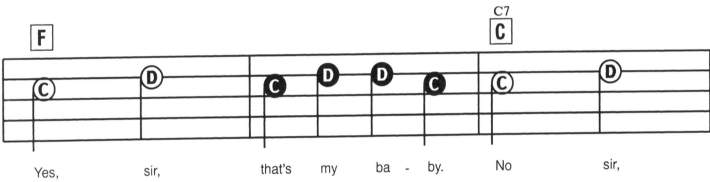

preach - er I'll say: _____

Yes, sir, that's my ba - by. No sir,

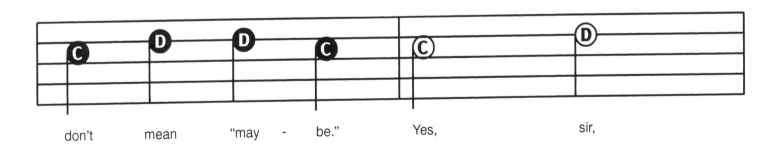

don't mean "may - be." Yes, sir,

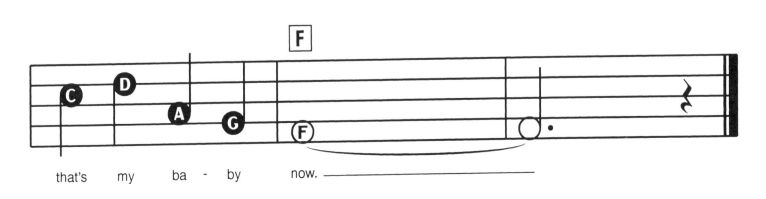

that's my ba - by now. _____

Yes! We Have No Bananas

Registration 5
Rhythm: March or Polka

By Frank Silver
and Irving Conn

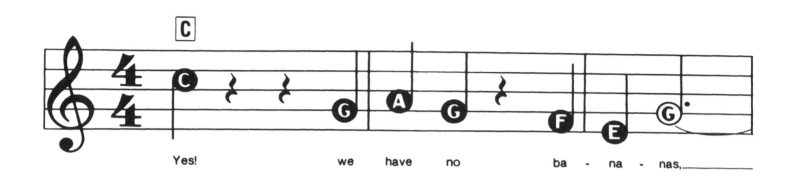

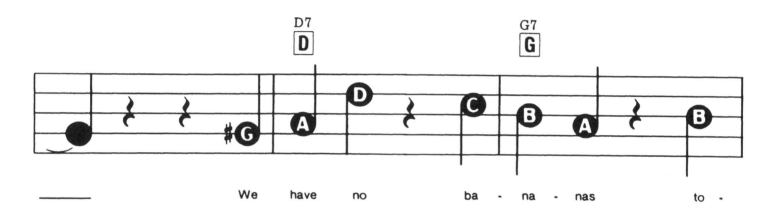

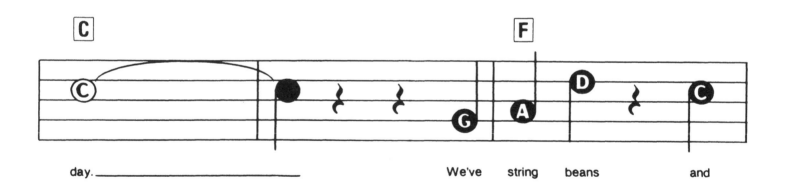

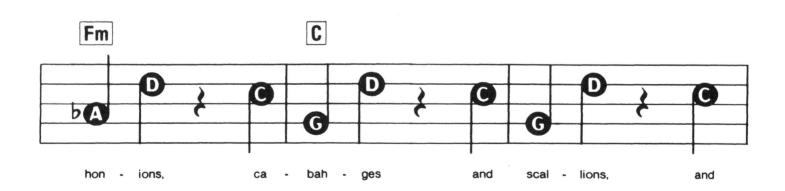

Copyright © 1923 Skidmore Music Company, Inc., New York
Copyright Renewed
International Copyright Secured All Rights Reserved
Used by Permission

221

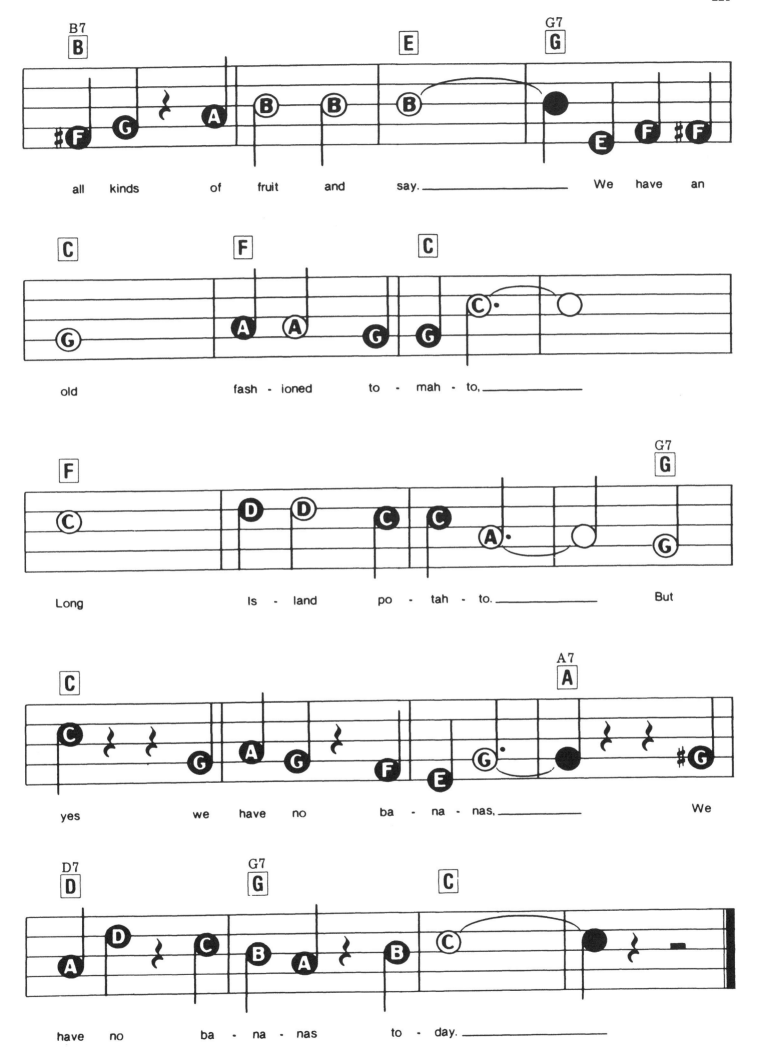

You're the Cream in My Coffee
from HOLD EVERYTHING

Registration 4
Rhythm: Swing or Fox Trot

Words and Music by B.G. DeSylva,
Lew Brown and Ray Henderson

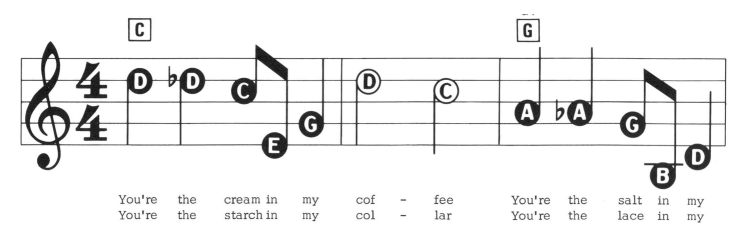

You're the cream in my cof - fee You're the salt in my
You're the starch in my col - lar You're the lace in my

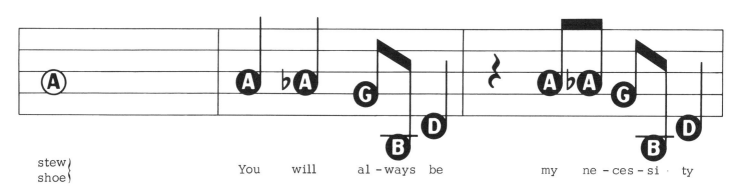

stew)
shoe)   You will al - ways be   my ne - ces - si - ty

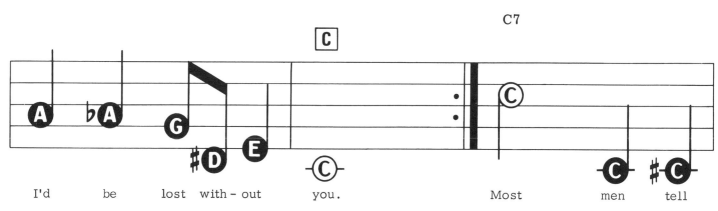

I'd be lost with - out you.   Most men tell

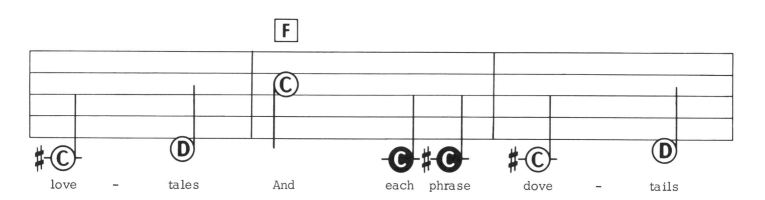

love - tales   And   each phrase dove - tails

Copyright © 1928 by Chappell & Co., Stephen Ballentine Music Publishing Co. and Ray Henderson Music Co.
Copyright Renewed
International Copyright Secured   All Rights Reserved

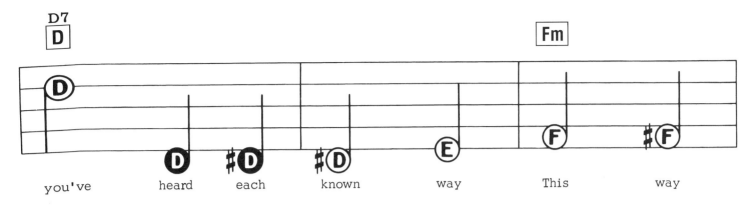

you've heard each known way This way

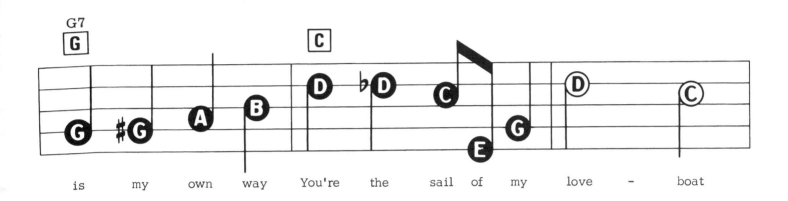

is my own way You're the sail of my love – boat

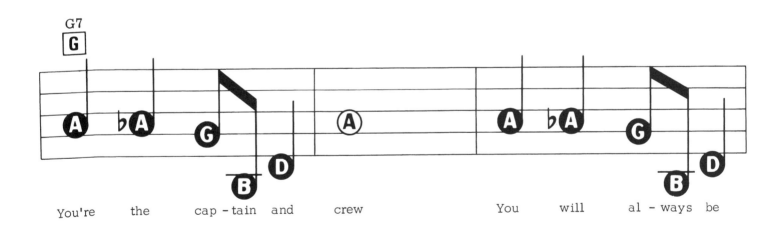

You're the cap - tain and crew You will al - ways be

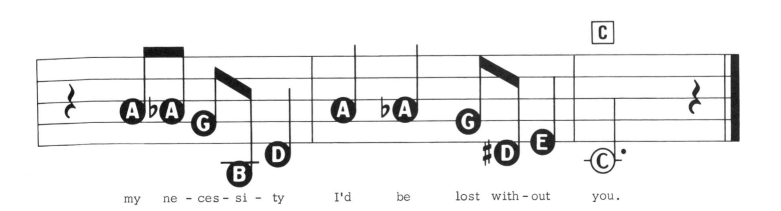

my ne - ces - si - ty I'd be lost with - out you.

Registration Guide

- Match the Registration number on the song to the corresponding numbered category below. Select and activate an instrumental sound available on your instrument.

- Choose an automatic rhythm appropriate to the mood and style of the song. (Consult your Owner's Guide for proper operation of automatic rhythm features.)

- Adjust the tempo and volume controls to comfortable settings.

Registration

1	Mellow	Flutes, Clarinet, Oboe, Flugel Horn, Trombone, French Horn, Organ Flutes
2	Ensemble	Brass Section, Sax Section, Wind Ensemble, Full Organ, Theater Organ
3	Strings	Violin, Viola, Cello, Fiddle, String Ensemble, Pizzicato, Organ Strings
4	Guitars	Acoustic/Electric Guitars, Banjo, Mandolin, Dulcimer, Ukulele, Hawaiian Guitar
5	Mallets	Vibraphone, Marimba, Xylophone, Steel Drums, Bells, Celesta, Chimes
6	Liturgical	Pipe Organ, Hand Bells, Vocal Ensemble, Choir, Organ Flutes
7	Bright	Saxophones, Trumpet, Mute Trumpet, Synth Leads, Jazz/Gospel Organs
8	Piano	Piano, Electric Piano, Honky Tonk Piano, Harpsichord, Clavi
9	Novelty	Melodic Percussion, Wah Trumpet, Synth, Whistle, Kazoo, Perc. Organ
10	Bellows	Accordion, French Accordion, Mussette, Harmonica, Pump Organ, Bagpipes